The Collected Letters of Major Thomas Harvey CVO DSO

THE COLLECTED
LETTERS OF
MAJOR THOMAS HARVEY
CVO DSO

SELECTED AND EDITED BY
DAVID AND KATHLEEN HARVEY

Edited, designed and produced by Tandem Publishing
http://tandempublishing.yolasite.com

ISBN: 979-83-00797-25-6

Contents

DAILY TELEGRAPH OBITUARY

21st June 2001

MAJOR THOMAS HARVEY, who has died aged 82, was formerly Private Secretary to the Queen (now the Queen Mother); he was appointed in 1946, when he was 28, two years after winning a DSO in Italy with the Scots Guards.

Harvey escorted the Queen on her public visits, assisted with a voluminous correspondence and kept her diary of engagements – an exacting task, given the multitude of deserving causes which appealed to the Queen for patronage. The job demanded a great capacity for hard work, diplomacy, common sense and writing ability, qualities that Harvey possessed in abundance.

He also accompanied the Royal Family on their visits overseas, such as their tour of South Africa in 1947. The journey began when the Royal party embarked on the *Vanguard* bound for Cape Town. Partnered by midshipmen, the Princesses ranged through the ship in a treasure hunt organised by the gunroom. Princess Elizabeth, a front runner until close to the end, was defeated by the final clue. Harvey won a bottle of port.

In the spring of 1949, Princess Margaret made her first solo trip abroad, a private educational visit to Italy. Harvey was among the welcoming party at Naples airport to greet her as she emerged from the Royal Viking aircraft.

It has been said that the trip was the inspiration for the film *Roman Holiday* (1953). The photographers snapped away excitedly when Harvey appeared on the beach wearing a shirt over his bathing trunks. The headlines the next day read: "Princess goes swimming with man in shirt-tails."

In November 1948, Prince Charles was born. Harvey wrote a diverting account of the occasion which he later presented to the Prince. When the birth was imminent, Queen Mary left

Marlborough House for the Palace accompanied by the Earl and Countess of Athlone. Unfortunately, the latter was taken ill after eating a bad oyster and the hapless doctor had to shuttle back and forth between his illustrious charges to ensure that the joyful event was not attended by one less felicitous.

Thomas Cockayne Harvey was born on August 22 1918 at Ickwell Bury, near Biggleswade, Bedfordshire. His father had won a DSO at Festubert in 1915.

Tom was educated at Radley and then at Balliol College, Oxford, where he read Modern Languages. An excellent golfer, he won a Blue and, but for the outbreak of war, would have captained the university team.

Playing against Cambridge in 1939 at Royal St George's, Sandwich, his opponent, Willie Whitelaw, was one up with one to play. Needing only to halve the last hole, Whitelaw topped his drive and landed in a bunker. Bernard Darwin, a partisan Cambridge supporter and later doyen of golf correspondents, jumped up and down in a paroxysm of rage, bellowing: "Bloody fool! Bloody fool! Always was a bloody fool! Always will be a bloody fool!" The match was drawn.

Harvey was already in the Scots Guards' supplementary reserve of officers and had begun preliminary training when war was declared. His first taste of active service came in April 1940 when he went to Norway with the 1st Battalion. The Allies were forced to abandon the campaign and early in June the battalion was evacuated.

After a year as an instructor at Sandhurst and a number of home postings, in 1944 he rejoined the 1st Battalion in the Apennines for the gruelling slog up the backbone of Italy.

On September 30, the battalion was ordered to attack Monte Catarelto, a formidable feature which dominated the Divisional axis and was defended by crack SS troops. Harvey led two assault companies up heavily wooded slopes, sparing his men the heaviest of the shelling and mortar fire. But once they were out of the trees, the summit was seen to be bare, affording cover only for the Spandau gunners concealed by a sunken track and stone walls.

Harvey led a bayonet charge which carried the crest and put the enemy to flight. The Germans launched three ferocious counter-attacks – at dusk, by moonlight and at dawn the next morning. All were beaten off. Harvey, although wounded, was to be found wherever the fighting was thickest, an inspiration to exhausted men beset by greatly superior numbers.

For his gallantry, Harvey was awarded the Distinguished Service Order. His citation declared: "By sheer personality, accompanied by utter disregard for his own safety, Major Harvey dominated the battlefield."

In April 1946, Harvey was released from the Army. After then spending nearly four years as Private Secretary to the Queen, in 1951 he was succeeded by Captain Oliver Dawnay. Appointed Extra Gentleman Usher to King George VI, he attended diplomatic functions but otherwise the position was undemanding. On the King's death in 1952, he became Extra Gentleman Usher to the Queen.

With three children to educate, Harvey decided to go into the City and in 1952 he became a partner in Mullens. He worked at the "short" end of the market and did the rounds of the banks and the discount houses.

For more than three decades, Harvey involved himself in golf at the highest level. In 1959, he became chairman of the Championship Committee of the Royal and Ancient, and was Captain of the Club in 1976. In 1977, at Turnberry, he presented the silver claret jug to Tom Watson after his victory over Jack Nicklaus.

Harvey retired from Mullens in 1978, but for a number of years he was a regional director of Lloyds Bank. He was also an energetic fund-raiser for Cumberland Lodge, in Windsor Great Park, a former residence of the Park Rangers that now provides a forum where students of different nationalities can meet for discussion and fellowship.

Tom Harvey was a man of many parts and a perfectionist in all of them. He had a gift for humorous wordplay, and for doggerel verse, composed on subjects as diverse as the Duke of Norfolk's arrangements for the coronation and Sir Solly Zuckerman's 80th birthday.

Harvey's house in Norfolk with its Elizabethan walled garden was the perfect complement to his good looks and patrician ease of manner. It was also the setting for many enjoyable parties at which he often played the piano.

In retirement, golf remained his great passion. The Royal West Norfolk course at Brancaster was probably his favourite place on earth. His marriage and his family were a source of immense happiness. He looked after his wife devotedly in her last illness and faced his own with characteristic forbearance and courage.

Harvey was appointed CVO in 1951. He married, in 1940, Lady Mary Coke, younger daughter of the 4th Earl of Leicester and a Woman of the Bedchamber to the Queen Mother. She died in 1993. They had a son and two daughters.

PREFACE

This book is a result of a chance discovery by my wife Kathleen whilst clearing out the cellar of my late parents' house in Norfolk of a Peter Jones plastic bag full of letters.

Despite my suggestion of "binning" it she persevered in typing them out, much of the content indecipherable, and putting the letters all in correct date order. For her it was a fantastic voyage of discovery of a life, much of which we were not aware of, which we now hope will be treasured by future family generations.

The letters are, of course, very personal and at times mundane but account should be taken of what was going on in the world outside and the need to protect Mary from the realities of the battlefield.

There are also many references to drinks parties and dances, but remember: not only was it wartime but how young they all were. Indeed, at the end of the war Tom was only twenty-six years old.

His account of the birth of Prince Charles is delightful and I suspect the only one of its time.

Tom Harvey's spellings, punctuation and usages have been retained from the original letters. Some letters have been lightly abridged.

My warmest thanks to Sam Carter (from Tandem Publishing, kindly introduced to us by Algy Cluff) for his enthusiastic support, but above all to Kathleen, who is entirely responsible for the whole project.

– David Harvey, 2024

most sacred personal feelings must be merged into this higher cause —— & it is my resolution that our love, & the great whole that those four little letters mean for us both, that our love shall in 1941 be heightened and rededicated, & purged, & purified by the fire of sacrifice and, perhaps, suffering. Be cheerful that so much may be required, for all, all is at stake, and the path of the brave is honourable.

God bless you, my Angel heart, and send you my love. and kisses till we're together again

from your adoring Tim.

BRITAIN
1939–1940

Rothschilds' tennis party.

Ringstead Bury
King's Lynn
June 29 1939

My dear Mary,

I did enjoy myself so much last Sunday: thank you very much for allowing me to invite myself so blatantly. I thought Sowley* perfectly divine, & as for those records they surpass one's wildest dreams (in the immortal phrase of Frances Day). What the Rothschilds & their entourage can have thought (a/ of my costume for & b/ of my performance at tennis) I shudder to think, though the two fitted in extremely well: I looked like a 50/- tailor's dummy & played like one! But for all that I enjoyed it vastly, & the last set with an iron racket (at least it felt like that) was a fitting end to a most delightful day.

I saw your Mother afterwards & she very kindly asked me to the Cobbolds' dance, but as I was rather afraid, we have got some people coming to stay here & I must be 'in residence'. As it is I have got to go up for a dance on 11 & must hare back to Ringstead† afterwards. Will you explain all this to your Mother, thanking her again, & apologising.

If you simply can't wait to set foot in Norfolk again, a supposition I strongly doubt, would you like to come here for the weekend of 28 July – on your way to Holkham‡ so to speak – & go straight on there afterwards. It may of course seem a little cramped after our vast rooms but your Grandpapa could be persuaded to give you a State room so that you didn't suffer too acutely from claustrophobia. Don't worry about this – but if it seems possible, beetle through a postcard, & the house is at your service. And talking of service we might have some tennis, & this time I shall wear white (or at any rate whitish) flannels, & will use

*   Mary and her parents' (Lord and Lady Coke's) house.
†   Tom's widowed mother's house in Norfolk.
‡   Mary's grandparents' house.

a racket of some substance more pliable than pig iron.

However until I hear from you or see you again I shall expect nothing – or to put it more continentally 'J'attendrai'.

With love from Tom

* * *

1ˢᵗ Bn. Scots Guards
Victoria Barracks
Windsor, August 15 pm

My dear Mary,
A line to tell you, (what my halting tongue can never say) how much I enjoyed our various parties together, & how I loved to have you with us at Ringstead.

Have just arrived here, very alarmed at the prospect of being back at school, & of doing an inordinate amount of work. No doubt when you next see me, I shall be more efficient than Lord Gort himself. I only hope you'll be able to recognise me behind the ginger moustache & ramrod spine that I propose to cultivate!

Do write if you have time, in the intervals of Norfolk gaiety & if at any time you can get over to see Mother she would adore it.

Goodbye, poppet, & all my love
from Tom

* * *

1ˢᵗ Bn Scots Guards
Victoria Barracks
Windsor, Aug 20 1939

My Dearest Maria,
Many thanks indeed for your letter, & its attendant frivolities, especially that elegant pen-portrait of my impending moustache.

Your imagination, my dear, is just too vivid!

Am having an idle morning, writing letters, & listening to swing on the Mess gramophone so if this letter is more than usually disjointed, you'll know it's because periodically I have to get up & truck round the room. (Yea, mama, break it up!). But I will try to summon my jitterbug brains, & tell you something of the life here.

To start with, it is most amusing because five or six of my fellow reserve officers have been in the last War, one is half blind & stone deaf, & another, Tommy MacDougall, has got a wooden leg!! Every morning we drill on the square, under a drill sergeant, perspiring (a nice refined word!) like a ship's stoker in a heat wave, doing everything wrong, & looking too idiotic for words. We all giggle feebly if we catch each other's eye; & to see one middle-aged subaltern with 5 medals, slow-marching in the style they abandoned 23 years ago is a sight, the sheer beauty & delight of which can seldom have been shared by all the gods of Olympus.

John* & I have had one or two games of golf, but the peak of my athletic prowess was reached yesterday, when I consented to play cricket for the Battalion. Tommy Bulkeley & I were the only officers playing, & unfortunately late – but we determined to make a suitably impressive entry. Unfortunately we mistook the turning, & leaving the car in a field we had to approach the pavilion from the rear stumbling over nettles, corrugated iron, & old bricks – looking exactly like two stained & weary explorers bursting through the jungle into the cool oasis beyond. The cricket itself was not uneventful because our side only made 16 – I was out first ball in the first innings, & second ball in the second innings – you can't have it fairer than that! However we had five of their wickets down for 6 runs, & but for a sparkling scoop of 12 by one of them we might have won not withstanding.

This morning I am so stiff that each step is a taste of hell, each movement a glimpse of purgatory.

---

* Tom's older brother, also in the Scots Guards; married to Anne.

So sorry to hear about David,* I do hope he is alright; otherwise we'll have him living on oranges too, & that will never do.

If the Maggot† is still around your engaging desolate countryside would you tell her from me that alas! I can't get up to Scotland in September; I've got to go to Pirbright, of all […] for a course on some ridiculous subject, & all frivolity is thereby precluded, as the centipede with corns used frequently to observe.

But I must stop and put some fertiliser on my upper lip.

So with all my love (& apologies for this interminable script)

from Tom

Lady Coke with her daughter Silvia and son David

---

* Flight Lt David Coke DFC: Mary's brother, RAF pilot.

† Maggot: Margaret Ogilvy (daughter of the Earl of Airlie), Mary's cousin.

Chelsea Barracks
London SW1
Aug 26 1939

My dearest Maria,

As you see from the address on this paper, the machinations of Hitler have caused me to be transferred here until further notice. So having celebrated my birthday* (& herewith many many thanks for all the sweet messages Mother gave me from you), I return to Windsor to find that a full blooded crisis had turned up in my absence. Hence my arrival here. Of course I know that as long as this 'emergency' lasts there's no chance of seeing you here but if you do come this way, or are passing through, then send me word & I will await upon you.

I hear that you & Jacqueline went to the theatre with Mother on Monday. You've no idea how she loves that sort of thing, & how good it is for her to see young cheerful creatures, when otherwise she would be alone. So whenever you've got nothing better to do, do just drop in & 'swing it' on the keys.

Rather a ridiculous and disjointed scrawl, I'm afraid, my dear; but I wanted to thank you for your messages, & let you know my whereabouts, in case there's a chance of a 'rendez vous'.

With all my love (& confusion to Hitler!)

from Tom

* * *

---

*   21st birthday.

1st Bn Scots Guards
Victoria Barracks
Windsor
Aug 31

To 'Just an old cow-hand
From the Rio Grande'
(Veide. The Sketch) Aug 30 1939*
It must, no doubt, be topical
to be tropical
But we're not in the least fond of cactus.
So in that respect you counteract us.
But one advantage of your dress is that
you will continue to talk through your hat.
It must be wretched
to be etched
& sketched
without a bronco
like getting dronco
without exhilaration,
like Prince Littler
without Ruritania
or Hitler
without mania.
But I have said enough
without getting tough.
But I never knew before how Earls
had granddaughters dressed up as cow-girls!

With apologies for this rot. From Tom

* * *

Pirbright Camp
Woking

My Dearest Maria,

Thank you so much for your letter – & that rude postcard which naturally enough I didn't think the least funny. To laugh at golf is surely blasphemy in one of its forms, & that is a crime no girl (not even a cow-girl) should ever commit. However I think I can see my way to forgiving you this time, tho' adding the strictest warning against any repetition!!

I don't know whether you gathered from one of my previous scrawls that life has been rather inactive.

[page here torn]

… limbs are numb, & my body bathed in (to you) 'perspiration'! As for the next ten weeks (starting from Monday) we are to have 7 parades a day, apart from routine work, so life to me no longer has any glamour. We must therefore meet at the earliest possible moment, so that you can restore my faith in civilization & existence.

Unless the War Office plans have been changed, your good brother Tommy is due here as Adjutant to our Training Battalion. I expect you've heard something about this, & I am hoping with every breath that it's true. It would be grand to have him here. As I say, the plans may have been changed, but before we came here, we were told by the C.O. that he was certainly going to do so.

At the moment I can't see my way to getting to Sowley, but as soon as there's the least hope, I will ring you up madly on the telephone. I've hardly been out of uniform for years & I get to dislike my appearance more & more. In another two months my horror of myself will reconcile me to the most violent of deaths!

Still, however one may joke, it is ghastly to think we are at war, & at war with people whom, but for their bestial leadership, we could & would like enormously. It's no good pretending that we've seen even a glimpse of war yet; & who knows what might not be the devastation & death we will have to face, before returning to a human and contented life. But tho' everyone thinks in the same way, it's not the least use doing it out loud, & a stream of flippancy is the best way to drown one's apprehensions. It is easy enough here, with crowds of other people, of one's own age, but for you it can't be too good; still, you have your music, & that is a joy forever – except when I'm there trespassing in the treble.

John & Anne are together again at Windsor, & he comes over here every day. Mother has arrived there this evening but I am on duty & can't leave the Camp – so I hang about in this Mess, which has been redecorated in the style of Beverley Hills, white stucco, black tiled roof & modernistic gables in the verandah, opening onto a lawn tipped with roses!

But next week I shan't even be able to do that.

No more now poppet; don't ever let yourself get depressed, but if you do, just remember the great motto, Hold Tight.

All my love Tom

* * *

Pirbright Camp
Woking
7.10.39

My Dearest Mary,
Thank you so much for your letter: I loved getting it, tho' was depressed to hear that life at home was so gloomy. Can't you possibly get away for a bit. I know the Masseys would adore to have you to stay for any time you liked; they've got a house at Wentworth, about 10 miles from here so, needless to say, it would suit me admirably!! What is more, I was with them last weekend, & Mrs. M told me she was thinking of taking a large country house (no names!) and converting it into a convalescent home for officers; & she asked me whether you would like to join up there

as a nurse or helper. I said I didn't know, but would pass on the information, in the hopes it might appeal to you. The house, by the way, is not far from Oxford.

What about it, Sister?

The news from here is nil, & seems to be of nothing except myself, with my alternate moods of cheerfulness & depression. At the moment, owing to many causes, chiefly the b ____ y [abbreviation for beastly] programme we have to do day after day, my mood is one of acute depression, so I shall say no more of it. But if you could tell me that there is a hope of us fore gathering

[page missing]

* * *

Pirbright Camp
Woking
26 [?]

My dearest Poppet,

I meant to write ages ago to say how much I enjoyed our week at home – but I've felt less like writing letters than ever, & besides that, there hasn't been much news.

I had a most successful day at Newmarket: I arrived there for tea, & on the Saturday we got about 470 pheasants and over 90 partridges, which was great fun. In fact so many cartridges did I fire that I felt violently sick after tea, & had to go to bed for the rest of the evening!! However I was none the worse for wear next morning, & was able to return here, rather dismally, for another week's training. Luckily this week hasn't been too bad: I haven't had to get up early, go out at night, or do P.T – none of the usual horrors in fact. But it all starts again tomorrow, so I am having a respectable and stately weekend in Pirbright, in preparation.

I believe that I am going to get a week again at Christmas – roughly from 20–28 – so whatever happens we must get together again, be it North or South. Still, I can let you know about that when I know more: & perhaps you can let me know what your plans are.

I saw John on Wednesday, he nipped over here for a second, & told me he'd had a wonderful shoot on Saturday. 808 pheasants, & the rest out of reach! His term has started by now, so I expect he is busy shaking the moth-balls out of his mortar board, & covering his fingers with coloured chalk from the blackboard.

Haven't heard a squeak from the Masseys[*] lately, but I think I shall ring them up tonight, and have a chat. It's such a striking day I can't believe they'll be away from 'The Knowe'.

Must stop now: am rather irritable, as I am trying to give up smoking for a bit, & I hate the effort!

But herewith all my love from Tom

* * *

Pirbright Camp
Woking
29th [?]

Dearest Maria,
It seems ages since I last heard your news, but I imagine that the intervals between delousing evacuees and sewing mattresses for troops (myself included) are very short, & deny you the chance of putting pen to paper. The same tends to apply to me, for I am treated here like a guardsman & work like a black all day. But the day seems to finish fairly early, about 4.30 & often one can then buzz off to play golf or see a flick. The blackout & the petrol rationing tend however to restrict our activities, same as everyone else's.

Still we do occasionally have first class 'concerts' here, & last Sunday we had the most excellent entertainment from Flanagan

---

[*]   Vincent Massey, future Governor-General of Canada.

& Allen, Nervo & Knox, Tommy Trinder, Will Fyffe, & Teddy Brown.

They all dined in Mess afterwards & were in frightfully good form. They're coming down again in 3 weeks' time, & we're due to play golf against them beforehand. It should be a lot of fun.

Must stop now; but you're sure to hear from me again, for as soon as I get a chance, I am going to descend on Sowley for a Saturday night. So prepare the sandbags!!

All my love & do write again soon.

From Tom

* * *

Pirbright Camp
Woking
Dec 13

My dearest Maria,

Thank you so much for your long and 'newsey' letter. You certainly seem to be working like a black behind your counter – and, 'when off', on the dance floors of the city, but no doubt the infatuation of Ginger and his pals for you, is sufficient reward. I trust the 'hop' went off alright and that there were no rows as to who should dance with whom, and how often. I should be heartbroken if one morning I saw in my Daily Mirror headlines that "Society Girls Manhandled in Boston – two-Step". "Corporals Duel for hand of Earl's canteen's granddaughter" etc etc. Can you imagine it!

Since I last wrote to you, I have become increasingly busier, because I know I have to instruct in Tactics, & also for the last ten days we've been rehearsing madly for a concert which we are giving tonight. How it will go off I can't imagine, but there always popular however bad. Some of our battalion 'artistes' are really marvellously good, so I hope they get a good reception.

I went up to London last week, for the first time for weeks, in order to dine, see a play, & dance. This we did quite successfully, until it was time for me to leave at 1.30, & motor back here in a car which 3 of us had hired, I had to hang about in an empty room at the Lansdowne till 3 am; we then set off in the car, & after an hour we had just gone about 5 miles – the fog was a blanket. That was 4 am. We turned back to catch a train from Waterloo – & at once had a puncture. There was no jack, & the chauffeur had to get out, find a 'phone' ring up his pal in Berkeley Square – he then arrived at 5 am, & we piled into his awful little bus. We just caught the 5.27 had a [missing material] …

2.15–4.30, had a night march from 5.30–7 & a rehearsal from 8–9.30, I then went to bed!! A nice restful way of spending an evening!

I take it you are still due to spend Christmas at Holkham – alas I don't get to Norfolk till the Thursday after; but I shall be there for over a week, & shall hope to see you more than somewhat.

Already our stay at Ringstead seems years ago, so you must come again and refresh my memory, if you will.

You might also nominate a Christmas present for yourself – so don't be bashful – I might easily take you at your word if you say "Really, I don't want anything, really"!!

Also, & this is most important, do let me know if & when you are returning from the North to London, & we'll meet. In any case, hurry back South; I am longing to see you again.

All my love (& a word of encouragement to Ginger)
from Tom

* * *

18a St James's Place,
S.W.1. Jan 28

My dearest Poppet,

Thank you so much for your letter; it was grand to hear from you again, that you'd enjoyed your Grand Tour. I was miserable at missing our party in London, and as I now have reason to believe that my days in this country are limited I am wondering how long I shall have to wait! Still, the canteen news sounds excellent, & perhaps London will soon see you again in its midst.

As you see from the address, I have left Pirbright, for good (for better, for worse!); this is my Grandmother's house, as she is 'evaporated' to the country, Mother and I have commandeered it from yesterday until further notice. In fact, if you want a depot from which to work at your canteen, you have but to say the word & the doors will be opened; even if I'm not here you & Mother can hold the fort.

Have had a hectic time since I last saw you: bitterly cold weather, & four times as much work to do, for there are so many officers 'in bed'. Had two days in bed myself after first inoculation last weekend, and all this week, have had a stinking cold, and the sorest throat I have ever known. Both are gradually going, but not as quick as I should like.

To my horror, Mother told me that she had offered you one of my newly hatched photographs – & I gather that your self-restraint and good manners prevented you from refusing with the eagerness and warmth which you no doubt felt – and so all I can do is to send you one. I won't, in days to come, be indiscreet enough to ask you what you did with it, and if it is picked up on the beach, or adorned with a calendar, & given to the village nurse, I shall not protest!!

Must stop now, & listen to Beethoven concert on wireless.

All my love and abject apologies for this 'worse than leaflet'
From Tom

The Goring Hotel
Belgravia
London SW1
12.2.40

Sweetheart,

I must write to you not only to thank you for our very happy week together, but also to get off my mind some of the many things I want to tell you. As you know I am a very reticent person at times, but as a rule I can express myself more surely on paper, so here goes. I write in all humility, and in great gratitude because I do feel that each of us looks on the other in the same way. So if I say anything the least bit presumptuous, don't be offended, will you?

My greatest trouble is that I am frightened – not of you but of myself. Being somewhat over introspective I keep wondering if it can be true that you and I are destined to love each other always, for we are both young and there is so much ahead of us. It is partly that, and partly the increased uncertainty of war which makes me so timid and hesitant. As I say, I am frightened of myself, for I know my weaknesses, & above all I hate appearing to be sincere about anything. I love being flippant!! So I have been thinking it over, and I am going to suggest, again in all humility that we adopt an alliance used by Kuniang and King Cophatina in the Daniel Vare* books. I shall buy some little object, break it and send you one half – as a pledge of our affection. Then, in time to come, if either of us seems to be drawn to someone else, (I really can't express what I mean!) then he (or she) can post the half of the pledge to the other one, as a sign for a meeting to talk things over. It sounds futile and sentimental, but it so to speak gives each other an option on the other!! That is why I spoke of humility; because your consent even to this little personal plan

---

*   Daniel Vare was an Italian diplomat and writer.

would be a tribute and an honour which I would always treasure, whatever our fate.

So, carissima mia, there is my plan: if you don't like it, do say so at once; if you do, then I will set about finding a suitable, quite cheap, possibly farcical, pledge.

I may yet funk posting this, but if I take the plunge, it will bring with it all my love
from Tom
P.S. This is, I think you will agree, strictly 'entre nous'.

* * *

The Goring Hotel
Belgravia
London SW1
16 [February or March?]

Darling,
Have been frantically busy & haven't yet had time to find anything suitable, but perhaps I shall later today. Was on guard Tuesday to Thursday, & enjoyed it all, except for the Dismounting which we did too futilely – in fact so badly that we laughed ourselves silly. To add to the upheaval we have been sent on Embarkation leave for 3 days, & the rush of getting the Company away as soon as we came off Guard was overwhelming. Added to that I had to compere a concert in the evening, & that had to be released at v. short notice. Reggie Forsythe played the Piano, & a Finnish blonde, v. glamorous, sang very sweetly. Later on we all dined at the Embassy, & the 'glamour' & I whirled round the floor like a Catherine Wheel. If I am on Guard next week (vaccination permitting), you must come & lunch, & I'll get Finlandia to come & croon to you as you drink your vodka.

No more now: in great haste. Am off to Woking for the weekend, & will be back on Monday. Mother has had flu but is much better, tho' still taking things easy.

All my love, Poppet
from Tom

* * *

1ˢᵗ Bn Scots Guards
27.3.40

My own Darling,
As you see, have arrived safely after the most ghastly journey – very long & stuffy, & of course for my sins, there was a howling baby in the compartment whose bottle was almost entirely emptied over my leg, & whose parents thought the best way of keeping it quiet was to wrap it up in a newspaper & let it fight its way out. The result of this devilish scheme was a cacophony of sound so shrill and rasping that my eardrums were slowly and mercilessly pounded to pulp. I would rather cross the Styx than face that awful trip again.

What heaven it has been together in London & at Ringstead. You seem to put up with all my tiresome eccentricities so sweetly that I just sit back in a 'bath' of delight and contentment – very selfish but extremely pleasant!

I hope Holkham is proving a congenial atmosphere, & that you've had some sailing.

No more now.
But all my love, sweetest poppet
from your Tom

Lord and Lady Leicester at Holkham during the war, with their granddaughters Anne Coke (Glenconner) and Carey Coke (Basset).

Norway

1940

Somewhere
Somewhere
NORWAY
14.4.40

My most precious Poppet
You must have been through a hell of disquiet and anxiety, hearing
no word from me for so long. But at last I am able to write and
say that I am in the best of health. I know you will realise that
I must tell you nothing – and so this letter will probably puzzle
you more than ever!! Are you still at Sowley or have you taken
up residence with Lavinia? Be sure and let me know as soon as
possible, and also tell me if anything has materialised about the
cooking lessons etc!! I can picture you with a cookery book in one
hand and a ladle in the other, stirring like mad, getting crosser
and crosser and greasier and greasier. Do try and do something
about it, as I know you will do it awfully well in no time.

   Darling, this must of necessity be a short and hopeless letter –
but later on I shall be able to say more. For now, this must be all.
But it brings with it a thousand hugs and kisses,

from your safe and sound ever-loving
Tom

* * *

Somewhere
Somewhere
NORWAY
20.4.40

My Darling of darlings
Again a line to tell you that I am still flourishing, and in the
best of spirits. We have still to be completely hush-hush about
everything, but I suppose it is inevitable though it makes letter

writing very difficult. All I can say, and that sounds trite and common place, is how much I long to be back with you to start our life and happiness together. The anticipation of all this being over and of our being able to settle down forever and forever is so thrilling that I can put up with almost anything for the moment.

In actual fact, life is not very hectic, but seems likely to become so for me as I have just been made Battalion Intelligence Officer …..only temporary I think, but might be fun. It seems rather a lot of work, but that said isn't altogether unwelcome.

My sweet Darling, I am going to stop now – I know its rather a horrid short letter ill written etc – but I gather the post leaves tonight, so I must catch it.

Meanwhile, until I write again, we shall communicate only in our imaginations – but as your pretty face appears in my inward eye, I find there, as the poet did, the bliss of solitude.

God bless you, sweetest Heart
from your loving Tom

* * *

As Usual
Norway
22.4.40

My most beloved and sweetest heart
For the first time I am going to force into the background the by now dull and obvious fact that I am still alive, and instead tell you a little news – tho' only a little!

I can't tell you where I am but only that it is the most wonderful scenery, all covered in a flaky blanket of snow. In the sun and blue sky it really looks too lovely. We have all been given a pair of skis for the duration, and this afternoon I am going to make my first venture on them – the most difficult and dangerous task I'm ever likely to have to face!

As for the journey here it was perfect. I can't tell you exactly where or how we came but we were most powerfully escorted by the Navy, and all together steaming through the sea, we looked a formidable array. On board our ship it was very peaceful basking in the sun, listening to the wireless but of course without any papers or crosswords. I haven't seen either since we left. We played a lot of bridge, at which I lost steadily and we also had a couple of ship's concerts organised by Jack Sanderson [?] and compered by yours truly. The tunes were really awfully good, considering they were unrehearsed and the variety of styles and regiments of the "artists" seem to be unending. I ran a little short of stories eventually, but luckily we had no time for a third concert before arriving.

I must say some of the other officers on the boat were a rum lot – whenever one went, one tripped over bundles of dropped aitches, and after 2 or 3 days of this company, one heard oneself saying, malgre soi, "What's your poison, old boy" when offering someone a drink. Still we got a lot of amusement and everybody is still in very good heart.

You've no idea how we're longing for news of home – it seems already ages and ages since we were in England and no sign of a paper or a letter yet. Still they'll be all the more welcome when they do arrive.

I shall be thrilled to see your handwriting again and to hear all you have to tell me. Darling, I do hope you really are keeping well and happy, seeing lots of friends, laughing and "swinging" as usual. For that is how I see you and that is the substance of the shadow which inspires me.

God bless you, Angel – Poppet
From your madly adoring
Tom

* * *

TCH and
Lionel
Massey

'Song for the Mess'
Norway, 1940

I've got Arctic circles under my eyes,
And the cold is making me blue.
But the sun comes out and warms my heart.
When I think of you.

The snow-clad mountains and the icebound fjords.
Make some at home seem untrue;
But I see the daffodils and smell the roses
When I think of You.
Buckingham Palace
Has Aurora Borealis
Beaten to a Frazzle.
And a crowd of gapers
At Norwegian papers.
Would make me give a fiver for a peep at Razzle.

Yes, I've got Arctic circles under my eyes,
And the cold is making me blue,
But the sun comes out and warms my heart
When I think of You.

The NAAFI can carry
The Café de Paris.
For only about two rounds.
And tho' it seemed silly.
The roar of Piccadilly.
Would be the most welcome and the best of sounds.
Yes, I've got Arctic circles under my eyes,
But I'm not by any means through,
For I'm inspired to grin and bear it,
When I think of You – my darling,
When I think of you.

Thomas C. Harvey, Scots Guards, Norway, 1940

* * *

2/LT. T.C. Harvey
First Bn Scots Guards
C/o Army Post office
April 28th

My most adorable
It is indeed a cruel fate which denies us even the consolation of each others letters and I feel sure that until one of my letters arrived you must have had a hellish time. But all is well, darling, and I can assure you that things are very very much better than I should ever have thought possible!!

I suppose it is useless to launch a tirade against the Army Post Office but you'd have thought that by now we should have received a post from England – however nothing of the kind has yet appeared and who know when it will?

Have a rather dry mouth and thick head this morning (Sunday) for last night several of us went to dine with the Navy and of course indulge very freely in their supplies of liquor. After dinner we had a film which inevitably had to stop because the machine broke down – after about ten minutes roaring like a siren.

Still it was an amusing change and very nice to invite us. This morning we had an outdoor service, under a bright blue sky and hot sun with aisles and pews of frozen glistening snow. It is always my fate on such occasions to get the giggles and the noise of the singing, and the snow falling off the roof and just missing the padre made me weak not so much with laughing as with the effort of suppressing it.

However I got through without loosing my name and enjoyed it. Our padre is a splendid person, very Scotch and most amusing – very tolerant of the somewhat un-churchly things said in the Mess. He has an excellent sense of humour and is a master at the three card trick. He's a great addition to the party.

I wrote a line to your grandfather just to tell him what little I could about his old Battalion. I hope he could read my writing; I must write to some other cronies and as there is a post leaving here after lunch I think I need to stop now.

So my very own and sweet girl, goodbye till my next letter. Give my love to all, like Tommy and Eliza when you see them, but be sure to keep almost all the love there is in this letter for yourself.

Bless you, my Darling.

from your Tom

* * *

Somewhere
somewhere
Bank Holiday

My most beloved darling,
I shudder to think how long it is since I last wrote to you, certainly it must be a fortnight and it feels like an age, for when I am writing to you I feel that we are together, talking and laughing and this delay in writing makes me feel as tho' I haven't seen you during all that time.

The trouble started as I say about a fortnight ago when some of us were whisked off at midnight on a destroyer for a dash of about 150 miles – into the very wilds of uncivilization; and here we still are uncomfortable in the extreme, ceaselessly on the alert but hitherto undisturbed.

The worst feature however of our isolation is that we've got no hope of getting your letters or of posting our own. None of us have yet heard a word from England since we left – but I have just seen a chance of getting this over to you in the near future and so we are all busily writing to make up for lost time. Alas, it may never reach you, but if it does, Darling, it brings with it a double ration of kisses and love, from your boy who for all his enforced silence, is thinking of you and praying for you and loving you all the time.

As for news, of course as usual I can tell you nothing; but in the late evening we can get the BBC News and hear the graphic start of the Blitzkrieg and its attendant excitements. What a time all of you at home must have been having, with the hopes and worries, the indignations and disappointments splashed in headlines over the papers. At least we've been spared all that.

One result of this sort of life we are leading is that I am getting quite acquainted with the arts (tho' here somewhat primitive) of the kitchen. I know exactly how long I like my eggs to be boiled and how to cook elementary dishes. It would indeed be an irony if, after this war, you were to emerge a hardened veteran of the Blitzkrieg and I, a qualified housewife!!

Have just had to suffer an interruption for about 3 hours, in order to take down in writing a summary of evidence in a legal case. A rather tricky business, particularly as we had to use an interpreter and everything had to be gone over several times. I find I am making no progress with the language, and would rather like a lesson book if you could get me one – but as long as one talks English as if one had no roof to ones mouth it equals in effect the most rhythmic and fluent Norwegian of any Ibsen.

Oh, how I am longing to hear all your news of the family, friends, any concerts you've been to, all those hundred and one little things which make up your daily life. I wish I could tell you more about myself – but at the same time I'm delighted that there isn't really much to tell. So I shall stop now as I must write a line to a few others in the hope of getting them to England somehow.

So my sweetest heart, goodbye for the moment and here's all my deepest and fondest love.

From your adoring boy
Tom

* * *

2/Lt T.C. Harvey
1st Bn Scots Guard
NWEF
May 27th

My own sweet Darling,
At last I can again write after a long and tedious interval. We have just had a week or so rather exhausting and futile activities and we returned to rest, and were greeted by the mail. My God, it was grand to get your lovely letters, photographs and cigarettes. Thank you so much and what cheered me up as much as anything

was to hear that some of my letters had succeeded in arriving. I hope this one does the same only about ten times as quick!

What a little Hun to go & get German Measles – I trust you were properly ashamed of yourself. Still, it was bad luck missing the week-end at Windsor, which should have been great fun. Perhaps by now it has taken place. I've heard from Mother, John and Anne by the same post as yours came by, and all sound very well, tho' poor old John sounds just a wee bit depressed by things. It wouldn't do him any good to come out here for all the one-horsed campaigns that have ever been fought this takes the toffee-apple. If David* did come out here he'd be given a terrific welcome, for we haven't seen a single one of his kind since we've been here. And you may imagine what that has meant. The whole thing here is just a bloody farce, and that's that!!

I am so glad Mother has been down to Sowley. I'm sure she loved it, as it must be perfect now that the summer is beginning. Here, too, it is perfectly heavenly and quite scorching during the day tho' at night we've lately found it a bit cold sleeping out. It must have been disappointing not to go to Lavinia's, but I do so sympathise with you over the expense, as the mere fact of being in London automatically sends up one's overdraft, even if one's staying at Buck house.

I gather from Mother that the Massey's convalescent home hadn't started when she last wrote, but now I imagine everything is different seeing that the war on the Western Front has began. Out here we have heard no news of it at all, except occasional rumours of more or less terrifying proportions. I fear the whole thing will be on a gigantic scale and must cause endless suffering, for no purpose. It's going to be a hell of a job straightening things out afterwards, but those of us who survive will have at least the incentive to try, for the incentive to make money will be success- fully stifled by the government!!

I suppose by now Anne is all set for the big event and the house

---

*   Flight Lt David Coke DFC, brother to Mary and pilot in the RAF.

littered with shapeless woollen comforts of negligible size. Poor girl! What a time for a first-born.

Well my Darling, I must be stopping now. You can't tell how thrilled and happy it made me to get your news and photographs, as it were, to be back with you again, hearing your laughter and seeing your twinkling eyes. And until I see them in person, here's all my fondest love; mind you have lots of fun and give my love to your Mother and Father and all our cronies.

God bless you my darling and bring us together soon.

from your adoring

Tom

* * *

2/Lt T.C. Harvey
First Bn Scots Guards
N.W.E.F.
2 June

My Darlingest
Another lovely bunch of letters & your parcel have reached me and brought with them a tremendous sense of happiness and joy. Your letters were perfect, just as I hoped they would be, cheerful, amusing, interesting and may I add, not unaffectionate!! Bless you a thousand times for them. As you will have gathered from my earlier letter – though in the same envelope – we were rather exhausted from our visit to the front and I don't think it's a secret to tell you that we fought a rear guard action on foot for nearly 100 miles. Now we are well back and I hope quite safe, eating decent food and actually sleeping in a bed! The way this campaign out here is being run gives the foot soldier a thankless and unin-spiring job, and I know we will all of us have some sharp words to say about it when we get home. Meanwhile all our thoughts and prayers are with you in France and England so close to that

vast unrelenting clouds sweeping over Western Europe, like a devouring host of ironclad, gigantic locusts. If the cause of Right can still mean anything, if justice and freedom can balance the welter of efficiently mobilised evil against which we are battering, then we must wish – and pray God it will be soon.

What fun you must have had with Sylvia* – I do so agree with you about that district; it sounds ideal, very incidentally the presence of the Red Barn will mean that we won't have to trek off to London every time we want a jam session. If I get home at all, we must have a week-end with Sylvia, and see what we can find. I heard from Mother who told me how much she was loving Sowley. Some talk I gather of you're both going to E.T. a splendid idea, which I hope can materialise tho' as you say it is impossible to make plans.

It really is most noble of your father to join the parashooters – half mooning† will at last come into its own. Personally I think the menace is somewhat overrated and the proportion of survivors very small, so long as precautions are made, and opposition can be on the spot quick enough. Three men on the spot with shotguns are worth a battalion half an hour later.

I'm glad David is in such a fine squadron – no more than what he deserves, but all the same very pleasant for him. Do give him my love when you next see him and say that a few of his Kill and Kiss out here would transform our life here. Perhaps by the time you get this you will have heard rumours of the Battalion – do let me know anything you hear as I shall want to compare it with what I know.

Well, my sweetestheart, I must write to John and Anne and to Mother, so I will stop now. Your letters, as I say, have been a real

---

*   Sylvia Combe: Mary's elder sister.
†   A rather dangerous, old-fashioned form of shooting.

inspiration to me and I thank you for them from the bottom of my heart.

Herewith all my deepest love, Darling Girl, from your ever adoring
Tom

P.S. I hope Totti [?] impressed you: now you should know the type to keep out of the house when we're married. Give her my love if you haven't already scratched her eyes out!!!

BACK IN BRITAIN
1940–1941

6.7.40
Homewood South Eden Park Road
Beckenham

Dearest Lady Coke,
How you and Lord Coke have allowed me to take Mary from
you I can't imagine – and my gratitude to you is as great and
inexplicable as my resolve to be worthy of her. She has I already
know, the sweetest and kindest nature in the world, and if only
I live up to her we shall have the most perfect life together. Alas!
That it should start in a hotel, and with the Damoclean sword
of invasion hanging over our foreheads – but surely all the more
reason and inspiration for courage and idealism.
   You, by allowing us to marry and by your unfailing kindness

and encouragement have given us both, and I promise we shall not betray your trust.

I feel most strongly and I am sure you will agree, that this country needs both individually and collectively to re-assume that it is and is worthy to be, both feared and respected. At the moment we are neither and look at the mess it has got us into. It is people like Mary and myself whose job it will be to share in that "renaissance" and it is you and Lord Coke whom we must thank for giving us the chance to make a home dedicated to a worthier England.

I hope this doesn't sound too pompous: I know it's what I feel, tho' heaven forbid that I should have to say it out loud!!

Again my fondest love
from
Tom

1ˢᵗ Bn Scots Guards
9.9.40*

My most precious Darling,
I do hope you arrived at Offley safely and without incident, after
the last hectic & horrid hours of Saturday & Sunday. Miserable
tho' I am at losing you for the time being, & furious with Hitler
for upsetting that glorious happiness of our midget flat, I can't
help feeling certain that for the moment this is not the place
for you – & the sweet way in which you agreed to go did make
our parting so much easier. Here the same aerial activity at night
continues to increase, & there is no doubt that it is better for me
to be on the spot in barracks.

You will be most grieved to hear that C/pl Boulton was killed
in London during Saturday's Air Raid. Such a charming and
splendid man, as we can ill spare – & such a waste too, as he
would have been a fine man in action.

Precautions have been relaxed here a little and I hope to get to
David's wedding this afternoon – advanced from Wednesday.

Well, my Darling, if it happens that the next week or so are
increasingly unpleasant, then even if we can't see it through
together, we can each of us so bear ourselves that, tho' apart, our
thoughts can meet in our imagination, and keep us both going.

Maybe I shall see you this week, maybe not; in any case we are
not going to let a little thing like being away from each other for
a short time, get us down, when whether we like it or not, we are
living 'in the breach of history', & seeing the fate of our world
being fought out above & around our heads. Thank God, you're
the sort of person who can see that: I love you more & more &
terribly terribly proud of you.

So God bless you, sweetest heart, and bring us together again
soon
from your Tom

---

*   TCH & Mary married in July 1940.

1st Bt Scots Guards
10.9.40

My Perfect Poppet,
I was so glad to get your telegram, saying you had arrived safely.
I trust your sudden appearance didn't cause too much chaos in
Chateau Pilkington. Give them all my love, & tell them how
grateful I am for their hospitality.

David's wedding was delightful & I thought that Patsie was
the sweetest little person, full of charm & immensely plucky. I
think it is a splendid plan she & David getting married, as they're
old friends and he will be able to replace, to a certain extent, the
happiness she lost so suddenly.

Again a somewhat sleepless night, but everyone in great form. I
got a letter from the agents to say that the Simms now want their
furniture, & so it looks as tho' the flat is gone. Luckily that isn't as
inconvenient as it might be; & as soon as this bit of trouble blows
over we can go somewhere else. I will pack up all your things &
keep them here until you tell me what you would like done to
them. It's a bore in a way, & if you don't want the stuff I could no
doubt arrange to leave it in the flat for a bit longer. In any case,
don't you bother to come up here & see about it as travelling is so
uncertain & I can cope with it all. Tonight I shall probably try to
ring you up, but even if I can't this will arrive – bringing with it
all my love and a million kisses, Darling,

from Tom

* * *

1st Bn Scots Guards
15.9.40

My own sweet Darling,
I trust you have arrived safely at Holkham, & find Grandpapa in

good order. As you know, ¼ of an hour after you left King's X the warning went, but even by then I was back in barracks, & the raid passed without incident. Since then we've had the usual alarms but no bombs anywhere near, tho' the whistling has lowered our heads on more than one occasion! This morning, in the trenches, we saw two parachutists coming down, who turned out to be Germans. One had his leg broken & was taken to hospital but the other was practically alright, & was brought to Barracks. He was a funny little chap, very subdued & polite, & very grateful to the Doctor for patching him up. So for him the war is over, altho' just before he left the sirens went again, so he isn't quite out of it yet!

Very little of interest has happened since I saw you. Boy[*] went up to London & had a frightful hangover next morning, after crawling round all the smartest air raid shelters in Mayfair. David, in desperation at not being able to get in touch with Patsy sent off a district message but within an hour she rang up, & all the effort had been wasted.

Have been busy playing backgammon with Hugh Rose, & have lost 5/-, altho' to start with I was 11/- up. In the middle, who should appear but Joe Airlie,[†] from the Tower. He seemed in very good form, & sent you all his love: he stayed and had a cup of tea but was expecting Jean[‡] to tea at the Tower & so had to hurry back. I gather that Margaret[§] has been packed off home: she hadn't really got a proper job, & was somewhat shattered by a bomb which fell only about 2 houses away.

Joe told me that Philip Blythedale has been killed & George Townshend seriously hurt in a motor smash somewhere: what a waste & a pity!!, except for the Mirror who can blare out some gruesome headline such as 'Two Guards Peers in fatal car crash'!

Well, my Darling, no more for the present. I do hope this gets

---

[*]   F. H. H. B. Harris.
[†]   David Ogilvie, 12th Earl of Airlie, known as Joe.
[‡]   Jean, eldest daughter of Joe Airlie.
[§]   Margaret (or Maggot or Maggie), 2nd daughter of Joe Airlie.

to you alright, with the least possible delay. In any case, it will keep my love & kisses as warm as in a thermos, so when the envelope is opened they'll come bubbling up to your lips.

God bless you, Maria from your Tom

* * *

1ˢᵗ Bn Scots Guards, 19/9/40

My Darling Maria

I do hope my letters are arriving safely: I had a lovely one from you just now, & delighted Norfolk is more or less up to Standard. I am glad you went over to see Mother & found her with plenty to do: the cocktail party sounded the greatest fun. I must say, miserable tho' I am at you being away from me, it really isn't very pleasant here, & it's worse in London. Not that so far the Barracks have been hit or anything of that kind, but it's tremendously noisy at night & already today we've had six warnings.

However the night before last I braved the metropolis & with Hugh Rose & Derek Hague, went to dine at the Dorchester, where we co-opted Jean Ogilvie, Peggy Clarke & a 'glamour' of Derek's: Jean & Niall Rankin appeared & also Boy, who got rather tight!!

It was great fun, & tho' the bombs were falling all round & we couldn't leave, we kept vastly amused. At one stage I played the Novachord, which was heaven, but they soon switched it off!! What fun it would have been if we're there together: as there were lots of laughs, & some of the old trouts sleeping in the foyer were worth a dozen in the Queen's Hotel. 'Potter' was also there, in very good form, tho' he's just had his jaw operated on, & is beginning a week's sick leave.

Yesterday evening we had a terrific game of squash – 4 of us – & all got frightfully hot & excited. I found I played better than expected, tho' far, far from the class of Tommy Bulkeley. The

All-Clear has just gone, so am off to pick up our things, which I may send to Holkham with a District Messenger. The Simms have taken their furniture away today – the bomb having gone off without damage.

So, Darling, until my next letter, here are all my kisses and love. As soon as it looks alright for you to come back or at any rate to meet in London, I will of course let you know. Pamela Vestey keeps appearing & causes Bill no little worry & anxiety. I can't tell you how grateful I am that you are wiser and more considerate.

God bless you, my very sweet Darling
from your loving Tom

* * *

1st Bn Scots Guards
21.9.40

My Darlingest Poppet,
Here I am, still safe & sound, unworried by 'whistlers' & not the least short of sleep. Your telegram arrived, & was duly answered tho' heaven knows when or ever, if my reply reached you.

Since I last wrote very little has happened, tho' I had the usual sleepless Picquet: it was made more tolerable by the fact we had a terrific bridge session in the Orderly Room, & I had a plate of sandwiches, a flask of whisky, a thermos of tea and a pile of novels to keep me going. Nothing exciting occurred, but as the All Clear didn't go till 5.45 I didn't get much sleep.

Last night we played some feeble tennis, & my usual brilliant play was not in evidence, tho' I was still, of course, outstanding.

The flat is now cleared out, & I have all your luggage here: tomorrow I will make a big effort to re-pack it all, and send it to Norfolk. The bomb is still sitting there, no doubt a dud: the wretched furniture remover pinched your wireless, & a bottle of whisky but the agent must repay us for that, & won't get paid until he does.

Have you written to Child's yet about opening an account, or are you going to leave it for the moment – let me know as I want to pay in some mun to your bank, whichever it is. I think it will be better to pay you what I would if there were housekeeping expenses, although you needn't spend it all!!

I hope Holkham isn't being too deadly, & that the family is in good form. By now you will know David's fate: I do hope he is back with you, shooting with one 12 bore instead of 8 machine guns. The smell of leave is being distantly wafted towards us again, but heaven knows whether it will ever get here. If ever we can get thro' on the telephone we can discuss it if there seems to be a chance. I try to get through, but it seems quite impossible.

Well, my love, no more now, keep happy and brave, & may God bless you from your Tom

* * *

1ˢᵗ Bn Scots Guards, 24.9.40

My Darling Poppet,
Thank you so much for your lovely cheerful letter. You will be thrilled to hear that various 'flaps' etc. are for the moment off, and I hope to get some leave sometime in October.

The new situation now that Ringstead is going to be let will need a little consideration, but we'll fix things up somehow.

My God, how I long to see you again, to laugh & love together: not that I would dream of wanting you here, where the nights grow longer and noisier, & where the sirens sound at least ½ a dozen times a day!! Still for all the roar and cacophony we are unmoved, & usually get a game of tennis in the evening. I never go to London now, but may have to go soon to get my hair cut etc – but the business of getting back, through the barrage & diversion, is to say the least tiresome.

Tim,* at the moment, is in bed, with a septic gland in his neck & is not at all well – he will probably have to have a minor operation. He's been very glum the last day or two, & has only just surrendered to the relaxation of his bed.

Darling, I must stop now & write to Mama: have had a most successful motor-bike ride & am quite an expert!!

Herewith a mass of hugs and kisses, sweetest heart, & won't I multiply them when I see you!!

Your adoring Tom

* * *

1ˢᵗ Bn Scots Guards
29.9.40

My Darlingest Poppet,
Thank you so much for your letters, which arrive with clockwork

---

*   Lieutenant Tim Mostyn.

Tommy and
Eliza Clyde

precision, & are most cheerful and amusing. By now you may be on your way to Eliza,* & I only hope I will be able to get over there, tho' at the moment Boy is on leave & Tim in hospital, so Jack & I are stooges for the moment.

John & I are miserable at Mother's ridiculous plan to P.G. with Phyllis – its' all part of her tiresome & stubborn idea that 'nobody wants her' heaven knows whether we can talk her out of it. If only she came to the Sunningdale – Ascot area, & possibly shared a little house with you there, we could see each other quite often, & I might even get a weekend from time to time. Do suggest it to her!

Yesterday, in a very cold wind, we played our last game of cricket, which we won, thanks to a sparkling century by George Mann. I was on Picquet on Friday & had a fairly quiet night – tho' the barrage is deafening from 8pm to 6am, every night, there is a constant shower of shrapnel & the usual whistlers.

Our tennis court was nearly cracked up on Thursday but the German again missed his mark and did no damage.

---

*   Eliza Wellesley daughter of the Duke of Wellington, married to Tommy Clyde (film producer) and very dearest friend of Mary. They both became godmothers to each other's first born: David (Harvey) and Jeremy Clyde (actor).

I spoke to John this morning on the telephone & he complained of a rather noisy night – I told him he ought to come here for a bit & get used to it!

He didn't seem any too certain where my guns were, & thought they might be in Windsor – in any case he is going to send them to Holkham, unless we can collect them from Eliza's.

How lovely it will be if we can see each other again this week: don't, darling, be disappointed if I can't make it, but I think I shall be able to, & will hire a car to come over & see you, as trains etc, are hopeless.

So, 'till then, Sweetest One herewith all my love and kisses
from Tom

David Coke and his brother Tommy

1ˢᵗ Bn Scots Guards
29.10.40 pm

My Darlingest Maria,
I am <u>so</u> sorry about Tuesday – I bogged it, for I was in London, & couldn't get hold of you to cancel my telegram. I have been in bed since Saturday evening with (?) – haha! – a chill – & as there was a Bn exercise all day today I thought it safer to put you off. I'm still not certain of a good day but will send you a wire – an impossibly difficult thing to do from here. Loved getting Tommy's* letter, & also heard from David† in great form & had a good shoot the other day.

Give my love to Eliza & Tommy. Am longing to see you again, Darling One, & will fix something just as soon as we can.

God Bless you,
from your loving Tom

* * *

1ˢᵗ Bn Scots Guards
1.1.41

My most Darling Girl
I do hope you have arrived safely after not too detestable journey – without damn my memory, a rug to keep you warm. As you no doubt discovered I had the most impossible time trying to get through to Holkham, & it was 3pm before I succeeded. I trust someone was there to welcome you.

I can't tell you, my Darling, how distressed I am that things are being so difficult, and the goal of a house of our own so desperately elusive – but I know that if we try hard enough and try not

---

*   Tommy and David Coke, Mary's brothers.
†   See above.

to care too much, then we're bound to get just what we want, and it'll be all the better for having had to struggle.

The day here has been very quiet and dull, everyone trying to recover from Hogmanay. I gather the party here was a terrific success, and the number of sore heads and disgruntled stomachs was legion. The Commanding Officer had the most appalling hang over and Boy has spent a large part of the day in bed – Sammy Stockton is definitely laid up, everyone else practically has taken the day off, with the result that the Mess looks more like the sitting room in a convalescent home at a Spa, than the hub of life of a first class fighting unit. However tomorrow we resume our normal duties, and I'm looking forward to a long night – no warning luckily.

Well, as we stand at the doorway of 1941, how can we tell what is the other side, waiting for us; possibly something so vast and malignant that even to contemplate it sends a shiver down our back. And yet, Darling, let us not have to face this as tho' it were directed solely against us, One menace alone, our particular tribulation. It is too great for that, and we could neither stand the stress nor face the fear by ourselves. Let us rather think of ourselves as a young pair, destined by fate, to take part in the most gigantic all enveloping tragedy in the world's history – in which individuals are both microscopic and yet all important. If we fail in courage, in resource or in resolve, we shall fail under the very eyes of History, and we shall fail for ever. Fate has staged a single performance of the Tragedy on a scale which Cecil de Mille multiplied by a million could not approach – and every single man or woman taking part must act perfectly – with no second chance – unless the whole production is to fail.

Even the most sacred personal feelings must be merged into this higher course – and it is my resolution that our love and the great whole that this four little letters mean for us both, that our love shall in 1941 be heightened and rededicated, purged, and purified by this fire of sacrifice and, perhaps, suffering. Be cheerful that so much might be required, for all, all is at stake, and the path of the brave is honourable.

God bless you, my Angel heart, and send you my love and kisses till we're together again.

From your adoring
Tom

* * *

SANDHURST 1941/2

We are the Officers of the OCTU
But we welcome everyone.
We hope our appearance hasn't shocked you,
We merely want to give you some fun.

Please don't think that we are barmy.
We merely want to make you laugh.
Try to forget all about the Army,
Pretend you've never heard of the Directing Staff.

Let PT stand for Perfect Torso.
PU for a Pair Undressed.
SAA for Sex appeal – and more so!
FE stands – well – for the rest!

Let CM stand for a Champagne Magnum,
BOR for the Bar of the Ritz.
CSM for Charlies with a sag in 'em,
MS stands for Military Shits!

But when we meet in the Halls of Study
Don't be flippant, coarse or rude.
Don't salute us with a "Hya Buddy",
Or you will be RTU'd!

Glossary of terms used above:
OCTU: Officer Cadet Training Unit.
PT: Physical Training.
PU: Pick-up truck.
SAA: Small Arms Ammunition.
FE: Field Engineering.
CM: Car Maintenance.
BOR = Battalion Orderly Room.
CSM: Company Sergeant Major.
MS: Military Secretary.
RTU: RETURN TO UNIT (Failed!)

Flight Lt David Coke DFC

Killed in action 9ᵗʰ December 1941

Flt. Lieut. D. A. COKE, R.A.F.V.R., 80 Sq. (since reported missing).

This officer participated in an attack on enemy transport on the El-Adem-Acroma road one day in November in which a large number of vehicles, tanks, and mechanized transport were bombed and machine-gunned. The damage inflicted played a very large part in the blocking of the road. By his skill and leadership Flt. Lieut. Coke contributed materially to the success achieved. In addition to the low flying machine-gunning operations which have been carried out, Flt. Lieut. Coke has led the squadron with great success in air combat. During an engagement two days later the squadron shared in the destruction of five Messerschmitt 109s.

FLIGHT LIEUT. THE HON. DAVID COKE

A correspondent writes:—

The death of Flight Lieutenant the Hon. David Coke, D.F.C., has caused bitter loss to his devoted family and to all his friends: from a rancher's camp in the middle west of America to a keeper's cottage in Scotland his loss will be felt, for to have known him was to have loved him. The memory of David, and for all he stood, his courage, his unselfishness, his valour, sportsmanship, and consideration to all men, will be a reward and an inspiration to all his friends. As a fighter pilot he joined the R.A.F. at the outbreak of war, and his career in the air was symbolic of his spirit. He was wounded in the Battle of Britain, and in February last year he went to the Middle East, where he fought in Greece and in Syria and finally in Libya, where he was awarded the D.F.C. His loss as a friend can never be replaced, but his memory will be an example of the very ideals for which we fight and shall uphold in the future. He gave his life as he would have lived, fearlessly, honourably, and nobly.

Eliza Clyde and her son Jeremy

Training Camp
1942–1943

4 S.G.
Royal School
Wanstead 25.2.42

My own sweet Darling,
It was lovely to hear your voice the other night, and to get your sweet letter. Yes, what a wonderful year we have had together, and though parting for the time being is a great and hard break to bear yet it throws into clear relief the happiness and fun and everything we've shared together. Now we must find our consolation elsewhere, I in my work, and you in looking after David. I only wish that I was as perfectly suited to being an Adjutant as you are to being the Mother of such a splendid boy. You really are the most wonderful, & natural Mother, & I can't say how much I love you for it. You're as good a Mother as you are a wife – I can't say or hope for higher than that.

I can see I am going to be very busy here, but most interesting and constructive work; furthermore my quarters (sleeping, not hind), are becoming increasingly comfortable & the gap between the comfort of Sandhurst & the austerity of Wanstead is being gradually and comparatively painlessly bridged. I like the Commanding Officer very much, somewhat serious-minded in office, but with a great twinkle out of it – & I feel sure we will get on splendidly together. At the moment Robin Whigham is still here & is most helpful & – he goes sometime on Friday, & then the full weight descends on me.

Corby* will appear today, a day late, but he has done well, & will be alright. No more news, now, my angel. I will write again soon. Meanwhile all my dearest love, and many many tremendous thanks for being such a darling, & making my life such a series of gloriously happy moments.

From your ever adoring Tom

---

*   Corby, his soldier servant.

R.S.W.

E 11

9th March 1942

My very sweet Darling,

What tremendous fun it was – lovely to see each other again. I hope you & Silvia got back alright, & none the worse for your activities. There's no news, so I won't write much, but as we're out from tomorrow till Wednesday & Saturday till Monday, I thought I'd write now just to say that I loved and enjoyed your birthday enormously. God bless you, my sweet, & may we spend as happy a time together soon.

From your adoring Tom

* * *

Royal School

Wanstead

24.3.42

My most Darling One,

I did so love getting down to see you last weekend, & was highly delighted to see David so well and flourishing. It was a real breath of fresh air, after the somehow dank atmosphere of separation at Wanstead.

I do so hope the move has gone off well – I am sure you were tired after all the hectic hours of packing and the fuss of the journey itself. Take it easy, all of you, for a day or two, & keep yourself and Susie* off the gin until you're quite OK again. It will be fun being with Sylvia, tho' none the less sad leaving Camberley with so many kind friends and happy memories. However all good things come to an end, as the actress said to the bishop.

---

*   Susie is the nanny.

No more now, my Darling. I will do my damnedest to get to the wedding on Saturday, & will bring Kuniang* who isn't really enjoying Wanstead & is getting dirtier and dirtier.

Bless you all, my Darlings, & my very deepest love from Tom

* * *

R.S.
W.
E.11.
8.4.42

My most precious Darling,

It was lovely getting down to see you last weekend – I think the cottage is too sweet, & I only hope we haven't crowded out Sylvia & Simon.† The male nit is certainly on top of the world, & I hope won't learn any nasty tricks from the female nit – or from his mother if it comes to that!

I had a very successful drive back – it was dark for an unpleasantly long time – but I never once got on the wrong road & was back in barracks at about 7.30. The car went very well, tho' I fear there isn't much petrol left. That night I went to Bn HQ & had a very good dinner, but got back rather late, so I was a bit short of sleep; but I made that up since!

I enclose a few railway vouchers which might be useful to you – particularly with all your illicit engagements in London and Brighton!

No more now: all my very dearest love to you & David & Susie – & to Sylvia who is so good to us.

From your ever adoring Tom

---

*   Kuniang is their Pekinese dog.
†   Simon and Sylvia (Mary's sister, sometimes written Silvia) Combe.

Marston
Bgd Comp
Near Frome
Somerset., 1.6.42

My own sweet Darling,

Thank you so much for your lovely letter; I fear this one is very late, but as you know we haven't exactly been very static since you left. We dashed off on this Exercise on Wednesday morning and we were at it until 6pm on Saturday: actually the Exercise itself was not particularly strenuous, tho' we didn't get much sleep & ate rather unpalatable food at rather odd intervals. Then we started moving off to this camp where we arrived at 3 in the morning – not the best time to reach a completely new home. However we settled down pretty well and had a good long lie in in the morning. Yesterday we continued fitting ourselves in, & today we are doing the same, and had a Commanding Officer's Parade this morning. The amount of work to be done in the near future is quite terrific, and I am pretty certain to have enough to keep me occupied.

Well done, David, to have learnt to say Da Da, those magic words which so delight his Father and make jealous his Mother!!

It shows a remarkably instinctive sense of discrimination, which will I hope, remain with him, and grow as he grows. Still, old girl, you'll get a look in one day, & I shall teach him at least to acknowledge your existence with a slight nod or a passing smile!

David Cuthbert joins the Bn on the 3, which will be great fun, also Bill Vestey. That sinister R.M.C. padre, Wilkinson, is in this Division – I saw him this morning. At all costs I must keep his saxophone out of the Camp!

Well, my Darling, thank you again & again for coming down all that way to see me: it was glorious to see you again, and to be together. Bless you both, and all my most devoted love

from your adoring Tom

Camp
4.6.42

My Sweetest heart,
A ton of thanks for your letter – how terrific David sounds, what a honey drop. No wonder his grandfather has fallen for him – I shall do the same myself a hundred fold when I get the chance. Give him a great big squeeze from me, & ask him not to forget me.

In great haste, so can't write much; but I believe I can get 48 hours leave soon, & I suggest spending it with Sylvia & Joscelyn* – I saw him today & that's OK. I might meet you in London, when I may have to go on duty, or else I'll fag you to camp – follow me here, I think it's better than stuffing in London.

So sit back & expect a wire, with luck – but don't count any unhatched hens!!

Herewith a load of love that makes the bombing of Essen look like a powder puff

from your adoring Tom

* * *

---

*   Hambro.

Camp
7.6.42

My own Darling,

Thank you so very very much for your letter, and all its cheerful news. I am so glad the weather is good with you: here it has been gloriously hot, a real heatwave, and a welcome change from the grim unceasing rain of Woolacombe. I've been very busy, but not unbearably so, and on Saturday p.m. I continued my work in shorts & a cotton shirt! We have attended a good many lectures and demonstrations – all of them having a somewhat Point-to-Point atmosphere, as there are so many friends to see. Unfortunately the petrol situation is bad, but this afternoon David Cuthbert & I cadged a lift off Tom Dundas and went to have tea with the Hambros. They are longing for you to come down, and are all ready to put us up: what I shall do is to take 48 hours leave when you're down here, & then to get over as much as I can. I shall be able to sleep out a good many nights, & can fag my stooge to do the early morning work. Jack & Rosie Hamilton also have a house quite near.

Bill Vestey arrived here this evening, and is, I think, looking forward to a pleasant change from the rather turgid waters of the 1st Bn. Luckily John Dalrymple is due to go and command it this week, which will be a welcome change and a long overdue improvement. I saw Hugo Waterhouse yesterday, who asked after you, but haven't yet seen Tommy, tho' hope to get hold of him during the next few days. I also saw Dick Westmacott, not looking very well, I thought; he tells me that he is learning to fly, for Army Cooperation. But there are still a lot of friends I haven't seen yet.

I'm so glad David is still flourishing so well, and enjoying the weather. He will become as brown as a berry. If you see Jack Leslie*

---

* Jack Leslie (and his wife Margot) was TCH's mother's first cousin, with their children Robin and Lavinia (Cholmondeley).

will you thank him for his letter – he sent me a press cutting in which he was described as the 'Norfolk archaeologist' – tell him from me that unless he pays up, I will send it to be pinned up on the bar at Whites.

I have a feeling that I may have to take my leave in August – I am not at all sure yet, but July has already got the reputation of being fairly busy, & I feel it will be better to get it over with & then relax. However, we'll see what your plans are, & how things are going.

No more now, Sweetest Heart. Herewith all my fondest love to you all at Holcombe. From your adoring Tom

* * *

Hell
17.6.42

My very own Darling,
I feel most ashamed at not having written to you before, but the conditions of discomfort are so unattractive that my weak and failing willpower has never yet enabled me to sit down on a wet chair, and write with a rusty nib a letter which I can't see, & the pages of which are blown across the dripping tent by gusts of rainsoaked wind.

Well, the journey down here was not too bad: Boy & I shared a first class carriage, & aided by cups of tea, & whisky & the wireless, we spent quite a good night. We were due to arrive at 5 am but luckily the train was late, & so it was light when we got in. The weather was still more or less OK, but once we were settled in the wind & rain started with a vengeance, and made life very difficult. We were due to do a Brigade scheme, but that had to be put off. However the next day it was better, and we did a 24 hr exercise until mid day yesterday, when we returned tired but none the worse for wear. The night before the exercise I dined (with Robert) with Tom Dundas at Bde HQ & had a very good evening. We have booked different rooms since I wired to you – Gerald Micklem's mother lives about 2 miles from here, & Victor & I went to have a bath there this evening (the first since last Friday for me!!) – She told us of a better place & so it's all fixed.

I am so longing to see you again – I am praying that I can get away a rather extra amount without completing losing my name – & the fact that you're going to Norfolk for about 2 months makes my claims even more worthy. I am however quite certain that the Commanding Officer, who is the soul of generosity, will be only too delighted.

Mrs Micklem is divine – a great fat Greek, who looks & talks exactly like Gerald & is frightfully tough. With her lives the most fantastic woman called Auntie – who swears like a trouper, drinks like a fish, smokes like a train & wears men's clothes – grey pin striped trousers with a seat baggy enough to stable an ox in. They're a heavenly pair!! The house is too awful, with painted knick knacks etc – and lumpy decorated fire-shields, but the two old trouts are very kind hearted, & worth a laugh a minute.

Tomorrow we are off into the blue for four days – quite what it will be like I can't think – great fun if fine, & unutterably bloody if wet.

However, Heigh ho till Thursday, & give David a tremendous hug from his father

from your ever loving Tom

* * *

M.B.C.
25.6.42

My most precious Darling,
A hurried line before I dash to bed to thank you a thousand thousand times for coming down here to see your tattered husband, and for making him think more & more every time he sees you, what a clever fellow he was to catch you! I adored, (more than that, only I haven't time to think of the word) every second of the time – which, in its beastly, jealous way, insisted on going twice as fast as usual. It's wonderful, isn't it, that not even the smell of weak old beer, not even the hiccups of sodden officers, no, not even the angry crush of crowds battering on our privacy and buttressing our privy, can drown the singing of our hearts when we're together.

Bless you, my most angelest sweet, and a tremendous jug for
David from your fatuously infatuated (flatulent)
Tom

* * *

Camp
30.6.42

My own precious Darling,
Thank you so very much for your lovely letter – I hear you were a great success & spoke beautifully capturing all hearts. Well done, I knew you would.

Very little news – my chief object is to bring you all my love on our second anniversary – a date I can never forget for it marks a beginning of such happiness as few can be lucky enough to have. Herewith all my fondest love to you – a little token will arrive with me on my leave, but the arcades of Frome have not yet tempted my purse!

Dashed over to see Silvia & Robin* yesterday after dinner, & also went on Sunday evening to see first & third Bn cricket match & dinner in evening. Great fun, but lost way on way back & I didn't get to bed 'till 2.15!! Work getting worse & worse & off on a 'stunt' on Thursday. However lovely weather. Many thanks for forage cap – it arrived safely & fits v well.

Give John & Anne my love – I expect to see him after his leave. Very worried about 2nd Bn, last heard of in Tobruk – fear very heavy casualties. What bad news from there.

I fear this is very disjointed & written in great haste. But my Love, it brings you my deepest thanks for our glorious two years together, for David & all he means to us, & for your unceasing love & gentleness to both him & me. Bless you a thousand times from your ever adoring Tom

* * *

M.B. Camp
5.7.42

My Darlingest Maria,

Thank you so much for your letter. I am so glad David is flourishing, & enjoying himself. I am not the least surprised to hear that Nanny & Florrie got on well together: two such gems could hardly fail to.

We have been on a 2 day Exercise, & got back at about 6.30 pm yesterday. Unfortunately it poured with rain most of the time, so we got rather cold and miserable. There was no question of sleeping or indeed of getting dry, and as the whole thing was in any case rather chaotic, no one was very sorry when it ended. We have another one on Tuesday, and then a pause until 20th.

My spies tell me that you lost your name badly for not answering the invitation to the Chobham party! I made what excuses I

---

*   Robin Muir and his sister Silvia Hambro.

could for you, & luckily they all realise that even my good influence and constant supervision over you, is not yet able to neutralise the inborn tendencies of your humble & vicious origins. I had all their sympathy – but naturally it was most vexing & humiliating to me!

Andy & Bridget went to the party & Brody pinched all the strawberries and ices which had been left for the Nelsons in gratitude for lending their house!! A & B both delighted & ate them all.

It really is insufferable! Robert is speechless. 'Louis' King is coming here today for a bit, & we'll be chasing him around. I hear he's been rather naughty at the 3rd Bn & so I shall have to bash him if he persists!! Who knows – I may be given a Chinese Army to command!! I saw Robin Muir for a second on Monday – he sent lots of love. Silvia & Jocelyn now on sick leave & so I can't have a bath for a month. Love, love & love again from Tom

* * *

M.B.C.
Nr F
S
15.7.42

My Angel One,
Well, it was fun, wasn't it – rather a flying visit, I fear, but still a lovely surprise, & all the better for being so sudden. I was so sorry you felt so miserable at the dance, & I must say the heat didn't suit me either – but after the constant open air in which I am compelled to live, the basement of a London hotel is bound to seem a little stuffy.

I had a v. good journey back & shared Tommy's taxi, bringing it on here afterwards. We had a fairly quiet day on Monday – a long conference on Tuesday am & off on a night scheme last night, getting back at about 10 am today. I haven't been to bed yet (3pm) & feel flourishing. Victor and I were off to bath with Sylvia after tea, but I gather Jocelyn left hospital for Lynton this morning.

I hope you found David well on your return – I am sure he gave you a great welcome. How is Kuniang – not too miz I hope. Her accident was heard of with the greatest sympathy by all her many friends.

Darling, I can't thank you enough for the lovely present of a ring – I am simply longing for it to be ready, & can hardly wait to put it on. Thank you a thousand billion times.

No more now – all my fondest love to you all from your adoring Tom

* * *

Marston B Camp
etc.
26.7.42

My most precious Darling,
It's awful to think how long it is since I last wrote to you – indeed spoke to you. I tried to ring you up last night, but there was no answer – so I imagine you were all on the razzle-dazzle in Hunstanton, a lure difficult to resist.

Most of this week has been taken up with an exercise – the last, thank Heaven, & on the whole a successful one. We spent a good many uncomfortable nights, but there were some moments of amusement, and that is more than one usually gets. However, as a result, I've got a streaming cold, so I suppose we got a lot of good out of it!

As you will have gathered, last week was an orgy of entertaining and dissipation. First, a farewell party at Bde HQ, then our own dinner party for the 1st & 3rd Bns on Friday, which was the greatest fun, & lots of good food about. Then on Saturday we had the Sports – crowds and crowds of Scots Guards Officers, many of whom you know & who asked tenderly after you. As I told you, the Chobham thugs were there – Andy with his arm in a sling – 'so as to be able to pinch the sugar' as Robert suggested!

David Wedderburn and I stayed until the early hours of the morning; so you can imagine that Monday morning was a rather dismal thought!

Next week we have the GOCs inspection on Wednesday, so we are all busy getting ready for that. Otherwise a fairly quiet week & I shall be able to catch an early train to London on the 1. What glorious fun it's going to be – I can't tell you how much I am looking forward to it.

I had a long talk with the Commanding Officer the other day, & he wants me to give up being Adjutant, & to command a Company. There is the prospect of a big re-shuffle, & I am to take over Victor's company in September when he goes to the Senior Officer's course! It is all very sudden & exciting. Nothing, as you know, would please me more than to get a company – tho' at the same time, I would like to have been so good an Adjutant that he was loath to part with me. But as he said himself, I am more of a Leader than a Staff Officer, & so he's giving me this wonderful chance. It's all very much in the air as yet, and no one knows a thing about it – you are the first to know, as I hope you always will be!! Perhaps by the time I get on leave, I shall know more about it, & can tell you all then. Think of it, a Company all of my very own!!

Well my sweetie pie – a bientot until Saturday and all my most terrific love to you all at Ringstead

from your adoring Tom

Dripping Tent
July 29

My Darling Sweet,

The condition of damp and darkness in which I am writing this make it impossible for me to read it, but I hope you will be able to! Your husband, you will be sorry to hear, has been up to no good during the last 24 hours, and tho' I am not exactly ashamed of myself, I reached considerable heights of gaiety. Last night I rang up Virginia* to ask her if I could have a bath & she said come on & dine, we are 14, & we're going to the Household Cavalry dance. So off I went, changed & bathed there, & was told they could put me up. In the party were Andrew & Debo, Freddy S, the Stavondales, John Fox S,† Billy, Mark, Antony Mildmay, the Scropes, & various others. We had a very good and rather noisy dinner & eventually got to the dance about 11.30. There I found Tommy & Eliza, Bet Barclay, Marjorie Peacock &, need I add, Gerry Balding with whom she appears to be living. The party was a tremendous success & went on & on & on. I'll have to tell you in person all the dirt when I see you!! Anyway at about 5.45 am I looked round for my party, & found the whole lot had gone! Wasn't that shaming – & I'd been in the room all the time – no funny stuff on the back stairs!! There was nothing for it but to join forces with Tommy & Eliza & go to the Station Hotel at York. I got a room, which I entered at 6.30 am, but naturally not even a toothbrush with me. When I woke up it appeared to be 12.30 – so I got up & dressed – still no ablution material – & then discovered it was only 09.30!! However I tottered downstairs where luckily I found Timmy Leatham who lent me his razor, sponge etc. I decided to stay & lunch with these lovely blondes, but had a very tedious wait until they appeared. My plan was to return to camp with Boy who was

---

*　　　Virginia Sykes.
†　　　John Fox-Strangeways.

coming from London at 3.25. This in fact was the only plan to come off, & I got back here for tea, went to bed for 1½ hours having reassured Corby of my innocence – & am now fit as a fiddle again! It was the longest, most complicated & exhausting bath I have ever had.

My Darling, I do wish you could have been there: I had a million enquiries after you, & messages of love, particularly from Eliza & Bet who are organising a terrific reception committee for you at Windsor. You can imagine my delight at seeing my two favourite blondes in one evening, & your suspicions are no doubt bubbling over like a kettle!! You really would have adored it as the room was full of your admirers. I do hope this doesn't sound horribly gloating: it was hell you're not being there, but I know you'll enjoy hearing all about it.

We're off on a 3 day exercise tomorrow, and as it never stops raining, I am not looking forward to it with anything but the keenest displeasure.

I must stop now, my love as it's just stopped raining & I may be able to slink to my tent without getting a soaking.

Bless you, angel one, and all my love to David
from your ever adoring Tom

* * *

M.B. Camp
12.8.42

My own sweet Darling,
What a perfect week it has been. Never have I seen you looking so well, in such good form or so sweet-natured and kind. That, coupled with my joy at seeing David growing up into such an

excellent person, gave me one of the happiest weeks of my life.

I do hope your journey to Holkham was a success and that Susie is none the worse for it. Also that the bombs are not paying unwelcome attentions.

I had quite a good journey to London. Jack & Rita were in the train as far as Cambridge, & talking to her was like having a tete a tete with a Stirling Bomber. More pleasant still, the Fullers got in at Wolferton; on their way to say goodbye to HM. Both in v. good form & really cheerful, considering all things. In London I had my hair cut, had some tea, saw Lord Raglan for a second, & then caught the 6 pm to Frome. I found everything much as usual on my return, rather more mud, & the dining tent had blown away while the Brigadier was having lunch. Lots of officers are away doing various jobs. Last night we had quite a good concert in the NAAFI, quite good tunes, pretty dresses and not a few presentable floozies – all of whom we entertained in the Mess afterwards.

Corby was much impressed by the pants!

All my love, Darling One, & a big hug for a little boy from your adoring Tom

* * *

M.B. Camp
15.8.42

My Honeypot,
I hope you are flourishing, and that Silvia is proving a good nursery maid. This filthy weather, which no doubt you are having as well, makes outdoor life a little difficult and unpleasant. No sign yet of Jocelyn and Silvia, but I understand they may be returning in the middle of next week. So with any luck I shall be able to have a bath sometime before my next leave.

Life is fairly quiet at the moment, as we are doing Company

training: in fact tonight I shall probably go to the cinema in Frome – a rather daring and risque plan, which will not, I trust, offend you.

The telephone keeps ringing as I write, and every time I answer it I have to get half out of my chair and make a grab. Either I catch it & pull it over, or I miss it & fall back. However by that time, my chair has retreated and I sit back on air. To save myself I clutch at the table which collapses. Thus you can see that it is a laborious process.

Am now in the act of ringing up Clyde & Profumo* to ask them to dine on Friday – a pretty unpleasant pair!

No more now. All my love to you all & a big hug for David.

From your adoring Tom

* * *

M.B. Camp
5.9.42

My very own Darling,

Thank you so much for your letter: so the rains have reached Norfolk at last. I was beginning to think that they would never move away, but remain overhead unloading their horrid waters. However, it has been a little better lately, tho' today there is rather a strong wind, and all the papers in the Office are blowing about like the cards in 'Alice'. Perhaps, like her, I shall suddenly wake up and find that the leaves are falling off the trees, and are tumbling about me.

We have had three RAF officers here this week – not a very exciting lot, but pleasant, and full of sympathy for our living conditions which they found incredible. I am afraid it was very dull for them here. This week I have had one or two 'nights out' – not in the military sense, for I dined with Sylvia on Wednesday &

---

*   Tommy Clyde and John Profumo.

with Dennis Fitzgerald last night. As a result I think I shall have a fairly quiet weekend – tho' I may try & get a bath on Sunday.

Sylvia & I made a plan that we would all go up to London for the weekend of Sept 20, & then meet you & bring you back with us to the Farm House. Don't you think that a good plan!

I saw Arthur Collins last night, who was up at Floors with Tommy & Jack Leslie: they must have had a very good party. The Commanding Officer & all our Majors have been away, & so Robert & I have been holding the fort. Boy returns tonight from Kimberley.

Next week I shall go off & try to find David a birthday present – tho' I fear Frome isn't any more likely to have a suitable toy than an iron foundry.

No more now! God bless you, my adorable love, and keep you & David as perfect as ever

from your Tom

* * *

M.B. Camp
10.9.42

My sweetest Darling,
I loved getting your happy and amusing letter and I fear my wire must have come as a horrid shock. The thing is that I have just heard that we may be going to Newmarket instead!! Can you beat it! Even this is not certain, so don't altogether cancel Lady S. It sounds a grand little house and even if it has to fall through, we'll find as nice a one in Newmarket. After all your sweating and struggling too – my poor Darling. However, don't be unduly

depressed yet, as it's still even money if not more that we should go to Kimberley. Try to postpone fixing anything too definite yet, & I will let you know as soon as I can. I am miserable that this doubt has cropped up – but I know one thing – & that is that somewhere, this winter, we'll have a home together, & it won't matter where!!

How sad about Alan – he was a great person. But as you say he is back with Dibs again and the two of them make a fine memory.

About our weekend, I may be a sucker, but when I say a weekend I mean a proper one, & I shall come up on the Friday, unless Col. Archie says 'No' – which I am sure he won't. I have booked a room at the Connaught for two nights & Sylvia & Jocelyn will be there with us. Then we will all come back together on Sunday evening. Let me know if there's anything you particularly like to do. This is a busy but rather amusing week. We're running what we call a Training Bee, showing the whole Bn what everyone else in the Bn is doing – sketches, demonstrations, instruction etc. There is one play emphasising Security which is the funniest thing I have ever seen. David Cuthbert has devised & written it & introduced various fatuous announcements (by the Police Sgt) about famous female film stars taking part. One of them is Ann Oomph Sheridan – & the Police Sgt. renders this as Ann Oop'em Sheridan or Ann A Hump Sheridan! The General, the Brigadier & all the boys have been over to see it and thoroughly enjoyed themselves. In the intervals I've been dictating operation orders for Exercise to a shorthand clerk, showing people round, firing Tommy guns & bathing with Sylvia! I shall be out on a 'stunt' from Monday to Thursday so don't attempt to get hold of me – but you might put Sylvia's telephone No on a p-c & send it to me.

No more now Darling, I hope David's present & wire arrived alright – a bit early I'm afraid but you can hold them up until Der Tag!

I am only so sad that I can't give 100% OK to the house – it might come off & it mightn't. But in either case we'll have one somewhere & that's what we want!

All my love, Darlingest Heart
from your devoted Tom

* * *

MB Camp
29.9.42

My sweetest Heart,
I got your letter, for which many thanks. Yes, it really was heavenly being with you again, and what fun we had: quite like old times and we were able to forget the war for once. I am sorry you had such a wretched journey back home – I can well believe it. My tooth is quite alright now, and no longer gives me any trouble: I have been making frantic efforts to get fit, and on Sunday David Cuthbert & I quite solemnly went for a run-march together. Of course Jocelyn would overtake us in a car – & the ensuing ribaldry was most acute. We both felt frightful, in spite of taking things very easily, and when we got back David found that half his stomach had fallen out & he has been excused all marching for 2 months!! I've done several runs and marches since you left and will soon get into the hang of things. I am enjoying the Company very much, & have ordered brother John to try and find out what likelihood there is of my getting a Company of my own in the near future.

I dined at Brigade on Saturday, & came back laden with the tenderest messages of love and devotion for you from John Mariott, our new commander. He was as charming and delightful as ever, and longing (rather more than I like!!) to see you again. I was fingering my horse whip from time to time – and am considering forbidding you ever to see him again!! But what a grand person. We are overjoyed to have him command us.

The Officers here have suddenly become fanatically 'charade minded', and for the last three nights, after dinner we have been acting the most ridiculous scenes. I have been a Company Sergeant Major, a cow, Dicky Buckle, Godfrey Winn, a baby in arms etc. Whilst others have been motorbicycle, all seven dwarfs. Ghandi, Queen Victoria, Lucretia Borgia, Sherlock Holmes, Goebbels & Colonel Bill. I must say it has been most amusing & a welcome ray of light amidst the sudden gloom of our tents. Today it is raining chiens et chats (or vice versa), and really is too wet to do anything.

I am delighted to hear that David is so flourishing – not that I doubted he would be for a moment. The little horse should help him to walk – but don't let him rely on it too much, or he will never learn!

Well, my Darling, again a million thanks and kisses for coming all that way to see the old boy: I hope and pray it won't be too long before we get settled together somewhere.

My address in Scotland will be

TCH

Scots Guards

Commando Depot

Achnacarry

Spean-Bridge

Inverness

Oceans of love to you and the children from your adoring

Tom

* * *

Officers' Mess
Commando Depot
Achnacarry
Spean-Bridge
Inverness-shire
10/10/42

My Darlingest Maria

You will feel it very remiss of me not writing to you more often, but really life here has been so unutterably ghastly and so ex-hausting that none of us have had the energy to put pen to paper.

Our day starts at 08.30 & we go flat out until 5.40 pm, doing the most appalling series of assault courses, PT stripped to the waist, & run-marches, all in tempestuous rain and oceans of mud. One reckons to be soaked to the skin all day. But in spite of everything we have so far survived, tho' loathing every minute of it. The instructors are, as you can expect, very much out for our blood, & have made our work as strenuous as possible – but so far they haven't really succeeded in defeating us, in spite of all their 'blah'. Yesterday was without exception the most hellish day I have ever spent, Norway included. We set out at 8.30 am for a 24 hr march, 7 miles along a road and 23 miles across the hills – some of them 3000 ft high. Between 9 am & 6 pm we had over 4 inches of rain. We were absolutely soaked to the skin and as we climbed higher the wind got stronger and stronger and colder and colder, it rained still harder, & we ploughed through swamps and burns, up and up, so cold that we couldn't stop, so wet that we couldn't eat our food. By about 2pm the cloud was so low & the chances of getting across the hills in daylight so remote that we turned back, down a burn for about 5 miles till we hit the road, and then marched 12 miles back to Camp, with a biting icy wind blowing in our kidneys. We got back at about 6.30 pm – & I must say now I am perfectly alright, with not even the sign of a sniff in the nose.

I have heard from Murray & am writing to take rooms there from November. I am afraid we can't have David (or Kuniang) there, but perhaps we will be able to find something better later on. In any case, moving Nanny & David at this time of year is pretty awful, and I feel, much as I long to be with them, that they would be better either at Ringstead or Holkham or the Red House. But there seems no reason why you & I shouldn't set up house at Parsonage Farm; anyhow I will write & see what the form is. I hope to get my leave at the end of this month & will come up to Norfolk – I don't mind where I stay – possibly a bit of both.

Well, my Darling One, no more now – but tons and tons of love to you all, from your devoted Commando

Tom

* * *

Scots Guards
6.1.43

My most Darling One,
The time is 04.am & I am just dashing off on a stunt. But before I go, in great haste, herewith a word of love & thanks for the lovely, blissful time we had together. I do so hope you did not have too ghastly a journey.

How wonderful it must have been to see David again. I am sure he is in roaring form, & thrilled to see his Mummy again.

Give him a big big hug from me – & my love to all the others. But keep a good whack of it for yourself.

Ever your adoring Tom

* * *

Longbridge Devirill
Warminster
9 Jan 43

My Angel of Angels,

Thank you so much for your long and amusing letter about your arriving at Holkham. I am thrilled to hear about David, and I am sure he is the picture of health. By now I expect he knows you quite well again, and you are having tremendous romps, though not, I trust, extending beyond the hour of bedtime!! The Hazards of the Pots sound too acute for words, and I hope the carpets in the Nursery are none the worse.

I adored your stories of Lady Leconfield. I am amazed that she has been allowed about for so long. Just Eliza's cup of tea: how lucky that you weren't there too!

You were no doubt rightly shocked by the audacity and presumption of my daring to consider myself even for a moment, as in any way suitable to be the next Conservative member of West Norfolk – & no doubt, nothing will come of it. But seeing that all my hopes are eventually in that direction, it would have been rather chicken-hearted to do nothing. I hope Mama heard some of what I said on the telephone, & looking forward to her answer. I feel just like fighting a spirited election at the moment, & could vent some of my angry feelings.

I hope your Father enjoyed his shoot with the Monarch, & is making a suitable effort to return the hospitality. If Jack Leslie comes over to shoot & if Mama's efforts are in any way hopeful, do mention it privately to him, as he may perhaps be able to help.

The Exercise which was just beginning as I wrote that scrubby little letter, went without much trouble – but next week looms up dreadfully, for we are turning night into day, and life is likely to be even more topsy turvy than usual. Boy has returned but is still far from well having lost two stone in weight. Not that that would do him any harm, but all the same, he is still fairly cheap. Robert has gone to his Battle School, so I am in sole and supreme command, which means all the more work for Col Archie.

I am going over to dine with Tom Dundas tonight to play bridge. It is so foul here that I am delighted to be going out.

Corby is very worried about a towel, which he says you pinched. After the experience of the green rug, your denials are worthless!

Bless you all, my Darlings, & a huge hug for the Boy

from your v. loving Tom

* * *

Longbridge D
W
14 Jan 43

My Angel Bee

I am so miserable to hear that you are having such a wretched time with that cold – & a temperature too. Promise me that you take good care of yourself and don't get up or go out too soon.

Our week is tottering along, tho' the worst is yet to come. Unfortunately it has been very cold and soaking wet, so already existing difficulties have been increased. We parade at 9 pm & work either till lunch at 12.30 or till late lunch at 2 or 3am. Then we carry on till about 5am & have dinner at 6am, followed by a rather drivelling conference. Then one can go to bed – but I always wake up between 3 & 4 pm, have a cup of tea in the Mess, & then back to bed, where I now am, the time being 5 pm. I am usually called about 7 pm & breakfast at 7.30 pm.

Well, my whirlwind political campaign seems to have blown itself out already. I wrote a long letter to Harry Lance explaining why I made the offer, but I doubt whether he will be particularly impressed. John Hope & I had a very pleasant evening with Tom

Dundas, playing a little bridge, & then adjourning to the piano. We stayed rather late, but were able to get up in our own time on Sunday morning. Corby is on leave!! So I am being looked after by someone else; I propose to bring Corby with me on my leave, & shall only decline to do so under most virulent protests. So will you warn the family: if I am to 'canvas', I must have clean buttons etc!! Do please also try & arrange for Mother to stay for 2 or 3 nights: if that is not possible I shall have to go & spend a night with her – but I would rather not, as I shall want to see as much as David as I can and we can't cart him about.

I am going to ask if I can take my leave on Monday, but I will send you a telegram. I hope it will be ok, I'm longing to see you all again.

I am sorry about the undercurrents of discontent at Holkham – it is a scandal as well as a tragedy; but what can one do. I suppose Aunt Marge would be equally powerless but it is high time someone said exactly what he thought.

I wrote to Jocelyn & Sylvia to thank them for the happy months we had together. I heard from Jocelyn who sends you all their love. He says the old cottage woman is very tiresome, & they are glad it won't be for long.

One thing for which you will no doubt be grateful is that I haven't so far had a single drink since we began to live at night & sleep all day! If I can get leave next week I may not be able to get away early enough to reach Norfolk the same day, but anyhow the details can wait.

I heard from Lord Bob's servant who told me that the discomfort & cold of Robert's course surpasses belief & I am afraid the old boy will be hating every minute of it.

I am sorry to hear about Tommy – perhaps he will be recuperating at Holkham when I get down, which would be tremendous fun. Have I got a dinner jacket available to wear in the evenings?

I must stop now & write to the Runt. You may, I hope, expect a wire from me very soon. Meanwhile, my beloved, herewith all my love to you all. Get better quick, & who knows, I may be ringing the front doorbell in no time.

From your very loving Tom

* * *

L.D.
W
23 Feb 43

My Beloved Heart,
Just a quick line to say I have arrived safely, in spite of the train to London being 1½ hrs late for no reason.

How grateful I am to the flu, not only for being so lenient to me but also for giving us such a heaven-sent extension of leave together. My Darling, I feel it very deeply that you are being called upon to embark again on the ship of motherhood – particularly as I know you so very much wanted to wait a little. I have been admiring your spirit more than I can say, and I am so proud to know that you have already found your sea-legs, & are watching out to sea, instead of casting longing, lingering, or embittered glances back to the shore. I am quite convinced that we are right – but it is your courage that has changed conviction into gladness.

And I must say, seeing beloved David, it would have been shabby of us to do the world out of another like him!*
Bless you both, my Darlings & a smother of kisses on you.

From your very own Tom

* * *

---

*   Daughter Caroline was born in September 1943!

School of Infantry
Barnard Castle
Co. Durham, May 8 1943

My darling Maria,
I arrived safely after a very comfortable journey. There are not a great many people here whom I know, about a dozen all together, but many of the others are nicer than I expected. Our quarters are not comfortable, tho' quite tolerable, & the work is interesting but in no sense physically hard. We do none of those frightful things I had half feared, and are treated half as children & half as senior officers. So things are really quite pleasant.

What fun we had on our leave. I do so hope you enjoyed it as much as I did, trailing round seeing my rather heterogeneous collection of friends.

I am longing to hear how you found David and Mother. The former is I am sure in great form, & I trust Mama is really better & taking things easy. Look after yourself too, & don't let that wretched tummy-pain go on bothering you.

What wonderful news from Africa – I can't wait to hear the full & final chapter. In great haste.

My love to you all & many big kisses from your adoring Tom

* * *

Derwent Mount
Castle Howard Road
Malton, July 5th

My Darling,
We arrived safely after a very good run, having spent a night on Doncaster Race Course. We found quite a good pub, not very far away, and had a pleasant dinner there, hitch-hiking both ways! Next morning, we were off at about 09.30 hrs (!), and arrived here

in time for tea. The Company billets are, on the whole, very good – one big house–& six Nissen Huts. We feed at a Central Mess, which is adequately furnished, & sleep in yet another house, all about five minutes walk from each other. My bedroom is a good one tho' not very exquisitely furnished – & it has running water.

Archie* has bade official farewell both to the officers & the men in two rather embarrassing speeches. We are having a little party to try & get him tight tonight, but I feel it will be a flop. Once Boy† has really taken over, things will be easier: for, at the moment, everyone feels a little awkward. I have no information yet about my own position, but I shall be most disappointed if it remains completely unchanged & without any prospect of improvement. However, we shall see.

I do hope your London visit was a success & that Mama enjoyed herself. Poor David must have been miserable at such sudden & complete desertion. I am sure his arrival at Holkham will be a "succes fou".

What a paradise we have been living in at Ringstead! The most perfect gift from Heaven one could ask for. Like all good things, it has at last ended – but it was wonderful & has given us both a lot to work & fight to get back to. Bless you always, my most darling person, & big kisses to David & Susie (& Kuni) from your ever loving Tom

*　*　*

Malton
Yorks, July 25

My Own Sweet Darling
My journey wasn't too bad and I got back in good time to have a hot bath before breakfast. When I got back I heard the sad truth

---

that we have got to send away almost the last of our men, and this morning we bade them farewell. It was a most bitter feeling, having to say goodbye to those very men who had made the Battalion such a good one. We've been training them for nearly two years, & those who went today were the cream. We were all of us deeply depressed; every one of us had a lump in his throat, and poor David was actually in tears. We crawled back to the mess and drank four bottles of champagne to try and cheer us up; but it will be just as bad tomorrow. All this, on top of the end of leave & the thought of not seeing you for so long is hardly the most cheerful influence – but by the time you get this letter I shall be in good spirits again, & finding plenty to do keep busy.

Five officers have gone, including Jack Sanderson, tho' of course there is always the faint possibility that they may not be wanted. I think I shall definitely get the Coy:[*] but no appointments are being made just yet.

What a lovely time we had: Darling thank you so much for always being so angelic to me. I trust little David is quite well again, & his usual blissful self. Will write again & to your Pa tomorrow. Meanwhile to bed.

Bless you all & a sea of love from

Tom

* * *

Malton 496
Yorks, July 28

My Darlingest Maria,
Thank you so much for your letter, & the enclosure from the garage. What a ghastly journey you must have had back from London. I do hope that you weren't too tired after it.

Since I last wrote, things have improved a little, and we hope to

---

*   Company.

get some men back in the near future. That has cheered everybody up, & last night we had the most excellent dinner. The General & John, the Brig, & all the Irish & Coldstream were there, and we had lots to eat & lots to drink. After a suitable interval after dinner, where we either played bridge, or poker, or the wildest form of billiard fives, I was ordered to sing my songs, including the one criticising the training of the Division. I refused at first & then said that if I were to sing it, its title could only be 'Prelude to a bowler-hat'. If anything this made it worse, as I at once thought the General must think that I meant a bowler hat for him. However he expressed himself wildly delighted, & as yet I haven't been given the sack! Boy is in London seeing the Lt-Col about our future, so I shall have more news later.

It occurred to me that 'Julian' is quite a good name for a boy – do you like it?

Nothing much doing at the moment – but as far as anything is certain, I am pretty sure I won't be off yet – certainly not on a draft, so that is most comforting.

What wonderful news it is: anything might happen in Italy at this stage. It really looks as tho' they are going to chuck their hand in.

I hope my leave situation won't be too bad. We are allowed to take 48 hours plus a weekend – so I can fit in one of these, & then just have seven days when next due – which is towards the end of October – a ghastly thought. I think it's best if I try & stick out August without seeing you, & then perhaps take two lots of leave fairly quickly. How is the house going?

Give David an enormous hug from me & keep a colossal one for your darling self.

From your very loving Tom

Malton
Yorks
1 August

My Darlingest One,

Thank you so much for your letters and the fruit, which was delicious tho' somewhat sweaty. The big news of the week is that I have definitely and officially got command of Right Flank & David is 2 1/c. Naturally I am delighted and only hope I can justify Boy's faith in me. I am not at all certain whether I shall in fact succeed in becoming a Major, but that is a comparatively small point. I went to see Ronnie* christen his godson in York Minster and came back loaded with messages for you – 'that woman' as he called you. He was his same delightful self & I was so pleased to be able to see them again. Last night the Sgts gave a dance, which was much nicer than usual, less drunken, less stuffy, and less long. During the day, three of us motored over to Ravenscar to bathe in the sea! We had to descend about 400 – 500 feet of steep cliffs, to the sea, which was icy cold, but the sun was lovely. After trudging all the way to the top I discovered that I had left my wrist watch on the shore, so we had to go all the way back again. However we found it – with the tide fast approaching. Tomorrow is marked by Sports–& I'm in charge of sideshows, to make money for the prisoners of war. We are having the usual items such as Aunt Sallies etc, & with luck and good weather we ought to be able to make quite a lot of money. I have got to go & have tea with old Col Malone, & play bowls with him afterwards. As I want to get some clothes out of them to dress up two C.S.M's† as fortune tellers, I hope the fatigue (in the military sense) will be worthwhile! I am so glad David is really better. Susie will be going for a holiday soon: give her my love & tell her to leave a little gin in London for my next leave.

---

*   Ronnie Pilkington.
†   Company Sergeant Major.

Masses of love to you both and many kisses from your
husband & father Tom

* * *

Malton
Yorks
7 Aug

My Darling Maria,
Thank you so very much for your sweet letter. I am so glad you
are keeping well; & that David is in his usual good form. I was
not the least surprised to hear that Sylvia has worked herself to
exhaustion point; but all the same the house must be charming
& I am longing to see it. I expect Nina & Dorothy are with you
now, doing yeoman work. Susie will be all the better for a good
holiday, & should come back quite refreshed & ready to compete
with the large increase in family. There have been various activities this week, mostly of a non-military nature – as I can't quite
remember when I last wrote to you, I'll start on Monday.

The side shows at the sports were a roaring success, and by dint
of raffling a bottle of whisky & a cake, and auctioning another
bottle & 2 cakes, plus the usual attractions we made £57. I
dressed up 2 of the C.S.Ms as fortune-tellers & in spite of their
shamefully obvious deceptions they did a roaring trade.

On Wednesday, a trio of Home Guard pundits came to dinner
& took all my money off me in no time. We played various futile
gambling games & I had a disastrous evening. The next night
there was a Guardsman's dance to which I went for about an
hour, but as there were only two pretty girls there, & they were
dancing with each other, I didn't get much of a look in. Three
men of ours returned yesterday, & as I went on the platform
I heard a shout & there was the Maggot arriving to stay with
Jean for a party at Sledmere tonight. You could have knocked me

down with a crowbar! She seemed very well & I am going to see them tomorrow after lunching with John. Tonight I am dining with Lady Grimthorpe, whose son is on leave or something. It all sounds very gay!! However next week we really get down to business & on Friday I am doing a scheme with Murray's tanks. Don't you feel just a tiny-weeny bit jealous??

I wrote at once about the car & I trust it is on its way up. I particularly wanted it to go by road, for if it breaks down, they will have to mend it. I am searching for the fruit box, as I should adore some more.

No more now, my honey bee, but lots and lots of love to you all & big hugs and kisses

from your adoring Tom

* * *

Malton
Yorks
Aug 11

My Darlingest Maria,

What a tale of woe about Dorothy. I do so hope she gets well quickly, & as you say, isn't put off forever from the idea of leaving home and coming to us. I am sure Nanny H is perfect and already quite a part of the family.

It is sweet of you to suggest such a lovely present. Actually, I am becoming more & more anxious to get a flying suit, or something like it, because now I am a Company Commander I shall have more opportunities for wearing it, & shall need it more, as I travel a good deal in windswept vehicles like Jeeps and carriers. If coupons are necessary I can supply them – but a little help towards the cost would be a lovely present. It would have to be a fairly big suit, which I could slip over my Battle-Dress instead of an overcoat.

As soon as I've finished this letter, I will ring up Tom Dundas.

I much enjoyed seeing the Lloyds & Maggot on Sunday, & found them all in very good form, tho' somewhat bleary after the terrific party at Sledmere.

There were apparently lots of lovelies there, & Lady Wey was being even more than usually blatant with the young ensigns.

Robert Cecil apparently looked like a month old corpse, while Rutland & Johnny M were both v. tight, the former revoltingly so. The gambling was colossal, with £200 banks running all the time. There is going to be another party next month to which I shall certainly go, so hold your hat on & expect the worst!!

Nothing very much on this week: & on the 20 we go into a tented camp for about 3 weeks. Suppose I can get away for September 14-17, how will that fit in with you. Then I can certainly get a night or two when the baby is born, while my leave will start either Oct 10 or Oct 17. Let me know when you would most like me around, & I will have no difficulty in arranging it.

The news is certainly staggeringly wonderful: & Churchill is no doubt planning even greater expeditions. I wish the weather would get better & we could bomb more. It is perfectly foul here today & quite cold.

I do hope the car will arrive soon.

Give David a big hug: bless you both, my Darlings & loads of love

from your loving Tom

* * *

Malton
Yorks
Aug 14

My Angel One,
I loved your letter with its tit-bits about David & the carrier-

pigeon. Funnily enough, one settled on Corby's bed on the same day. What a good plan it would be to train them to fly backwards & forwards between us. I am sure you had a good laugh at Diana: I must say she sounds a most unattractive sort of woman, but no doubt most amusing for a short time. Roger would have been in his element!

Nothing much has happened since I last wrote, except that I got rather tight last night dining (+ Boy) with Jimmy Lewis. I've had to go a bit easy on it today!

I wish I could be sharing with you a greater part of the burden of waiting, which, you have to bear alone for the next month. You are wonderful to write so cheerfully and to keep so good tempered and happy: I do pray that the time will pass quickly, so that before you know it's happened, there is a tiny squeaking person lying in your arms.

Wasn't it fine news about Antony Lyell,* an abject lesson to all Company Commanders, but one that isn't easy to follow. The war is certainly going better than ever before, & now that we're started strafing Italy again, we can expect some big headlines in the near future.

The weather is foul – raining like hell. Camp will be detestable if this goes on: also it has been rather cold. Everyone is away and it is rather squalid and miserable here. I may go to a flick tonight if I can get in. Janet has been here for a few days, in great form, but without very much gossip. She says Susan & Pretslik are madly in love & completely on air, & which is such a good thing.

No more now, darling Heart, but loads of love & kisses to you both

from your ever adoring Tom

---

* Anthony Lyell was Lord Lyell, killed in action in N. Africa aged twenty-nine; he was awarded the VC.

Malton
Yorks
Aug 19

My Beloved One,

Thank you a thousand times for your lovely birthday letter, and its message of love. It is very sad that we can't spend it together, but I shall be with you again as soon as I can, tho' I fear recent 'legislation' on leave will make it rather a flying visit. I shall take 48 hrs from 11 to the 13 & then a weekend after the baby is born. I am sure Boy will give me a little compassionate leave as well – I trust it won't be too bad. I'll postpone my 7 days to suit you.

We have just come back from a short, and very dull exercise, & we go to camp tomorrow. You can address your letters as before: for we collect them daily. I am luckily getting a little jaunt for my birthday, by being sent to Kirkcudbright to watch the tanks shooting. I go tomorrow & get back on Sunday. I am hoping that brother John will go too: so it might be quite fun. The fruit has arrived and is delicious. Thank you so much: I've sent back the boxes. How I should have loved to see David having his first real trit-trot. Do keep him at it as he will love it so. Give him a great big hug from his fast-aging father.

Things certainly do seem to be hotting up and Sicily is a great victory. It looks as though we'll have a winter full of exciting news. On a smaller scale, I have very little other news, but will write again on Sunday, after my tour. Bless you, my darlings and again my thanks for your love and good wishes

from your devoted Tom

* * *

Frinber Camp
As from Malton
Yorks
Aug 21

My Darling One,
As you will see my trip to Scotland has fallen through: John has
to go on a course starting early on Monday and there was really
no point in my going with anyone else. So I have stayed here and
am writing this from the tent which is undeservedly dignified
by the name of Company Office. I am going to dine with John
tonight, however, so I shall be able to keep in touch with the
glamour and comforts of civilisation. I must try and get hold of
Virginia at Sledmere which is only a couple of miles away: as in a
week's time I will be greatly in need of a bath. I have just taken to
smoking my pipe again and am very glad to have done so, altho'
it is an infernal nuisance to carry.

I can't think when I can get to London to buy David a birthday
present, or even to do some things for myself. The whole question
of the exact dates of my privilege leave is bound to be uncertain:
but I take it that you won't be back in Norfolk till the last week in
October. It may be that I shall have to take my leave sooner and
spend it at Windsor, but I shall try not to if I can help it. Tom
Dundas is trying to get the films done, but hasn't quite finished
the roll yet, so I'm afraid it won't be ready for some time.

I haven't got a good recent photograph of either you or David,
so do try & persuade your father to take one. The weather is still
unbelievable – pouring rain and sultry. I do hope it will get a little
better soon.

No more now, my Sweet Heart: but herewith all my fondest
love:

God bless you both my Darlings from your loving Tom
P.S. Send back any you don't want!!

Malton
Yorks Aug 22

My Darlings,
Thank you a thousand times for your telegram: it arrived safely
& made my day for me. I arrived to dine with John last night &
found a very gay, mixed party, which included Barbadee & Kay.
B. was very gushing & asked tenderly after you, & wished you
luck with the new baby. The lovely Lady Evrington was not there,
alas!!

We had 2 good films & altogether a delightful birthday party.

Herewith the coupons, which I fear I forgot before. I dread to
think what you must have been thinking of me.

A world of love, my precious ones
from Tom

* * *

Malton
Yorks 26 August

My Angel
A very hurried line in a damp and cold tent to tell you that all
is well, & that I loved getting your long letter. Lock up all your
valuables while Malise is about, & don't cash a cheque for him!!

The new and blasted regulations don't permit me now to take
48 hours with a weekend, which is most inconvenient of them.
But I will wrangle all I can. Anyhow 11–13 is a certainty.

The conditions are too foul for writing any more: do ring up
Mama & tell her my news. I will write to her when the sun comes
out.

A million blessings on your lovely head and to my Darling
David

from your loving Tom

Malton
Yorks
Sept 43

My Darling One,
It was lovely to hear your voice & with it such thrilling news –
that junior is really and truly going to make his appearance on
Tuesday. I can't tell you how wonderful I think you have been –
always so calm and good tempered, cheerful and uncomplaining.
I take my hat right off to you!!

It was a blissful weekend, wasn't it – with the little man at the
height of his form. I dined with David Robarts, Humphrey Legge,
and a funny little man, rather ferret-faced and moustached, who
was on the boat with you coming back from Egypt. A very typical,
common, sea-voyage acquaintance!

I went over with Dereck, Rosse & Dundas to an 8 Corps party
with Michael Fitzalan-Howard, and saw a lot of friends. But at
the moment am training hard & trying to get to bed early. Am
just off for a 10 mile march.

Isn't the news much better!

Well, my angel heart, God bless you in this new great venture
which you are having to face alone. I shall appear with you very
soon, and in my prayers and thoughts I will be with you all the
time – so that, my Darling, in spirit, I will be holding your hand.
Bless you, a thousand times, & good luck

from your adoring & undeservedly lucky Tom

* * *

Malton
Yorks Sept 1

My Darling Heart

To expatiate on the inconstancy and fickleness of Fate has been the desire of many people for all time – but the latest blow we have suffered here is so crippling that we none of us have quite fully realised what it is all about. The Bn has been suddenly and summarily disbanded.

Without warning, & for inadequate reasons, we were told that we were to disappear into thin air, & be replaced by the 3rd Irish, commanded by Joe Vandeleur. Col Boy loses his command David goes to the 3rd Bn, & what must be one of the happiest and best battalions in the Army, is wiped out by a stroke of the pen. As it is, we still have to leave 2 Companies here, and it was difficult for me to decide what I should do. Originally Boy was not going to leave me here as he felt I could never be a Major with so many Irish majors in the offing: & he was going to leave a more junior captain who was not, so to speak, expecting promotion. However I decided that my place was with the Company, who are none too happy anyway, & so I am staying up here. You can imagine that after all our ups and downs, this comes as the final mockery. If one felt it was a helpful & necessary step, it wouldn't have been so bad – as it is, one seems to be the victim of unassailable and distant incompetence.

We all got very tight last night & look like staying so for some time. Do write to Boy & sympathise – for if anyone has suffered a dirty, underhand blow, it is he. He has taken it magnificently & been an example to us all.

So glad about the car: I was sure it would be alright. I think, tho' I am not sure yet, that I shall be able to add 48 hours leave to my weekend: but I will let you know as soon as possible.

Some of us are going out shooting this pm just to cheer our-selves up.

All my love to you & David, my Darlings
from your adoring and devoted Tom

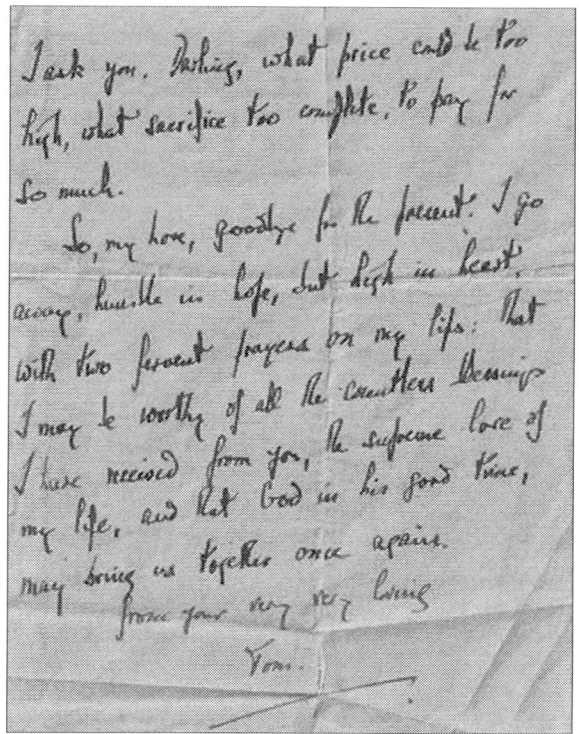

Malton
Yorks
5 Sep 43

My Darling Angel
Thank you so much for your long letter and the divine photograph
of the 'nits'. I thoroughly approve of your plan, as I too was rather
dreading what your journeys might be like. Provided Bullman,
or whatever his name is, is really good, and that Maxwell can
recommend him, I should certainly do it. Anyhow by now you
will have written to me, having made up your mind.
 As you can well picture, this last week has been appalling: and

at 8.30 this morning the last of our erstwhile comrades steamed out of Malton station. There has been an endless succession of really good, rowdy farewell parties: & last night, Joe Vandeleur's first with us, was made hideous for several hours, just below his bedroom. Everyone is still furious at the whole affair, even Col Bill, who let us down badly, is now beginning to see what an ass he has made of himself. However it's too late now: & the upshot of it is that my Company & Dereck's are both very strong, & full of excellent men. But that is only a partial consolation.

I had a very nice dinner a deux with Tom Dundas one night, who was in his usual charming form.

I have asked brother John to be a godfather & he has accepted – so that makes two. I thought the Hambro godparents were terrific – either millionaires or ex boy friends.

I think that with luck I should arrive at Hunston about 8am on Saturday, have breakfast & bath at Ringstead & then come over in time for the shoot. I very much want to go back via London on Tuesday, as there are certain things I just must do.

So glad about the car. It is neither licensed nor insured. The man has the book.

I have bought, & will bring with me £18.18 worth of alcohol!!
Bless you, my Darlings, & a tremendous hug for 'the boy'
from your ever loving Tom

* * *

Officers' Mess
Commando Dept
Achnacarry, Spean-Bridge
Inverness-shire 6 October

My Darlingest Maria
It is quite unbelievably bloody here, & we are chased about all day at the double, by the toughest & most unpleasant (generally

speaking) collection of thugs one could ever wish to meet. Our first day we did a run-march of 7 miles in 64 minutes, followed by 3 assault courses and yesterday we did 10 miles in 89 minutes. Some platoons were even quicker – but those times were quick enough for us. The discomfort is supreme. In fact the only redeeming feature is that there are lots of us in the same boat.

I have written to Murray Sinclair asking him if he is likely to be leaving his house, so that will give you some idea of where we move to. No more now.

Bless you all, my darling, & lots of love
from your adoring Tom

* * *

3rd Battalion Irish Guards
Oct 7

My Darling
Welcome home! How thrilled you must be to get back, & to be in your own room again, with David and Nanny, & all the familiar sounds, smells and voices. Not too tired, I hope, after your long journey – nor little Caroline upset by a long drive and new surroundings. I expect she slept like a mouse all the time, except for the important hours of meals – and as long as they appear at the right time, I doubt if she cares much where she is. I am writing this in my bedroom just before retiring – & I do hope it arrives in time – I have been dreadfully naughty about writing – but having been able to talk to you once or twice and having been terribly busy into the bargain I fear I've not done so. It's not a bit excusable, particularly as I have recently attended one or two parties which I should have better renounced in favour of pen, paper and writing desk.

As you know we got back on Saturday night, & promptly got busy tidying up etc. On Monday night I dined with John at Div

HQ, which was v. pleasant but rather late. Cols Bill & Archie were due to come up on Tuesday, so Dereck & I were busy plotting our plots and laying our snares. They dully arrived and all was well – we defeated Archie handsomely and he withdrew to Pirbright extremely unsuccessful and angry. That night David W & I dined with Dereck & I am ashamed to say got awfully tight – so much so that we gatecrashed Bde HQ at about 12.30 & caused considerable dismay & consternation. However as David had just become a Father, our odd behaviour was excused – tho' much ribald comment has since reached us. David passed clean out & I had to undress him. The next morning I was as fresh as a daisy & went into York to listen to the Army Commander. He was a most impressive and likeable personality, and just exactly the idea of all of us of what we should wish our Army Commander to be. It was a great fillip to everyone.

That night I dined with Fisher-Rowe – luckily a fairly respectable party. I was over with the 3rd Bn today, watching their training – & shall be out with Hambro & his crowd tomorrow & Saturday.

My majority is definite & I am crowned not only with crowns but a good deal of leg-pulling. I am afraid it may not last for very long, but I shall fight like a tiger to keep it!

Poor Stukes has been killed – & the 2nd Bn have had some more nasty knocks. Hugh Rose was not with them and may be coming home.

We go to camp for a week but fate has kindly decreed that it shall be during my leave: a great blessing as it will be most uncomfortable.

Am off early tomorrow, so I will say goodbye now. My Darling, I can't tell you how thrilled I am with Caroline, and with the thought that you are really getting on well & home again. Be a good girl & take things easy for just a little longer than you really want to.

Give David a big kiss & tell him to be nice to his sister.

Bless you, all my darlings, from Tom

3rd Battalion Irish Guards
October 12 1943

My Darling Love,
It seems to be unaccountably difficult to sit down & write – tho'
Heaven knows why. I wish I knew your telephone number – but
I have a call in to Holkham at the moment, so I hope I shall
have been able to speak to you before you get this. I can't wait
to have the news of your arrival, of how you are, & how darling
David welcomed you. What bliss it must be for you to be back
at home, & how I long, to the depth of my soul, to be back with
you again on Saturday. I plan to catch the 11.55 from L'pool St.
on Saturday & will go to any station you like – either Holkham
or B'ham Mkt. I must get to London somehow & am, alas! busy
Training on Friday night. But I hope to get to London about 7
am, – wash & shave & shop, & then home with all speed. It is
terrible to have only 7 days, but they will be such heaven that one
dare not grumble.

We have had one or two more parties – woe to my night's sleep
– one for the third Bn on Sunday & one in the Company last
night. Tomorrow Dereck has a cocktail party & hence to Div
HQ. Tomorrow I get up at 6.15 to watch some training – in
which Hambro figures largely. He is dining with me on Thursday.
I saw John & Anne for a second on Sunday – she was in good
form, but not looking too well as she has a stinking cold.

The news is full of one's friends being killed, & one has need
these days of all one's courage and belief. Walter White-Thomson
& Eddie Anson are two sad losses – both due, so tragically, to
accidents.

I expect the big shoot is on now – I trust a success. The Brig.
was heart-broken that he couldn't attend.

I'm bringing you as a little thank-offering a 25lb Ham!! So if I
fail to arrive, just ring up the Police, who will no doubt pick me
up on York platform.

Angel Heart, I can't wait to be with you again. In great haste, so that the intervening days may fly.

A million kisses on your beloved heads from your very own

Tom

* * *

3rd Battalion Irish Guards
Oct 31

My Darlingest of Loves,
It is awful to think that I left you a week ago after such a really lovely leave and haven't yet written to you. It must seem piggish of me, and I am most ashamed of myself: but the usual excuses of being busy all day and having no facilities to write in the evening are all I can toot out. However here goes, for a really long letter: tho' there is precious little news.

Apart from the ordinary, but enormous pleasures of being on leave, I was particularly delighted to be able to see with my own eyes that both you and Caroline are really getting on well now, and progressing by leaps and bounds. I do so hope, Darling, that the improvements of your sleeping and her feeding are maintained, & that by now she weighs innumerable pounds & you sleep for 11 hours a day. I thought the christening was lovely, & such good behaviours by the two nits I have never seen. We shall have to go & live in a church, if we ever want any peace & quiet.

My journey back was very long and tedious However we eventually got back & next a.m. I went to Camp, where I found, as well as ourselves, the 2nd Irish, who include Eddie Tyler, one of the O'Cocks (yours, I wonder?) & many other very pleasant people. That very night we were on an all-night exercise, which was a severe shock to my nervous system, but we survived alright.

During the last night, the Brigs came to dine, & after dinner the Scots Guards pipers played to the High Table of 'nobs': meanwhile Edward Fisher-Rowe and I, who were slightly high by then, were dressing ourselves up as Irish Guards pipers in saffron kilts (back to front) & we wrote out an absurd Programme concluding with 'Brig on the Dancing Girls' – signed Paddy O'Flaherty, Pipe Major, and Jock McFrigget, Pipe Minor. When we entered no one had read the programme, nor suspected we were phoney – so our rather drunken entry, followed by excruciating noises caused a deadly hush which luckily broke into loud laughter a moment later. I am sorry to say Edward is leaving to go as Chief Instructor to the Trd Bn: he will be a great loss, and it seems altogether ridiculous. This afternoon I have got to take the Cy onto the Wolds to dig in for a scheme – we come back at about 6 pm & go out again at 3 am, which is an ugly hour. Luckily it should be over easily by lunch on Monday, & it gives one a good excuse for doing nothing else. There is still no definite news about our future. I gather Boy, Michael, Bobby, Jock & Co are all on their way, or soon will be. I have lost Ian Tait which is very sad.

Well, my angel, thank you a million times for my lovely leave – it was a tremendous joy & thrill to be with you all again – a real home of love and laughter.

Bless you all my Darlings from your very loving Tom

* * *

Malton
Yorks
Nov 3

My Darling Maria,

Thank you so much for your long letter and the dirty washing. I heard an excellent talk, for 2 hrs 50 minutes by Oliver Leese on Alamein – Tunis – Sicily. He seemed just the same as ever, and more energetic if anything. Last night I walked down to the pub to dine with George and Maisi – I can't spell it – who are both in great form, and very amusing – half the humour unconscious. Let me know exactly what dates are best for your visit, as I shall have to book a room, for instance I could meet you in London for the weekend Dec 3/4. Travel up on Sunday afternoon (5th) & you could stay till the 10th when we could again go to London, or if you prefer stay here. It will be tremendous fun – tho' life up here is pretty deadly, & very cold – so bring the Mink and plenty of winter woollies!!

Tomorrow I'm forsaking the full ditchwater of military routine, and am going shooting with old Major Hall – the usual Bde HQ party, great fun.

Let me know if the shoes have arrived from Poulsen – if not, write to them yourself and ask them to hurry up.

Otherwise there's very little news, so I'll stop & write again later. In case I forget, could you bring my leather waistcoat & send me your photographs which I left behind. Also do ask your Father if he can possibly sell me 100 cartridges, or if not ask Tommy. It is so impossible here–& I need so few compared with what they shoot off in one drive!

Bless you all, my honeypots,
from your loving Tom

3rd Battalion Irish Guards
Nov 7

My darling Love,

I am so glad to hear that you are all well and happy, and that Caroline is making such good progress. Of course she's a darling, as any baby of yours must always be. I expect I will soon get your answer about the proposed dates for your visit here.

Actually, since I last wrote we have both been invited to the Christmas Ball at Sledmere on December 11th, a Saturday, which may be rather fun and I have provisionally accepted. It is Virginia's last appearance before 'going into Purdah' – so it is sure to be rather a good party.

Also Dereck and I are planning to give a cocktail party in your honour, so we'll have a lot of fun one way or another.

This week has been pretty dull, and the weather has become very cold in the last 24 hours. I went out shooting with the Brig on Thursday, but we had a rotten day. However we had an enormous lunch, & that on top of Edward Fisher Rowe's farewell party made me feel rather rotten! However I stopped it in time, & now feel perfectly alright. Yesterday, being bored to distraction by the thought of a weekend in Malton, I took my Company Cook, Sgt Finlayson, over to Ganton to play golf, & thoroughly enjoyed it. Though I didn't play very well, & played better than I thought I would, & felt like hitting the ball properly, even tho' I didn't very often.

Eddie Moss has returned from his leave, having just got engaged to Bridget Coke!! He is frightfully pleased with himself, but a little dubious of Dick, as well he might be. However he is getting married on the 18th of next month, & the occasion naturally gives the Brig tremendous opportunities for being giggly and smutty!

I am doing nothing about the announcement of the christening. I think it is a waste of money. John sent the draft on to me, and I have torn it up.

Did you hear the New York Symphony Selection broadcast at 12.15 today (Sunday). They played two movements of the Bruch's Violin Concerto with a Russian called Nelsen (or some such name) as the soloist. I was most impressed by both.

Do let me know when you hear from Silvia – I think probably she will fill the house up but you never know, as she can't say no to anybody. It certainly would be better to move if she does but it would be an awful nuisance.

Well, my angel, no more now. I can't tell you how much I long to have you up here with me again. It won't be long now. Give the babies big kisses from me & tell them to be good, also my love to Susie

from your very loving Tom

* * *

Malton
Yorks, Nov 15

My Darling Maria,
It was a bitter blow that the 3rd Bn party came at a time which was no use to you. I felt very lonely without you and although I managed to enjoy myself enormously, it was not and could never be quite the same. However, needless to say, with Eliza, Isabelle and the Brig there, there was a good deal of unseemly mirth and badinage, and I laughed a good deal throughout the evening.

To begin at the beginning: I motored down with Berteley Villiers and we arrived at Thoresby about tea time. The house has to be seen to be believed – complete St Pancras outside, and more ghastly inside than words can say. Vast deal sideboards with black garlands of grapes (wooden) rising to a peak of vulgarity – faded blue cloth on the walls, cheap gilt, stone halls with pseudo-gothics balustrades, cheap armour, massive concrete coats of arms, trowels left over from laying foundation stones, the freedom of Brighton in a glass meat-safe, and pictures one more ghastly than the other, yellow faded landscapes in revolting and colossal frames. To cap it all, mine host the Earl Manvers, a slobbering, lecherous dirty old man, shuffling after the girls to pinch their bums, his lips quivering and slobbering, his beaky fingers itching convulsively: and a veteran drunk of a butler, swaying through the ill-lit passages, offering titled guests a 'quick one' on the sly.

But it was a marvellous party, masses of people – lovely girls!, and unbelievable food, in unending quantities, ham, partridges, oysters, souffles, rum punch and so on ad infinitum. The belle of the ball was undoubtedly the Duchess of Portland, a wonderful, Queen Elizabeth like figure, with the proportions of a goddess, who waltzed serenely round the room, sweeping all before her. The organisation was terrific, trains and buses and taxis flying back and forth, disgorging vast cargoes of young women, collecting them again, and finally carrying them back to London.

Endless people asked after you & send their love, Elizabeths Maclean and Townshend, Anne Harvey, Claude[*], Willie & Celia[†], Neville & Poppy[‡] & countless others. People were much cheered by the news of George Johnson's arrival in England, and Dermot & Simon Ramsay's return to the 2nd Bn. How sad about David Loder: I gather also that Sammy Howlsworth was very badly wounded. Today I see that Pam Barton has lost her life – the war is indeed no respecter of persons.

I can't wait to hear what luck you have had, if any, about houses. Tommy & Eliza were most sympathetic: they & Robert & Janet are arranging an evening for us, which should be terrific.

---

[*]   Claude Dunbar.
[†]   W. & C. Whitelaw.
[‡]   N. and P. Wigram.

I forgot to tell you that I gave a pint of blood to the Trans-fusion people the other day: a performance I anticipated with considerable displeasure, but which turned out to be as easy as pie. There were several bets as to whether in fact I possessed as much as a whole pint of blood, so the doubting Thomases were well confounded!!

I hear the family are as divine and well as ever, and Susie bearing up like a 2 year old. I hear that your Father's latest craze is to engage a couple – he'll probably pick a pair of professional thieves.

Nothing very exciting promises this week. It now looks more certain that we shall be staying here permanently, which is most satisfactory. Nothing is definite yet, but things look better.

Bless you all, my Burnham Darlings, and a hug of big kisses all round

from your ever loving Tom

* * *

Malton
Yorks Nov 23

My Darling Heart,
I am a boor not to have written for so long: however our tele-phone call was lovely and clear, and I was able to feel once again that I was beside the fire in the drawing room of the Manor. How I wish I were. Still, we'll have a blissful ten days together, which I am looking forward to madly. In fact, apart from anything else, and to continue your pretty little metaphors, my Panzer Divi-sions are straining at the leash! It was a very sad family occasion, David's memorial service, but beautifully done. A lovely old English church, with the Christchurch choir & Tommy Arm-strong at the organ. Their house is quite the loveliest little Manor I have ever seen, and I am keeping in touch in case they want to sell it. It would no doubt be frightfully expensive but I believe

if it was really possible, we might coax some money out of my grandmother.

I get great consolation and help in these times from trying to say my prayers and think of things of the Spirit – and tho' I fail hopelessly, I do feel that tremendous strength could be obtained if only one were worthy of it. At the moment, the pendulum of our fate is swinging in the other way, and it now looks as though we shall in fact be relieved. However it is still very vague: & the moment I hear I can let you know if there is any likelihood of my departing, so that you can come & stay with me. That is why in many ways I am glad you will be at Holkham for a bit, so that you won't be too tied, & can come & be with me if time is getting short. In any case, I would get leave as well.

Must stop now & go to dinner.

Bless you all, my dearest loves and very much adoring love

from Tom

* * *

Malton
Yorks
Dec 15

My Darling Love,

I should have written to you far far sooner, my Darling, to thank you for the lovely time we have just had together. But the moment you left, life became a complete turmoil, the upshot of which is that we move to Pirbright on Friday, and on Monday or Tuesday I shall be appearing at Holkham to spend Christmas and the New Year with you!! So you can imagine that the last few days have been pretty hectic. Well, as you know, I have been waiting to go away for four years, and now that I am, secretly I am relieved, for the only justification of the wonderful life we have had together and the adorable family we have raised, is our determination to fight against our evil enemy: and the more we have enjoyed those blessings, and the more we love them, the more it is our duty to do our part in restoring them to others in the world, and safeguarding them for David's lifetime and Caroline's. So I know that you will not be unhappy, but rather thankful that the Almighty has given us such great happiness together that we can be absolutely certain in our own minds that this war is worth fighting & worth winning.

The Brig's farewell party developed, I am ashamed to say, into the most colossal blind, as far as the Right Flank Officers were concerned. Tim was fighting everybody, Eddie was too tight to be able to talk, David was terribly ill, and Sacha*, unable to find his way to bed, slept in a field for ¾ of an hour!! Next morning the chaos was indescribable.

When I get to London on Friday I will try to ring you up: but remember to be careful what you say!!

Bless you my honeypot, and all my love to the chicks from
Tom

* * *

Pirbright Camp
Woking

I ask you, Darling, what price could be too high, what sacrifice too complete, to pay for so much.

So, my Love, goodbye for the present. I go away, humble in hope, but high in heart, with two fervent prayers on my lips: that I may be worthy of all the countless blessings I have received from you, the supreme love of my life, and that God in his good time, may bring us together once again.

From your very very loving
Tom

---

*   Sacha Carnegie.

Pirbright Camp
Woking
Jan 6 [1944]

My Darlingest Heart,
I am not writing a long letter, tho' I will before I go. This is just
to thank you, with love and also with admiration, for the perfect
happiness of our leave together. I could not have enjoyed it, had
you not been so splendid. I hope I will talk to you before you get
this, so just give the nits a big kiss each: & you will get another
letter with, I hope, some news in it!!

A million blessings on you all
from your adorer-in-chief Tom

* * *

*Towards the end of 1943, the 4th Bn Scots Guards had to be frag-
mented in order to reinforce the two Battalions in Italy. This involved
the formation of a Composite Battalion, with a Company from the
Coldstream Guards and a Company from the Irish Guards.*

*A song to commemorate this situation had the following title and
chorus:*

"Compos-ite Mentis"

We're the Micks, and the Jocks, and the Coalies,
The Composite Batallion de Luxe.
With a mixture of the Holy of Holies,
And the unholiest of Holy flukes.

But 'Nemo me impune lacessit's got
With 'Nulli secundum' the Hun on the spot.
'Quis separabit'? It will take a lot,
'Cos we're 'Tria Juncta in-you-know What.'

BY AIR MAIL

AIR LETTER

IF ANYTHING IS ENCLOSED
THIS LETTER WILL BE SENT
BY ORDINARY MAIL.

The Lady Mary Harvey

Holkham Hall

Wells

Norfolk   England

← Second fold here →

The following Certificate must be signed by the writer :—

I certify on my honour that the contents of this envelope
refer to nothing but private and family matters.

Signature }
Name only

ITALY
1944–1945

Somewhere
21 Jan 44

My Darling Maria

I do hope this manages to arrive in the not too distant future, though I have no idea when. We are all very well and comfortable and cheerful. The weather wasn't too nice to start with, but it is lovely now, and we all did PT this morning. I have been playing a little bridge and Bill* and I have been quite a hot combination. Tim† and Sacha‡ and David§ are all in good form, and Corby has been enjoying himself enormously. I have been reading a good many books, some good and others definitely poor. I do hope the luggage I sent home has arrived alright: I seem to have everything I want with me, except a fountain pen, so I am borrowing Bill's to write this.

It will be a wonderful moment when I first get your letters – not yet, I fear, and hear all your news – I am sure the family are all very flourishing. Give them all my love, and also to anyone else you see, as I am not writing any other letters at the moment. The news still seems to be pretty good at the moment. I hope I will be able to deliver Sylvia's parcels to Simon. I had a letter from Boo the other day and I have an awful feeling I never answered it – also I never adequately thanked Robert and Janet.¶ Do "drop them a line" will you? I hope the names of some of the Company have arrived with you. I would be grateful if you could keep in touch. Get Mother to help you.

Bless you, my Darling, look after yourselves and keep well and happy.

From your very very loving,
Tom

---

*   Vestey, TCH's 2nd in Command.
†   Mostyn.
‡   Carnegie.
§   Tylden-Wright. These last three were TCH's platoon commanders.
¶   Crichton-Stuart.

28 January
Major TC Harvey
Scots Guards
Comp No 1 IRTD, CMF

My darling Love

As you will see I have arrived very safely and in tremendous form. The journey, no details of which can I give you, went off without a hitch and I wasn't even seasick, in spite of pretty rough weather at times, and an obstinate refusal to wear my "anti seasick" plaster. I played quite a lot of bridge on the way, and read a lot of books, so the time passed very quickly. The general conditions are pretty primitive here, though we ourselves are quite comfortable. The civilian squalor and apathy are widespread and not very inspiring. We marched for twelve miles last night in lovely weather, but the hot smells of hay, cattle and humanity which engulfed us as we passed through the villages, was a striking contrast with the cool night air. No news yet of Sacha's baby which is very worrying for him: I do hope we hear soon. I have seen Harriet and John Haslewood and also Eric McKenzie who arrived here today and seems to be in very good form and most helpful – tell Tommy that I have seen him and he will pass on the news. I fear that Peter Atkinson-Clark and Tommy Marsham-Townsend have been killed, but don't talk of it until it appears officially. Poor Tommy was shortly due to come home, and had booked his passage. Needless to say we get a lot of laughs from the civilians, all moping about except for a few officials who wear enormous tawdry caps and overcoats, beneath which they gesticulate and chatter madly with no effect. We waited for over four hours for an engine, and when at last it came, it coupled up and went straight off with the result that more than half the passengers were in danger of being stranded. The frantic race began, but everyone luckily managed to catch up without much difficulty. The little boys run in and out of the trains making faces at the police who are quite unable to cope and just mope when the onlookers laugh. You can write to me at this address and even if I am not here they can send it on. David W. is commanding the 1st Bn. I did write before but I fear it will take ages to arrive: I do so hope this won't take long for it is loaded with messages of love to you all. I long to hear your news and will write again when I can.

Bless all of you, my Darlings, big kisses to David and Caroline, messages to all the family, and my most devoted love to your beloved self, from your ever adoring Tom

* * *

Major TC Harvey
No(1) Gds Bn No IRTD
CMF, 1 Feb 44

My Darling Heart

I sent off a rather scrubby little cable about 3 days ago, which I hope didn't take too long to arrive. In it I gave you what is likely to be my next address and where I imagine I shall be fairly soon. All seems to be going pretty well here, and at the moment we are busy getting fit and shaking off the cobwebs of inactivity. We are settling down very well on the whole, and the weather has been very good, tho' cold at night. The dirt of the local inhabitants is rather worse than in peace time, but they seem to be fairly well fed. They scream at each other all day long and pester one with demands for 'cigaretta' or 'caramelli', especially the most diminutive and grubby little urchins who have a pronounced partiality for cigars. Their ideas of personal hygiene are somewhat limited, with the result that it is as well to walk delicately through the streets. We have been doing a good deal of hill climbing, and although it is hot and tiring work, the air is lovely and clean at the top, and a welcome change from the dusty aromatic smells of Italian domestic quarters.

My efforts to learn Italian have, I fear, peterd [*sic.*] out very quickly, but I must resume them again. I am going to try and get you some silk stockings tho' I've forgotten your size and am told that their quality is not very good. However I hope some will arrive with you soon, and that you have good weather in which to display them. I hope that all money matters are alright, and that you do not spend too much of your own, for mine is there for you to use. I think it might be quite a good idea to take out an insurance policy for Caroline similar to that of David's and in addition to the one that Mother has given her. I am sure the babies are in tremendous form and a great blessing to you all. Any new photographs that you get I should love to have. I am not expecting any mail for some time yet as I have very little faith in the APO number which I gave to you. It seems rather pointless to write to any other member of the family yet whilst there is still no news – but I am writing to John, giving various bits of regimental news which would bore you to tears. So will you tell Mother that she must regard this letter as half hers and that I will write to her separately later on. Give lots of love to Susie, and also to Eliza whose "blessed burden" is not I hope proving too tiresome: tell Tommy that the Bn is quite different from when he knew it, with many new faces. Tell Silvia that I am not likely to be seeing Simon for some time, so that for the time being I am hanging on to the cigarettes. I have done what I can to get the sweaters to John Nelson, but that isn't particularly easy either. The men are busy washing their clothes today, a sight which I feel their wives could hardly bear in silence. But here they have the excellent tradition that the women do all the work, and they walk up the mountains in bare feet, with 2, 3 or 4 cwt sacks on their heads. The men just look on. You might practise it a little as I shall want you to carry my golf clubs in that way!!

Bless you, my Darlings, and all my love from your most
devoted and ever loving
Tom

2ⁿᵈ Bn Scots Guards
CMF
8 Feb 44

My Darling Maria
You are a clever girl – your letter dated 24 Jan arrived safe and
sound on 4 Feb, and filled everyone else with envy. I was thrilled
to get one so soon, as I was not expecting it, and now I can hardly
wait for another. I do so hope mine have been arriving alright,
as I have written quite a lot, tho' I fear with little news. It was
a great pleasure to see Boy* again; he and his merry men are in
tremendous form. We all went to dine with him last night, and
had a very good dinner, followed by some revolting local cognac
which tasted of caramel. The village in which we are is no more
and no less squalid than the others, and most of the houses are
in a pretty good shambles. We lodge chez an old Contessa and
her derelict husband and the house tends to become a screaming
parrot-house of local contention and arbitration. Eggs and things
aren't very easily acquired and are very expensive but I have had
one the last two mornings. The dust on the roads is horrid and
the weather pretty cold, but so far not wet. I hope you had a good
visit to Ringstead and found Mama in good order. I fear she may
be a little hurt that I haven't written to her but as you know there
aren't a lot of letter forms available and I haven't had one to spare.
I will send her one of my next ones, I am so glad to hear that
David and Caroline are in such good form, and are getting more
and more fun everyday. I wish I could find little presents for them
but it would be hopeless. I am on the track of silk stockings but
I don't know if they're any good or what size you want. I haven't
yet had the chance of a shopping tour yet. Bobby went to Naples
the other day and saw a man whipping a horse. So he seized the
whip and beat the wop about the head. Not far from here there
are a mass of wild fowl, teal, widgeon and mallard and Hugh

---

*   Harris.

Rose and Jock have got several. Gerald Potter is in the next village and I hope to see him today; tell Frank Cringle that I have seen him, I must stop now, my Darling: it was a tremendous joy to get your lovely cheerful letter, with all the news. Give the babies lots and lots of love and kisses from me, and also my love to Susie and everyone else. We have had a great welcome here and great things are expected of us, so I hope and pray that we shall justify that confidence.

God bless you all,
From your most deeply devoted lover and husband
Tom

* * *

Major TC Harvey
2nd Bn Scots Guards
CMF
15 Feb 44

My Darling and Most Precious Maria
We have just returned from the line after a few days of comparative discomfort but relatively little danger. Sacha was unfortunately wounded tho' very slightly, and I am due to visit him today to find out what exactly is the matter. I understand that he won't be away for very long. I wish we could find out about his baby, for that would be a tremendous weight off his mind. So far I haven't got any other of your letters but I know there are lots on the way. I have sent you some silk stockings (2 prs) and some sort of undies tho' I have no idea whether they will be of any use to you. I have got my eye on some more, but it isn't always easy to have the ready money. I am writing this letter, sitting in the sun on the balcony of our mess. The house belongs to a somewhat down-at-heel Count and his wife who to judge by the frenzied screaming of their conversation, must be permanently on the point of hitting

each other. The rooms which we have got are all on the sunless side, so at the moment they are rather bleak. But sitting out here one gets lovely and warm. Tim is very seedy with a sort of Gippy Tummy, I only hope he doesn't take too long to get over it. Not having so far been able to get around much I haven't been able to find many old friends or acquaintances – but I have seen Nugent Head and Robin Mays-Smith whom John knows, Jack Profumo, Peter Marsham, Max Niven and Johnny Drury-Lowe. It is far more difficult to get news of the war out here than at home, tho' possibly what one does hear is more reliable. I am afraid there has been some disappointment at home, but taking into account the extraordinary difficulties of the country I feel that things are going pretty well on the whole. Today I am going to Sorrento for the night with Richard Coke, and will do some hospitalising on the way, in Naples. One often finds several friends and it cheers them up to see fresh faces, however dismal in themselves. I shall be writing to Mother tomorrow, but give her all my love. The weather is gradually improving here, tho' one still has bouts of torrential rain.

I imagine you are very busy planning summer suitings for David and Caroline and making them look too sweet – the sailor suit in particular should be most fetching. What fun you will be having with them as the weather gets better. I do hope Eliza is bearing up well and not having a wretched time; I fear Silvia will be worrying over Simon, but I have heard no news of him so that is a good sign. I may pick up some gossip today and I will write it all to you if it is not too indiscreet. So, my love, enough until then. Give the darling babies lots of love from their Daddy and keep for yourself all the blessings in the world.

From your most loving Tom

* * *

118

Major TC Harvey
2nd Bn Scots Guards
CMF
February 18

My Darling Love
I have just got your letter dated February 8 and February 10 &
one from mother dated Feb 11 which is wonderfully quick. I'm
so sorry to hear that little David's foot is again giving him trouble.
It will be a confounded nuisance for him to have to stomp about
in plaster. I do so hope it gets well quickly. I have no idea when
my parcels to you will arrive; I am sending off another today,
some stuff to make underwear and with a little lace coat which I
thought you could cut up for petticoat trimming. Later on I will
try to get you some material for a dress but the difficulty here is to
get money. The shops in Naples all filled with things that haven't
been seen in London for years & they make Aspreys look like a
bucket shop. I hope this little parcel may arrive for your birthday,
bringing with it all my love and wishes for many many happy
returns. I will write to you a birthday letter later so I trust it will
arrive in time. I saw Bill Sidney[*] in the hospital today. Very well
indeed and only slightly wounded – do tell Jacqueline.[†] He has
a slight flesh wound in the behind, and is certainly in the right
place very safe, comfortable and well looked after.

Also I saw Peter Wakefield, the son of the vicar at Hunstanton – so do get mother to pass on the news. He has been pretty
badly wounded – with a gash in one leg, and injury to both eyes.
However his eyes are getting better and he is likely to return to
England soon. He was very cheerful, smoking cigarettes and
joking. When I left him he was just about to have his first shave

---

*   Was to win the VC (a great boost for the morale of the Grenadier
Guards). He became the 1st Viscount De L'Isle and last Governor-General of
Canada.
    †   His wife.

for a week by an Italian barber. He was wounded by a mortar at the Factory in the Beachhead and was not picked up for 3 hours – but now he is getting along fine and looking forward to getting home.

Richard Coke has just got the MC, which is a splendid effort and well deserved. Have had lovely peaceful time lately, and am hoping, rather against hope that it will last.

Give my love to all at home and big hugs and kisses to the nit-pots. Your letters, my Darling, are the loveliest treat in the world; they bring you so close and I hear the Italian piazzas ringing with the voices of those I love.

Bless you my angels from your ever loving Tom

* * *

Major TC Harvey
2nd Bn Scots Guards
24 Feb 44

My Most Darling Maria
I have just had another batch of letters from you, some early ones addressed to IRTD and another dated 13 Feb. I am so delighted to hear that you are all keeping well, and that the nit pots are being good and happy. As you can guess from the pencil, since I last wrote we have moved to less comfortable surroundings, tho' on the whole things are not too bad. You will however be very sorry to hear that Boy has been very badly wounded. They operated on him very quickly and he survived the operation – but he is still very ill and the Doctor can't make any promises for a week yet. It really is bad luck on him, as it is the end of a second brief spell of command: I haven't been able to go and see him yet, but at the first opportunity I will. Sacha is getting along well tho' again I haven't been able to see him recently. I have been able to get the Overseas news in the evenings and also

odd programmes like Hardey's Half Hour – which brings one very close to home. Reading materials are however always very welcome, and anything you send out, no matter how trashy but preferably not too trashy, will be a great blessing. I gather that the W Derbyshire election has been a real music hall turn with Billy in the middle of it. Mother tells me that he has been conspiring with the Fermoys so I can see myself being involved in similarly unseemly brawls in the future. I have now had 2 letters from Mother and one from John, both in good form I thought. I gather from her that you vamped Maurice F quite shamelessly and completely captivated him – what with that and your secret drinking with Susie, my absence seems to be having disastrous consequences: I am daily awaiting to hear of a queue of Polish airmen outside the front door, but I suppose that not even my best friends would dare tell me. I very much fear that my parcels of stuffs will take months to arrive and will not reach you until long after your birthday: and even my next letter may be late, so I think it safer to wish you many happiest returns of the day now. 7th March '20 has proved a happy day for many people but for no one has it been more heaven-sent than for me. But it's ridiculous having to celebrate such an occasion apart, and so will somehow have to fix things out here so that we can be together again next year – and I hope long before. The war seems to be boiling up at your end, and the feelings of everybody must be rising daily. I only hope that a pervading spirit of resolve is the dominant feeling – to get it over quick, like a visit to the dentist and then go out and have a whacking great lunch! Give David and Caroline lots of love from their Daddy, with an extra big goodnight Poof for David. Bless you, my Darling Heart, and may all goodness and happiness smile upon you.

From your ever loving and devoted Tom

* * *

Major TC Harvey
1st Bn Scots Guards
CMF, 28 Feb 44

My Most Darling Maria
I got your letter dated 18th on the 26th and was delighted to hear of your successful visit to London. You certainly seem to have struck a good bargain with your fur coat, and it should at least be able to last you until such time as the Harvey millions can rise to a mink. What fun it must have been seeing Lotus Blossom again, and having a real good gossip. Harry sounds an excellent person. It was very clever of you to avoid the bombing, which seems to have sharpened up a good deal. I should be inclined to avoid it as much as possible for the time being. The Dusgate house, I must say sounds ideal, and I should snap it up if you can, and if it really is as good as it sounds. We can afford to pay a little more now, and I can't believe that they will want such an awful lot. I can't wait to hear what luck you have had, but letters are very good and I will soon know. I expect you heard that Harry Hardcastle* invited John and Anne and the children to go to Australia with them: but naturally enough John wants to see the war through first. I believe they'd do the job very well, not that I'd care for it, particularly with that couple. One is too liable to become a slave and lose all hope of a free and easy family life. From here there is little news, as we have been out of touch for some time. Boy is still alive, but still very ill. Alice Martyn writes that she is sharing a flat with another Wren called Rosie who knows me. I can't think who it can be. Thank you so much for ordering the cigarettes – I hope they manage to arrive ok. I am not expecting any parcels for some time yet. Give the nits lots and lots of love, also to Susie, Pa and Ma, Roger, Eliza and Silvia. If this letter too arrives in time, it brings a million kisses for your birthday and tons and tons of love from your ever devoted and adoring Tom

---

*   Regimental name for the Duke of Gloucester.

Major TC Harvey
1st Bn Scots Guards
CMF
2 March 44

My Very Darling Maria

Having just had my daily wash and shave, tho' I fear, nothing more extensive than that, I feel clean and tidy enough to put pen to paper once again, though I fear with little news. You will probably have heard by now that Boy died of his wounds a few days ago: and you will have gathered that from the first his chances of survival were terribly slight. The Doctors have said that had he lived he would have been an invalid for all time, and that is some consolation. For all his superficial mannerisms and exaggerations, I was most awfully fond of him and we have had great fun together, and I shall miss him very much. He never really had the chance to get into his stride and lead the Bn into the attack – but had he, I am sure he would have done splendidly.

I am still sitting in my little hole, with nothing much to complain about, except the weather which tends to be pretty wet, bringing with it the usual accompaniment of mud. I am keeping extremely well, as I always do, much to my annoyance, in conditions of discomfort. But it is a great blessing, as everything is so much easier if one is feeling well. Sitting here surrounded by olive trees, orange groves and, at intervals flowering cherries, one can understand the appeal of a peace time Italy. But then, and now even more, one sees that it is a beauty of facade, hiding both poverty and ugliness, incompetence and corruption. At the moment I am reading an amusing but rather trashy "romantic history" about Lady Hamilton (Miledi), which naturally talks a good deal about Naples and Caserta, and other places I have visited. In those days, of course, the contrasts were even deeper, as in every country then, but here they seem to have remained constant almost without change. Most evenings I manage to get on the wireless, the African Overseas Service from London, and its news, particularly a day to day summary of events with comments by appropriate experts, is really extraordinarily good – far better than the banal cliches of the normal service.

Did you ever get a lot of addresses of some of the men's next of kin. I do hope so, and always that you will make a big effort to write to each one and make contact: you have no idea the extent to which the men are inclined to worry about their wives – their jobs, their children, their money, the Americans and the whole bag of tricks: and it might well be that you could be of enormous help and comfort to some of them. I expect that you keep in touch with Pamela Vestey. Bill and I hardly ever meet as we function alternately, I hope to get a letter today, bringing all your news. Give masses and masses of kisses to the beloved nits and keep the biggest one, my Darling, for yourself to press against your lovely lips.

Ever your loving and adoring Tom

* * *

Major TC Harvey
1st Bn Scots Guards
CMF
9 March 44

My Darling Love
I am horrified to hear that my letters are taking so long to get to you: I have been trying to write regularly at least twice a week, but they don't seem to have arrived. I have just got yours dated 28th Feb and also the APO letters. We have just come out of the line after a long and rainy spell, but we are now in a most delectable place and one well worth waiting for. The Coy* is billed in very nice houses, and we have got a Coy Officers Mess

---

*   Company.

in one of the Palazzos. Tho' it isn't as yet very well furnished, it is highly luxurious with electric light etc – and we have employed an Italian chef at vast expense. The estate consists of about 15 acres of orange groves, lemon groves and vineyards which reach right to the edge of the cliffs – then break off with a sheer drop hundreds of feet into the blue blue sea below. We have limitless oranges and lemons and grapefruit, so with rum and gin and various wines and brandy we manage to have a high old time – or will have when we get organised. David Cuthbert blew in to see me yesterday when I was in bed, full of news. David W's[*] death, coming on top of Boy's is a damnable blow, and one's feelings for Patsy are beyond expression: he had done superlatively well, and was hit by a stray shell, when he was way out of the front line. One just has to be thick skinned about these things in war time, but that has been almost more than I can bear. Simon, I have invited to dine tonight, tho' I haven't seen him yet. It will be lovely to see him again, and you can picture us beating up the local lovelies together. One thing is certain we must both "hit the town" together – or otherwise one of us will be forever at a disadvantage!!

After the discomfort of the last few weeks – I never once took off my leather waistcoat, leave alone anything below it – it is bliss to be back in civilisation, eating good food, drinking less good wine, and generally tasting the joys of peace: later on I hope to broaden the perspective a little, doing some sight seeing, Pompeii one afternoon and then perhaps Capri, and also who knows, perhaps a few Marquesas and Contessas all of whom are already lined up by David Cuthbert!!

The news of you all at home is lovely to hear, and my heart thrills to hear of David's and Caroline's good progress and sweet (?) temper. The 8th Army dance sounds great fun, and I have no doubt that the bronzed heroes made excellent dancing partners. Greater temptation comes your way than mine – for here it is

---

[*]   Lt Col. David Wedderburn.

125

lamentably scarce! Perhaps by now you have heard definite news of the house – I do so hope you have managed to clinch the deal, as we can get any furniture we need from our various ancestral homes. I am sending you a "crate" (only 1 doz.) of lemons, tho' I doubt if they'll survive. I do so hope my silks and satins reach you soon. Alas! I spent 7th March in a most unsuitable way, and it was difficult to picture the previous years without what the cheaper novelists call "a wry smile". I trust, my Darling, that you did manage to have a very happy birthday and that David gave you a present! Bless you all, my loves, and a million kisses on your heads.

From your loving and devoted Tom

* * *

Major TC Harvey
1st Bn Scots Guards
CMF
17th March 44

My Most Darling Love
I was simply thrilled to hear that you have got the house: many congratulations, how happy you must be. £3 a week sounds marvellously cheap – you know you have full access to my account, so be sure and make good use of it whenever you want. Although I am writing in pencil, I am still in the arms of civilisation, and having a lovely peaceful time. Before leaving our billets, we had two whacking dinner parties, the last one including Georges Burns and Montague. Our food was superb, lovely sauce with the fish, tender lamb with delicious vegetables including potatoes fried in breadcrumbs with a sprinkling of cheese (try it) and orange souffle, made to perfection. Bill produced a wealth of genuine liqueurs so a good time was had by all! Now, tho' the Company has less good billets, the officers are in a lovely little

house, recently built very well "appointed" with a superb view. The owner, who is away, is a man of astounding culture, and a most comprehensive and cosmopolitan library, first class books in every language, Huxley, Dickens, Thackeray and a splendid wireless (*Scheherazade* is now on) and also a gramophone with lots of symphonies and a piano. We have to use the central mess for food, except breakfasts so we aren't eating so well, but we are most cosy. Yesterday Bill and I and Bobby Petre went over to Pompeii and saw the ruined city, which is fascinating – particularly the interior decoration of some of the better preserved private houses. The nearest equivalent to the style is that of the Adams, who got their inspiration from Pompeii. In one room the walls are decorated with exquisite miniature friezes painted on walls of red, black and gold – the red colouring made from sea-shells and the gold or yellow from egg yolks. One can still see the marks of the chariot wheels, the grooves for the sliding doors of the shops and the complete layout of the Baths, hot and cold – drying rooms etc, all exquisitely decorated and floored with marble – I am taking the Company over tomorrow. Last night, Cuthbert, Bill and I dined at Positano, a gem of a town, cut in the side of precipitous cliffs, and tumbling awkwardly down to the sea, like a straggling waterfall. Unfortunately it was pouring with rain where we came out of dinner so the drive back in our open jeep was rather a wet affair. I must tell you, my heart leapt when I saw in the library here a copy of a Leonardo Treatise on Water – but it is not the Holkham one, although that is referred to in the text, it seems that our Patrone is a marine engineer, tho' he must be a considerable scholar and sociologist as well!! My Italian is awful and I am making no headway: I am most ashamed and am resolving to do better. I still haven't managed to see Simon, we have missed each other at every turn, and now he is in the throws of St Patrick's Day orgies, however, I am going over to stay a night with him on Saturday, so we shall have a terrific reunion. I am so happy to hear the nit-pots are so flourishing – bless them:

David will probably hate his new home to start with but he'll soon settle down. I got a letter from Mother postmarked 11th on the 15th – quick work. It is lovely when they come so quick as one feels really near and in touch. Bless you, my Heart's Darling, and a million kisses to you and the babies from your ever loving and devoted Tom

* * *

12 March 44
Major TC Harvey
1st Bn Scots Guards CMF

My Darlingest Maria

My new address will doubtless cause you tremendous surprise, but I am only one of many to leave my old address, and I am taking all the "circus" with me. Territorially there is almost no change, in fact we are hoping to keep our present lovely billets, but I fear we shall not be allowed to: John Dalrymple is at present commanding, though final appointments haven't yet been made. Such a change has been becoming inevitable for some time, and the sooner it is completed the better. I haven't yet managed to see Simon, which is maddening, but I shall be dining with him one day next week. I saw Ronnie Strutt who dined with Simon last night, and said he was in tremendous form, in a luxurious hotel. I must say that we are living like fighting cocks, thanks to our Italian chef: we have Baba Rhum, omelette aux asperges (eggs at 1/-) and many other delicacies – while our landlord plies us with lovely oranges, which we either devour or use for cocktails. I only wish I could send you some, but they would all go bad. Tonight we have got a large dinner party – 11 people – and so everyone has gone out to tea except me: I am sitting alone writing, munching a bar of chocolate, and smoking a cigarette. Last night we had a 1/2 Bn party, very good considering how many people were there, plenty to drink and the usual licentious songs and acts to follow. I hammered away, as usual at a semi-derelict piano, and again this morning, at church, but on that occasion in a rather more subdued strain. I have just got your letter dated 5th, when you were still unaware of the many tragic deaths, notably David and Boy both of whom are irreplaceable – the former particularly, as he was an inspired commander, in addition to being one of the most delightful people I have ever known. My God, what a price we are paying for victory.

The weather has become wet and miserable again, and we are lucky to be in good homes. I am so glad you are writing to the wives, as they love it so, and several of the men have heard from their wives saying so. By now David will have his foot out of plaster, and I hope all the better for a rest. I am sure he got immense pleasure out of it, while it lasted. The house too – what your suspense has been I dare not think, as I am on a tenterhook myself. I do hope you have managed to get it, as it sounds perfection itself. I must write to John now: I have heard from him several times and also an airgraph from Mrs M. I told Archie Pearson to ask you for £12 for photographs, and I can collect the money here from the men. So for now, Darling, I'll say good bye with much love and many kisses to you all. I hear Caroline is a poppit – bless her. I can't wait to see the photographs.

Bless you and all my love from your own, Tom

* * *

Major TC Harvey
1st Bn Scots Guards
CMF
21 March

My Most Darling Maria
I have just got your very sweet and understanding letter dated 12th

March. I knew well that all of you at home would be as heart-broken at our sad losses as we ourselves are: but your philosophy is absolutely right, and we must all keep going at all costs and at any price. I too had great difficulty in telling Patsy how much I grieved for her – one's heart aches with sorrow and helplessness. But I'm going to snap out of it and tell you of all my doings, for as you must know one tries to keep things going as if nothing had happened. Since I last wrote to you, my most pleasant day has been last Saturday when I went over to dine and spend the night with Simon and his Bn. I found them all installed in a palatial hotel, and Simon himself in terrific form, looking awfully well. As you know he did brilliantly and everyone is very sorry that he didn't get a medal. On arriving I went with him up to Col. Andrew's room where we consumed dollops of whisky, and had a long snake about simply everyone and everything. To my mind Andrew Scott is one of the wonderful people I've ever met, a superb and brilliant commanding officer in battle and the most entertaining and delightful host imaginable. What he must feel about David I shudder to think – but he was reluctant to talk about it. We then went and had a most excellent dinner, with Jim Egan and John Haslewood in great form. After dinner I met Geoff Todd who sent you lots of love. I thought him charming: he is out here chaperoning the band, and finding it a rather tedious job, I should imagine. By way of an after dinner "spectacle", Vesuvius kindly started to erupt, and we had a magnificent view of its flaming cauldron, overflowing down the sides in streams of molten fire. Tonight, as I write, it is as good as ever. However to get back to Simon – we gossiped until about 11 and then to bed to be called in the morning with a delicious breakfast in bed. I had to leave early as Bill and I were due to visit hospitals in Naples, but we made a plan to meet again this week. Bill and I then bounced off in a fiendish truck along equally fiendish roads to visit hospitals and then home via Pompeii where we stopped to look at the new Cathedral. It is a superb and lavishly decorated affair in beautiful tho' ornate taste with the most lovely High Altar and a mass of small side Chapels, each with a fine modern painting as reredos and exquisite mosaics on the domed ceilings. The cathedral is vast in height and its domes are in pairs, the lower being open, to reveal a higher, both painted in lovely blues and whites, and often with the most intricate and delicate designs, superimposed by St Andrews' crosses of silver and crystal – the whole effect being most impressive, but providing to my mind a rather unhealthy contrast with the squalor and poverty outside. Next door, there is an orphanage for little girls which we also visited. I bought a little bib there for Caroline, which I will be sending along: also a little pair of gloves for David, leather with string backs. Among the rooms we saw, was one of "Sacred and Profane Objects presented by the Faithful". The sacred objects were mostly Chalices, Pixes etc. many of them extremely fine. The profane objects were mostly swords and epaulettes, but the most incongruous was the Silver Cup presented to the winner by the Hankow Golf Club in 1897 – a Mr FP Johnson, who poor wretch, had surrendered his most precious possession and thus, no doubt, saved his soul! You might look out a few of my prizes, if any, and dispose of them accordingly. We are still having a lovely time, tho' it clearly can't last forever. I do so adore getting all your letters, with the news of the babies and the house and everything. Mind that, as well, you keep me in touch with all the social low-down – and in particular the doings of my well-loved blondes. Norfolk seems to have its share of parties still, and I can see you're becoming quite the "Wing-co's floozie". What heaven it will be to have your own house: I'm sure you can't wait to get settled in. I must say au revoir now, my angel heart. Give little David and little Caroline big big hugs from me, and may a million blessings light upon you all. Bless you, and my most devoted love from Tom

* * *

Major TC Harvey
1st Bn Scots Guards
CMF
24 March 44

My Darling Heart,
I got your letter dated 15th a couple of days ago and was thrilled
to hear how well the house is getting along. It must have been
a pleasant change for you both to go to Ringstead, and I only
hope David behaved himself. I expect that there will be one or
two tantrums in the new house at first but that should all wear
off! Since I last wrote to you, very little of note has occurred, as
I am glad to say we are still in our nice quiet billets. The main
interest at present is the Eruption, which is rapidly becoming
rather a bore. Yesterday I had one of the worst days driving I
have ever known – in an open jeep. I drove over to Avellino, via
Naples (a distance of over 70 miles) and soon after passing thro'
Naples we got enveloped in an appalling snowstorm, with an
icy wind and negligible visibility. It was a long and most tedious
drive – by about 15.30h we had finished our business, so I took
Eustace Balfour to have tea with the 24 Canadian nurses with
whom we travelled out – security hasn't allowed me to mention
them before – a very pleasant and cheerful collection who helped
to make our voyage reasonably tolerable. However they gave us a
great welcome and we stayed to tea, so that it was 18.00h before
we started back. By now the snow (which incidentally was black
to start with) had cleared and we drove back in fine style, on the
way getting a simply superb view of Vesuvius. High up in pitch
black sky there was a steady red glow from the crater, and then
very often a gigantic billow of smoke would burst out, floodlit by
red flames, and silhouetted against the sky like some unearthly
and colossal plume. To add to the effect, great forks of lightning
flickered and flashed in and out and showers of sparks shot up
high into the sky. But unfortunately as we approached Pompeii,

the scene was clouded and we found ourselves in a whirling fog, first of stinging, hail-like rubble and then of a fine powdery dust – and that sand storm of pulverised sulphur followed us all the way home and is with us still. It comes through the windows, it comes under the doors, up through the floors, everywhere in fact and we are all beginning to look like grey creatures from another world. This morning the visibility varies from 50x to 100x and the whole earth, trees, paths, houses, cars, beasts and men are covered in a coating of thin grey powder!! You can imagine how glad we were to get back, to a warm fire, round which Eustace and I sat with first a whisky and water and then tea and fried eggs!

I have written a marching song for the 2nd Front and have been trying to write it down, and here is my unaided effort – though I doubt if you can make much sense of it – the base for the beginning is C E F F# G G C etc.

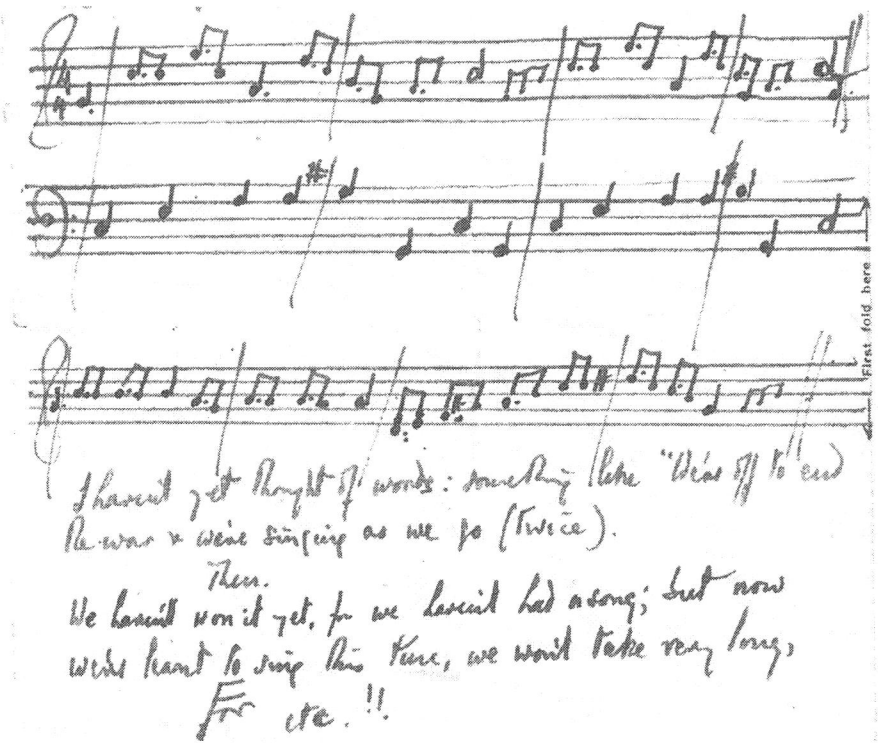

I haven't yet thought of words: something like "We're off to end the war and we're singing as we go" (twice).

Then,

"We haven't won it yet, for we haven't had a song; but now We've learnt to sing this time, we won't take very long"

For etc!!"

If you can get that published I'll buy you a new toothbrush – but don't be had for a sucker!!

Bless you, my angels one and all, and a million kisses from your loving (and should I say Lara-ing) Tom

* * *

26 March 44
Major TC Harvey
1st Bn Scots Guards
CMF

My Darlingest Love

Tonight is Sunday evening and I am sitting beside the fire, writing this on my knee. Our Italian landlord and his wife and mother are also sitting here, reading our papers and chatting away. He talks English as well as French, but normally we talk together in French. I have been trying to get Winston's speech on the wireless, but without success. Since I last wrote our chief incident has been the continued inconvenience of Vesuvius, which has converted the whole countryside into a complete grey-green desert. The dust still gets into one's eyes and throat, but it is certainly better and will I hope remain so. But with at least 2 inches of dust everywhere, the gales of icy wind which have swept us lately become like tropical sandstorms – in fact the weather is perfectly and absolutely pestilential and has increased my dislike of this horrid country by about 100%. You'd think that here at this time of year we'd be basking in the sun – but not a bit of it.

Today I got your letter posted on the 21ˢᵗ which was very quick – but I fear you still did not know my new address. However by now you should: Guy Taylor arrived the other day and is a great addition. I haven't been able to see Simon again, which is most disappointing and I was unable to get to the dance which they gave last night, and which I believe was a great success.

Instead I had an awful day driving in the Jeep for miles and miles along the dust and cinder strewn roads, with the coldest wind blowing it into one's face and freezing one at the same time. When we got back we found that our journey had been all in vain and I just hadn't got the energy to turn out again. Instead I went to bed early and stayed there until 9.45! David Cuthbert has been staying here this weekend but I have hardly seen him. On Friday night we went to gamble in Positano – chemin de fer – and it wasn't long before I lost my allotted portion – however I then stopped and resisted the temptation of trying to get it back. Various others played poker, and we all enjoyed ourselves, it being a change from the normal. I am heartbroken at not taking a lot of money off fat Italian black-marketeers, but I can't honestly say that I expected to. It will be just as well to get it straight about the rent of P. W. – but don't lose a good house for the sake of a few pounds. It must be unbearable at Holkham with your father making such a fool of himself. I should certainly allow yourself to lose your temper one day, as it is high time someone told him how ridiculous he was being.

I am in great haste to catch the post so I must stop now. Give the chickadees lots and lots of kisses from me and also, my Darling, my devoted love to your beloved self from your ever adoring, Tom

* * *

Major TC Harvey
1st Bn Scots Guards
CHF, 28 March 44

My Precious Darling

I am writing this from a new 'home', which at first we feared would be less nice than our late one, but which has turned out to be surprisingly civilised. For one thing, the country people are clean, healthy and sturdy, and the air is much cleaner than the dust-ridden environs of Vesuvius. The peasants here all wear traditional dress, the men, long black capes with fur collars, the women broad bell-bottomed skirts, embroidered bodices with a high, tight waist and brightly coloured shawls over their heads. Both men and women wear full length white stockings, gartered criss-cross, often in pretty colours. They work like blacks in the fields all day, hoeing and digging – tho' instead of spades they use things like this which they wield high above their heads and bring cracking down into the soil. They seem to work in parties of eight, which with their variegated coloured dresses, leave delightful splashes of white, red, green and yellow, along the bare slopes, and among the olive trees. Today Bill and I were clambering over high and distant hills, miles from anywhere and of the five Italians we found and spoke to, 4 spoke excellent American-English having lived for years in Connecticut or New York!! Our present landlord is a prince who was educated at Wellington and is now a prisoner of war. His house is charming and very English with a superb squash court and a swimming bath! We played squash last night, but the rackets gave out almost at once, and are now in the hands of the cobbler, who I hope will make them fairly serviceable. The wind is still cold as ice and very strong, so that the swimming pool is still merely an object of academic inspection. But we are surprising well found, tho' the demands of strenuous training do not permit very much "luxuriating".

I haven't had a letter from you since I last wrote, or one from Mother for some time – nor I fear have I been able to write to her but I will very soon. I do hope the beloved children are really well and happy and that they are being at any rate fairly good. I will send them their gloves and bib as soon as I can. Mind that you secure the house alright; no doubt your parents will say we can't afford the extra money but rather than lose such a fine opportunity, I am sure we can. I am paid at such a vast rate nowadays! I wasn't able to get to Simon's party which was very sad – but it happened at a hectic time – and I just couldn't make it. I do hope I shall be able to see the old boy, and use him as a Mercury. Derek hasn't arrived yet, but Col Guy is here in great form tho' suffering from near flu.

Well, my love, it is dinner time. Bless you all a thousand million times, and a heap of kisses on your heads, from your every loving and devoted Tom

* * *

Major TC Harvey
1st Bn Scots Guards
CMF
2 April 44

My Darlingest Love
I had a lovely bunch of letters from you, dated I think, 18th, 22th and 24th. I am delighted to hear that the parcels have arrived and are acceptable. I hope to get a day off again this week and I will see if I can pick up any other little tit bits. Please don't have any nonsense from Boodles – I wrote to him resigning when I was at Malton and instructed my bankers not to pay. If there is any trouble let me know, and I will write him a stinker – and if necessary you can always write to David Robarts to complain. With reference to our combined incomes, I have at my hand the

latest statement from the CGA which divides our incomes into two headings – one taxed (at source) and the other, untaxed.

For Taxed I have	£314.15/-6		
You have	£148.18/-6	Total	£463/. 14
Untaxed	I have £171/.16		
You have	£62/.15	Total	£234/.11

And Army Pay which they estimated at £300 but which will in fact be nearer £500 – in other words the total is nearer £1200 – of course the untaxed has still to be taxed and they reckon my 43/44 liability will be at least £125 and possibly £280. However enough of that for the time being. I am very boldly addressing this to the new home, and I am very envious of a wretched little airmail card seeing it before I do. How blissful you must be, installed and domiciled on your own. I know the house well by sight, standing on that little hill, with the wood behind it, and lavender fields all around.

We are still at peace in our ducal or is it princely – residence and I am writing this on the patio with the sun shining hard for a change. There is desperately little news as I haven't been about at all lately, having been training etc instead. What a tremendous effort of Bill Sidney's wasn't it. I had no idea it was en l'air, I have seen him once since hospital and he is now quite recovered.

A short letter now – I will write again soon. Bless you, all my pretty Darlings, and a million kisses to you all. From your ever loving and devoted Tom

* * *

Major TC Harvey
1st Bn Scots Guards
CMF
6 April 44

My Beloved Darling

It seems ages since I last wrote to you, and my last letter was very dull and empty of news. But since I last wrote I have been successful in getting a night off and thoroughly enjoyed myself, although I spent most of the time driving the Jeep. I left here after lunch on Monday and did some hurried shopping for you in Naples – among the rather mouldy things I got for you, was a length of rather pretty lame stuff, to make up into "an evening smoking" or coatee. My adviser, however, insisted that you had only short very puffy sleeves and the coat cut a la smoking, so I hope it will be alright. That done, I resumed my travels and had the most lovely drive along the Pompeii Estrada; it was like slicing through a cake of pink icing, for on either side of the road there were sweeping fields of almond blossom, with Vesuvius rising up on one side, and the other side falling away into the deep blue of the sea. The weather was perfect, and the whole effect quite wonderful until one arrived into the dust belt where a blight seems to have descended blanketing the whole prospect with a drab and colourless powder. Eventually I reached Simon, who gave me a wonderful reception, in spite of the fact that I arrived suddenly and unannounced. As usual, the excellence of the wine, the food and the accommodation was supreme, and after a really good gossip I tottered off to bed to sleep the sleep of the semi-tight, until my breakfast was wafted into me at 9am by the ubiquitous and unequalled Gray, unfortunately I had to leave soon after, but I gave Simon my few humble trinkets for you. On the way back I stopped to buy you a sort of negligee, dressing gown affair, which I trust will be of some use, and as I was lunching with Hugh Rose afterwards I have given it to him either to give to you or to Tommy. I then set off on my way back and stopped on the way at Bill Sidney's cocktail party. I found him in terrific form, and giving full justice to the occasion. Boy Brooke was there, also very cheerful and pleasant – in fact all the Grenadiers were there, smugly basking in reflected glory. I got back safely in time for dinner, having thoroughly enjoyed my lightning tour. I also managed to acquire some "buckchee" stores including a jeep and a trailer!! Last night I fear I again indulged myself somewhat with the result that I lost a lot of money at poker. Mercifully I woke up feeling very well so I was able to face my losses without undue remorse. We have, in this superb house of ours, a lovely dining room with a vast table which we load with fruit and nuts and flowers and surround with eighteen or twenty chairs. We have one or two pipers in after dinner who play interminably but add a very welcome atmosphere of regimental tradition. On Sunday we are planning to have a Company party, which involves a good many scrounging parties and may, I fear, have disastrous results which will bring the pock-marked pundits of AMGOT* running round like women shoppers round a street accident. However there is little enough amusement for the chaps and a really good blind will do them all a lot of good. The photographs have arrived, and I am delighted with them: particularly the ones of David in the garden, playing with the hoses. The indoor ones are not so good, for in some he looks as tho' he's been nosing his way into a large jar of strawberry jam and in others, as though he is running an enormous temperature. What fun they must be and what a nightmare it is, never knowing what David's going to say next or how he may insult some aged or otherwise venerable visitor. I am sure he does it on purpose, and gets immense pleasure from seeing you "puce up" with embarrassment. Were it not for the miners, one would say that the war is approaching a grim but successful climax – but the latter adjective is undoubtedly being prejudiced by their behaviour. No one would deny that they have

---

*   Allied Military Government of Occupied Territories.

had grievances in the past, but no more than many others, and there must be some clever enemy agents at work amongst them, corrupting this community life. It is difficult to know how to treat them – certainly the unions have no control over their members.

Well, my angel, I must stop now. Give the babies many big hugs and kisses from me, and my love to Susie. I can't wait to hear about the house and all the tit-bits; I think you have been very clever about the rent, and will make you my business manager!

For yourself, my Darling, a million kisses and blessings be upon you.

From your ever-loving and devoted Tom

* * *

Major TC Harvey
1st Bn Scots Guards
CMF, 13 April 44

My Beloved Maria
Jack Sanderson brought me some very nice cigarettes, and I got Lewis's parcel yesterday, so I am very flush with cigarettes, and they are most welcome. There seems to be very little news since I last wrote, and luckily the weather has improved a good deal so that makes life a lot easier. I haven't heard from you from the new house yet, but am eagerly awaiting the stories of your "flit" and the reactions of the children. I feel sure they played up really naughtily and made life as difficult as they could for you and Susie. I am sorry to hear that the car is behaving badly – it has never done anything else, but it would be very difficult and expensive to replace it now. They ought to allow you a good deal of petrol to get to Hunstanton and it is a lovely excuse to pop in at Ringstead and take Mama in with you. Everyone here is very well: We had our landlord, the Italian Duke, in to dinner one night – and he arrived at 6.30 instead of 7.30 to find only Bobby

Petre in the mess: it was up to Bobby to entertain him, and so royally did he do it that he (Bobby) got very tight in the process and started insulting the wretched man, calling him a "something fascist" and every other abusive name under the sun. However during dinner everything calmed down – I should have said that all conversation had to be in French, which made things all the more grotesque. During dinner, George Burns aided by wine and thereby inspired to talk with verve rather more than fluency, got going in the best tradition of French without Tears and made some superb statements – in particular by confessing his surprise at a piece of news with the phrase "Voila une nouvelle chose sur moi". Bill and I, who must in fact have sounded just as funny, got hopeless giggles – but that was nothing to the convulsions which shook us when George proceeded to translate the Pipers' programme into French. The Diable in the Kitchen was easy enough, Le Diable dans la cuisine, and the 79th's Farewell to Gibraltar was equally so – tho' both slightly ludicrous – but when he came to tackle Tail Toddler and started muttering about "queue" and "enfants mechant comme ca" it was too much for us. However, George was very good-humoured about our ribaldry and never laughed at us even when we got into equally deep waters. I thoroughly enjoyed the evening and it was most interesting to hear the point of view of the traditional Italian monarchist as opposed to the clever little Socialist whom we met in Sorrento. The Duke's view was that Mussolini in the early years promised to give Italy just what she needed, organisation, reform, efficiency. But as he gradually became more extreme, so equally gradually he became more powerful – until the time came when the desire to get rid of him couldn't overthrow his carefully arranged precautions. I personally don't think that the argument absolves the educated classes of responsibility, and further if they had shown themselves more interested in the reform and welfare of the masses, the masses in their turn would have had a reasonable alternative to which to turn.

Well my love, I must stop now, as for a miraculous change I have some work to do – I hope it won't be very long before you get my latest batch of shoppings, and with it many unwritten messages of love to you all.

Bless you all, my Darlings, from your ever devoted Tom

* * *

Major TC Harvey
1st Bn Scots Guards
CMF
15 April '44

My Darling Maria

What fun the house sounds! I am so glad Susie is better and that David takes a good view of his new home: that must make things a good deal easier – for you will be having enough to occupy your hours in the kitchen without any additional worries. I imagine that housekeeping must be very complicated now – even more so than before – but I hope you will be getting plenty of extra goodies from Holkham to help you out. You will be sure to use my account whenever you want, won't you – because that's what it's there for – and any largish unusual expenditure can be met from it. I have had two letters from Mother recently, and was so glad that John managed to get home for his birthday. The old boy must be out of touch by now, I expect, or at any rate becoming so rapidly. I am writing this out of doors at 5.30pm, after a boiling hot day, spent in the hills. The country looks superb, and the carpets of violets and primroses more numerous than ever. But the sun is tiring a little now, and a colder wind fanning the writing paper rather tiresomely. I must stop and put my scarf on. The strikes seem to go on steadily which seems a pity: people out here tend to get rather angry about them: apart from them, Robert Helpmann's Hamlet seems to be the next best headliner. Sacha is

143

now almost recovered and indeed may be back with us very soon. Derek is here in great form, and he and Col Guy and Freddy Fermor-Hesketh swap some red hot reminiscences of the old Cairo days and others!! Dick Twining's widow, Lorna, comes up once a week with a canteen, and provides an astounding glimpse of civilisation and English beauty – much in contrast with the raddled produce of Italy. I have only just met her, and haven't had a chance to talk to her about Dick. I heard from Summers(?) the other day asking us to Oxford again – so I must write to him and explain the impossibility of it.

It is getting so cold and drafty that I really must stop. I haven't had a letter very lately – but I think a batch may come up any time. I won't wait for it, but will answer it in another letter. By the way, I adore the photographs: I think I forgot to tell you.

Bless you, all my Darling ones, and a million kisses to you all.

From your ever loving and devoted Tom

* * *

Major TC Harvey
1st Bn Scots Guards
CMF
17 April 44

My Darling Maria

The last letter I got from you was dated 4th April, when you had had to put off your flit owing to Susie's 'hangover'. Poor Darling, I do hope she is alright again and drinking in little sips rather than great huge gollops! I know your first letter from Peddars Way will be full of excitements and I can't wait to get it. Letters lately have been on the scarce side, and so I am a bit out of touch with things: equally I have not been able to write very much lately but I hope to have a good session tonight before dinner. The weather has improved on the whole very quickly and we have had one or two really hot days, which have sent the snow scurrying off from the top of most of the hills. Naturally enough the flowers are a good deal later here, and the sides of the hills are now a mass of primroses, snowdrops and miniature lupins. The buildings in which I am writing were part of an experimental agricultural college, and certainly the fields around seem to have been cultivated with rather more method and on more up-to-date lines than most of the country. However the Germans didn't want us to have much winter accommodation so they dynamited the village for four days, leaving only the church standing, with a note pinned on the door saying "we leave you this for your Xmas services – and for your casualties"! I As a result, the locals have no great feelings of affection for their late ally, and do in fact help our side on every possible occasion, often at considerable risk. In return, we feed them. Several of them have instilled the military tradition to the full, and bring their hand smartly up to the peak of their cloth caps or homburg, when an officer passes. Life is, in fact, very peaceful. Sgt Watson told me that his wife had heard from you, and how pleased she was. I think their financial arrangements are being rather difficult. I am delighted to hear about my bank balance: since being here I have spent about £45, which will be deducted sooner or later, I imagine, in smug self-defence that most of it went not on entertaining sumptuous signorinas, as you allege, but on draping your exquisite figure with materials worthy of the task! Corby asks often after you all – he couldn't help noticing how you studiously refrain from ever mentioning Kuniang – but I explained that such was your jealousy that you would never dream of bringing up her name, for fear of diverting from yourself the hourly attention of my thoughts! Col Guy is very well and makes a grand commanding officer – very sound and the greatest fun, which is the perfect combination. Derek is completely mislaid and so Jack is acting for him. Unfortunately we have no piano on which to make the night hideous. Sacha reports that he is very much better and may be quite alright soon: I am trying to arrange for him to get back here, and I think it will be possible.

It is ages since I wrote to Mother, but I know you will give her all my news. Give the babies a lovely big hug each from me: I think the gloves I have sent to David will fit him when he goes to school – but never mind. The 1st parcel from Lewis arrived this week – many thanks. Could you get me some batteries for my tiny torch – the one from Asprey's? Also, 'War and Peace' and any other good book.

Bless you, angel blossom, and a million kisses on your lips from your adorer Tom

* * *

Major TC Harvey
1st Bn Scots Guards
CMF
28 April 44

My Darling Sweetestheart

I got your letter dated 21st April on the 26th which is lovely and quick and made me feel so up to date and in touch. I must say the house sounds divine, and you must be blissful to be settled there. I too more than I dare say, long for the thought of being with you again, and with my beloved babies, but perhaps now it won't be too terribly long. Daily I await news of the Second Front, for grim tho' it will surely be, it alone can shorten the hours of our separation.

The weather during the last two days has been unutterably foul, biting wind and ceaseless rain, making life very uncomfortable. Today it is sunny again tho' not yet as boiling as it was. I am thinking of taking some leave – 4 days next week with Bobby Petre: tho' we haven't yet decided where to go to. However, I can assure your anxious mind that it will all be "clean, ship-shape and above board", and that all the stories of dusky alluring contessas are too remote from me to be of any academic interest!! The cigarettes are coming thro' well now but I think that 100 per fortnight is enough: the tobacco however will be most welcome but I gather that that is in hand. I was most grateful for your books and those from Mother: I read them during the two bad days of rain and enjoyed them enormously. You remember Humphrey Sumner[*] at Oxford? I see he has published his "Survey of Russian History" – do try and get it for me, will you Darling? – there is much in it that one should read and remember.

More and more of the men come up and tell me how grateful their wives are for your letters – so do keep up the good work: it will be much more difficult for you with so much domestic toil on your hands, but I know it's worth it, and they seem to appreciate it enormously. I am sorry news from RHQ is so scarce: I wrote Archie P a long letter the other day, with very little in it: I feel very guilty at not yet having written to either Tommy or your parents, but I will in due course. There is so little to say and I tell you everything: it seems so silly to have to write the same "nothings" in a dozen different letters.[†] I heard from Boo, a typical Boo letter, very hard to read, but full of amusing remarks. I must write to her today.

Tommy Bulkeley, our Brigade Major, has astounded us all by getting married yesterday! An amazing effort tho' heaven knows where he's going to spend his honey-moon. Apparently his lady arrived not so long ago, was seen by Bobby Petre, who put them in touch, and before you could say "knife", they'd got married. I think it shows great enterprise. Apparently she's with some mobile hospital or something of the sort.

I am now able to reveal the comparatively dull news that our first visits to the line were in the area of the Lower Garighano near Minturno! By the way, I trust that you are taking great steps

---

[*]   Historian.
[†]   All letters were censored (see image on p.110).

147

towards editing and publishing my latest epoch making song – the song of Victory on the March! I should send it personally to Monty – whose unlimited conceit and unbridled power will cause and enable him to have it published and played ad nauseam!! It needs a lot doing to it, but I do think it's quite a catchy tune, tho' no doubt a crib of something else. Still, the army needs a good song, and there's no harm in trying!

Bless you, my angels three, and a big kiss to Susie from your ever very loving Tom

* * *

Major TC Harvey
1st Bn Scots Guards
CMF
3 May 44

My Darling Maria
I got your letter about Simon's home-coming a couple of days ago – and by now I hope you have got the things I sent with him – also the parcel I gave to Hugh Rose. What a bore Rowena* being in bed: poor little things they do seem to catch everything – but at any rate its quite a good thing to get over the troubles when still young. What a monkey David is hiding the key – I am sure he's got you all absolutely taped, and knows he can get away with murder! I go off on leave tomorrow with Bobby, though we are not yet certain where we are going to; certainly Naples first and then either Capri or Ravello which is where the Grimthorpes have their lovely villa. However if the weather stays as perfect as it is today, it will be lovely everywhere – but is strange to think that 3 days ago we were having snow! I heard from Mother, who told me that her share of Lila's will was about £54.000, and as usual she hinted at giving us more money: but I told her that we already

---

*   Combe, daughter of Silvia and Simon.

took so much and that if she took over 100% expenses of Ringstead that would be quite enough. With her rotten eyesight there are masses of little extra luxuries that she ought to have, though heaven knows she would never admit it. The house sounds more divine every time you write – do send me some photographs of it so that I can picture you all in and around it. I am sure you have made it charming inside, with your impeccable taste, and I can picture you sitting in your very ritzy bedroom – suitably draped in the silks and satins which I have sent to you. I think that my leave will probably cost me most of my month's allowance so there may not be any more parcels for a while – also I want to get something for Mother – but have got no ideas. Do think of something and let me know what you suggest.

I feel that if your great plans for my political future are to materialise successfully, I shall have to try and acquire some useful knowledge of agriculture and get to know what the farmers are thinking and what their views and difficulties are: Maurice Fermoy and Gunston might be able to help by recommending certain books etc – and if Maurice meant what he said, he might like to write me a letter sometime. I have no idea what the conditions are going to be like after the war, but I think the best course would normally be to wait for a year or two and then, having acquired some experience and knowledge, and possibly one or two minor directorships thrown in (!), one could set about winning the constituency. If, however, after the war, my chances are better of getting in at once (ex-soldier, young man, new blood blah blah blah) then it would perhaps be best to charge straight into it. Allan Jacobs is very sound, and knows the form backwards and he can always give you a reasoned opinion. But I don't suppose any of these people want to take me on out of the blue, and personally I should prefer to wait a little – except as I say if Labour looked like getting in as a reaction against Maurice Fermoy. Susan Maxwell too is very much in the know, and ought to be most helpful. I should love to attend the committee meetings – its high time Lance got the boot, he always was useless and always will be, and nothing creates greater chaos or a graver menace than senile, pompous incompetence seated in "The Chair". He is too old to be persuaded, too pompous to be criticised and too stupid to be snubbed.

I've only just got your letter about your party at Apple tree – or Appleby – Appleton that's it. You must have thought it very boorish of me not to congratulate you on being such a "succes fou". I am sure it was a delightful evening – and I've no doubt that T.M.* have been jitterbugging ever since. It has struck me that the Marlboro' girl was a bit quick in laying her egg, wasn't she. On the assumption that she was, I have just composed the following libellous doggerel, which should not repeat not be repeated.

> The senior Malborough girlie
> Always seemed to me terribly surly,
> But such was her hustle
> For Lootenant Russell
> That the baby was born two months early.

Not very good, nor very kind!

Bless you all my Darlings – the sight of David's scrawl at the bottom of your letter brought quite a lump to my throat.

Oceans of love and kisses to you all, from Tom

* * *

---

*   Their Majesties the King and Queen of Norway, then resident in Appleton House on the Sandringham Estate.

Major TC Harvey
1st Bn Scots Guards
CMF
7 May 44

My Darling of Darlings
Here I am on leave in the most wonderful place in the world –
Capri. How I long for you to be here with me! But perhaps one
day we will be able to come here together, for surely it is the home
of all romance. But there is so much to tell you that I must start
from the beginning. On Thursday morning Bobby and I set off
with two jeeps, a trailer, and two henchmen. We pottered about
collecting rations and things, but got to Naples about 4pm. There
we installed ourselves in a hotel, cashed our cheques, and then
joined forces with Mark Kerr (Diana's brother) and one other, &
went to the Allied Officers Club, where we dined and drank and
watched the dancing. Then on with some sailors to their club
until about 11:30, when we went to bed. Up early next morning
– the hotel was ghastly like all British Officers amenities, & off
at 9:00 AM to Massa Lubrense beyond Sorrento. We had no idea
whether we could get a boat to Capri, no idea where to stay, or
even if we would be allowed to land, as the US AAF have taken
over the whole place – restaurants, hotels, amenities, everything.
However our late liaison officer, Boogie di Bugnano has a villa,
& we hoped we might contact him. Massa Lubrense is a tiny
fishing village, & the prospects didn't look too good: however the
usual conclave of seedy Italian children besieged us with advice
and help & eventually we got hold of a little rowing boat with
a "crew" of four: into this we piled with our rations, luggage, 1
henchman, Bobby & I & off we went. Halfway there, we hoisted
a sail and spun along at great speed. It was a heavenly day: deep
clear blue water and an underlying pleasure of uncertainty and
general fun. We chatted to the fishermen, one of whom had been
in New Zealand for 20 years and we munched some food. As

we approached the harbour we began to look out for military police, but there was no sign of any & we then got ashore. But our troubles weren't over – because neither of us could remember Boogie's proper name, & although we had vague knowledge of where his villa was, that was all. So we climbed into a taxi and went off to the main hotel, which was of course out of the question for us. After a lot of to'& froing we got fixed up in a very pleasant little pension & there we domiciled ourselves & fed. The great problem now was how to find Boogie & after endless fruitless inquiries, we accosted a fairly respectable couple – who eventually guessed whom we were after. They took us into their Tennis Club & a few moments later Boogie himself appeared so there was great rejoicing. It was then about 6:30 PM, so we had some drinks, we dined in the pension and then to one of the "bars" where we drank steadily but safely!! Boogie stayed the night and next morning we moved up here to the villa. Now I must try to describe it. It stands on the tip of the island nearest to the mainland right on the edge of the cliff, with a sheer drop of 400 feet into the blue blue sea below; in fact from the garden, the sea seems to extend under the house. The house itself is white, square and classical and very big. The front door is of wrought iron, and you enter a cool marble hall with one big grill door on the left and the marble staircase on the right. Through the hall on the left is the "salon". It is a long room, the length of the Library at Holkham and half as wide again. The walls are white, the floor marble and carpeted. There are 4 pillars in the centre, supporting a low domed ceiling – and the pillars and the walls have a plain pattern of gold mosaic. In the centre on the right is the fireplace with an excellent, simple, classical chimney piece – the furniture is French Louis Quinze, Seize & Empire, tho' there are easy chairs, tables of drinks – though not many alas, in fact all the affluence of a comfortable house. It is full of flowers, lilies, blossoms, wild Capri flowers and overhanging all a faint smell of incense. It's just beautifully cool, while outside the warm breeze & hot sun lap around one like a delicious bath. We share a bedroom – in which I'm writing now (8:30 PM), with a view I cannot describe – facing Vesuvius – but so high & as it were detached, that one feels like a god looking down on all the white specks of sailing boats and the silver waves of faster craft. The whole island is a mass of lilac, verbena, honeysuckle and lilies – and to breathe the atmosphere is a taste of heaven. We are quite on our own, far from our hooligan allies – bless 'em all the same – in fact it is a perfect leave – perfect save for your absence. Bobby and I went to the Blue Grotto on 1st day – you enter lying flat in a little boat – through a tiny hole in the cliff & there you are in an enormous cavern. The light from outside enters under the water giving it an unearthly but very lovely transparent blue – so clear, so pure like liquid sapphire. We spend our time lolling about, sun bathing, sipping wine, listening to the gramophone, sleeping, eating, reading. Our host's brother, a diplomat, is as charming as Boogie & frightfully interesting – I will write you a sea-letter about it all. Tomorrow is our last day and we are going to sail, if it is fine. Then we give Boogie and Alex dinner at the Tennis Club and off early next morning. Never have I been more tempted to go absent. But it has been a wonderful few days and I hope to come back if I get another leave – better still to bring you here. For badly though I've described it, dull and insipid as my words are, compared with the exquisite reality of the place, at least you can be sure that it will be a setting worthy of you and one in which we can make up for some of the things which we have had to miss!

Bless you all, my angels three, I will write again soon from
your ever adoring and now Capri-cious Tom

* * *

153

Villa Fersen[*]
Capri
May 8th

My Darling Love

Such notepaper can hardly be resisted, tho' I fear it may take some time to reach you by surface mail. My airmails will have told you how our visit finished up – it is our last day today, and our programme is very full, so that this is my last chance of writing to you. I should first of all describe our hosts. Boogie, the younger brother was an Italian fighter pilot until the armistice, when he escaped from Rome and joined the Allies, to be liaison officer with 201 Bde. He is a most amusing person a great "dolce far niente" man, dabbling in cooking, gardening, arranging the house, in fact a typical, charming, lazy and cultured Italian aristocrat. His older brother, Alex (aged 35) was a professional diplomat, and made a very skilful escape from Brussels when the armistice was signed. He has been in consulates in New York, San Sebastian etc and is most interesting about the rise and decline of Fascism. Like everyone else, he claims that it started well, and once es-tablished it became tyrannical and corrupt. The good things it did, like land reclamation and youth education were spoilt by the corruption of the officials – they all had to have their pickings, and so the expenditure of public money was doubly increased. As for the war, the plan of the High Command was to start it in 1943/44. In 1938 the Italian Army had big manoeuvres, and although they only had one motorised brigade, they ran out of petrol after 5 days, and everyone had to go home!! Mussolini called a conference of all the Service chiefs and inaugurated a 4 year plan for the setting up of factories to build armaments. Then Germany could no longer wait, and when in May 1940 France was prostrate, Mussolini scrapped the whole 4 year plan seriously believing that the war would only last another 20 days. Basing his

*   Now Villa Lysis.

whole strategy on this one assumption, he declared war and on the 21st day had nothing left. Alex believes that latterly syphilis has soften M's brain, and that he was totally insane – he used to rave about fighting a war and even against the Italians, if necessary. The tragedy was that the stupid little king, who could have opposed him and would have had the support of the nation, did nothing – or worse still acquiesced. Queerly enough, Ciano* in his heart of hearts was pro-British – but he was such a bounder and so rotten that he allied himself to the War Party in order to keep his "pickings" – but at private parties he used to go about praising the British and the Americans! What a mess they have got themselves into. This villa, which I described rather feebly in my first letter, was built by Boogie's uncle who sounds a superb rake – he was very queer, and "came over all Chinese" building himself an exquisite opium den, where he puffed away at every sort of drug and holding the most primitive and Priapian orgies – as his choice of paintings books and statuary bear testimony most vividly. However by the age of 35 his vices had exhausted him so he left the villa, and its lovely belongings to Boogie.

Unfortunately he had most of his real treasures in his apartment in Rome, so heavens knows what will happen to them. The news from occupied territory all sounds very encouraging, tho' of course one can never be certain. Stories from German hopelessness, of the enthusiasm for us of the occupied countries, have to be compared with the undoubtedly gigantic strength and ingenuity of the defences – but the general view seems to be that; for all the difficulties & bloodshed, the end of the war against Germany should come fairly quickly. Here at Capri we have absolutely no news of anything, which is lovely. Cut off from everything except sunshine, warmth, beauty, comfort and laughter, we have drunk deeply at the cool sparkling well of peace and have been refreshed to the depths of our soul.

My Darling, I must stop now. We have to go down to the

* Galeazzo Ciano, Italian Foreign Minister and Mussolini's son-in-law.

harbour to meet the boat which we ordered – send it away with our servant and the luggage and then find ourselves a sailing boat. Our jeeps will then meet us at Sorrento, and then back to the Bn. If I don't stop now, I shall not be able to post the letter tomorrow.

So until my next letter, a million blessings on your fairy head, and lots of big hugs and kisses to the nit-pots

From your ever adoring

Tom

* * *

Major TC Harvey
1st Bn Scots Guards
CMF
12 May 44

My Darling One

You will see by the date that I am back from my leave, and am now sitting peacefully out of doors writing this, in the after breakfast sun. Our last day at Capri came up to the highest expectations. We walked leisurely down to the harbour, and set about booking a sailing boat in which to meander round the Island. As you know, any form of transaction with a member of the Latin races is invariably preceded by tremendous chi-chi – waving of hands, communal advice and counter-advice, haggling, refusal and final agreement. One boat is too slow, another already reserved, a third is selected, terms arranged and then it is declared unseaworthy. However, eventually we got one, we piled in and rowed around to the private landing stage to pick up Alex and the lunch. It was a lovely day, hot sun and fresh wind and off we went. The highlight was when Bobby was sick!! However he recovered at once. After about 3 and a half hours we got put ashore on the south side, near Gracie Fields' villa, and then Boogie and I went off to see the Monastery, while Bobby and Alec walked back to the villa to tidy themselves up for dinner at the Tennis Club. It is a fine old monastery, still dilapidated after being a ruin for many years – but in 1933 a few monks settled there and have done wonders in reconstruction. The church is baroque and there is a lovely large cloister, the pillars of which were brought from a roman villa. Best of all was the little garden, full of exquisite flowers, perched on top of the cliff. Then to the Tennis Club, where Bobby and I entertained our hosts with a very good dinner. Very replete, we went early to bed, as we had to get up at 5.30am to catch the boat to Sorrento where our fleet of cars met us. In Sorrento I couldn't resist getting you a night-dress which took my fancy, and also a little smock for Caroline which will fit her one day. I do hope they arrive alright, and also that by now you have got the dressing gown thing. I fear all the things I get for you will be too long, but my advisers tell me that a hem is an effective and simple remedy! Lunch in Naples and back here for dinner, a perfect leave. I found 3 letters from you, and was so sorry to hear my mail is being slow; perhaps it's better now. I am full of admiration at your resolve to open the bazaar at Norwich – what an ordeal. How are you to begin – I suggest either "Ladies and Gentlemen as the only titled inmate of the Home" or alternatively "My friends and fellow bastards". Don't however fail to end up as follows "And so, Ladies and Gentlemen, I throw myself upon your generosity: today dawns the age of universal consent. Let it never be said that any Norfolk girl from whatever stratum of society, whose ambition it was to become an unmarried mother was ever thwarted by a lack of public sympathy or a scarcity of private subscription"! That ought to keep you clear of public engagements for some time. Seriously though, I think it's a great effort and I am proud of you. So glad the poppleberries are well – they sound so sweet. Send more photographs when you can Darling. Parcels and cigarettes come through luvla now. Bless you, all my loves and a million kisses from your ever loving Tom

Major TC Harvey
1ˢᵗ Bn Scots Guards
CMF
May 20ᵗʰ

My Darling Maria

I am terribly ashamed at not having written to you for so long – particularly as you will, I know, have been imagining awful things, tho' I trust the date and tenor of my last letter were not overlooked by you. I have in fact no news, since I got back from leave. I succeeded in getting somewhat sunburnt during a hot spell – but it has clouded over a bit since, and we have had a certain amount of rain. Today I am taking the officers into Naples for dinner, to celebrate David's 21ˢᵗ birthday, which was yesterday. We'll go off sometime after lunch, taking with us drivers as a wise precaution. Bill has just come back from the local town where he found the most fascinating children's sun hats and I shall certainly get some for David. Is he wearing a sailor suit yet – because I can get him a little white round cap like an American sailor: he'd look an absolute dream in one. I have got several lovely letters from you lately, and also from Mother and Silvia – will you thank the latter very much, and tell her that I will try to write soon. What fun having Simon back – I do so hope it's true about his M.C as he thoroughly deserved one.* The news about Tommy is very exciting and I think worth accepting if he can really get to know something about large scale farming in Australia. For after all, his whole life now should be devoted to making himself fit to run Holkham on really up-to-date and efficient lines and he might learn his stuff there as well as anywhere. Before I forget, could you try to send me some hair oil – preferably a bottle or two of

---

* In a separate letter to his mother, not included in this volume, TCH wrote: 'Simon [Combe] was taken prisoner, shot his guards, seized an abandoned carrier and drove back to the lines, picking up Rorie Stuart-Richardson (badly wounded) on the way! A splendid effort!'

that wonderful stuff that Simon uses. It is good of you to take so much trouble about getting me books – I hear from Oxford that Humphrey Sumner has now been appointed Professor of History at Edinburgh, so I fear he may be more elusive than ever. After the spate of Capri news, I am absolutely stuck for anything to say. The war news is of course thrilling but I don't propose to discuss it, no doubt the papers are more than sufficiently full of it for your liking. We had an out of door Bob Hope film the other night – the machine wouldn't work to start with, but eventually it got going and we laughed a lot. It was called "They've got me covered" and was full of ridiculous situations and wisecracks.

We are now in K.D.* which is lovely and cool: tho' my million dollar legs have fallen in value somewhat and might be described as "bayonets sticking out of kit bags". I have had one or two sessions on the piano with Jack Sanderson, which we enjoy if no one else does. The great difficulty of life in tents is that there is no place big enough for recreation under cover – but provided the weather keeps fine, one can manage pretty well. I will let you know how our party tonight progresses, and you can expect a little parcel of hats sometime.

Meanwhile, my Love, a million blessings on you all and lots and lots of hugs to the babies. From your ever devoted Tom

* * *

Major TC Harvey
1st Bn Scots Guards
CMF
22 May 44

My Beloved Maria
Your letter written on May 13th, when you heard news of the Italian offensive was the most perfect and lovely thing I have ever

---

*   Khaki drill.

read; I can't begin to tell you how deeply it affected me – and it was in every way the ideal letter to receive on going into battle. Although, as you can gather, my time is not yet come, I suppose it may do at any moment and I shall be reading your letter again and again. Thank you a million times, my Darling, and May God strengthen me to be worthy of you.

As I told you in my last letter, we all went off to Naples the other day, to celebrate David's 21st birthday. We met at the Officer's Club at about 6:15, Bill arriving with his last bottle of liqueur Brandy and 6 lbs of strawberries – tiny wild ones, sweet as sugar. After some preliminary cocktails, we sat down to dinner which was on the whole very good, and helped on its way by 4 bottles of wine. Then we got down to the strawberries, eating 1 lb each and covering them with ice cream and sugar. Then on to the brandy, which we quickly and lovingly demolished – as Oscar Wilde said "Each man kills the thing he loves" – well we killed that bottle good and proper. Then upstairs to watch the dancing – our efforts to cut in were too late as it was the last dance! – and then at 9:30 the club closed. So we drove back in our jeeps – Sasha, David and I singing the whole way non-stop for 2 hours.

We had fixed up some deck tennis in the olive grove where our tents are and I have just been playing a four; great fun and good exercise, stripped to the waist in the in the evening sun. We are busy organising sports & fun for the men, & tomorrow we are having a sort of Coy. Rodeo, followed by a sing song. Our last Coy. party became a very drunken affair, so I trust this one will be more respectable. Then on Thursday we are going to have an officers Cocktail Party – & needless to say Col Guy has sent out press gangs to the girls. It is rumoured that Marlene Dietrich will be in the neighbourhood and we are trying hard to get her!! Willie Lindsay & Johnny Drury-Lowe have been over, as we are quite close to them. I shall see a lot of friends on Thursday, & will have lots of gossip to tell you. I have heard some good scandal about Carolyn Howard which you no doubt have heard ages ago:

otherwise one doesn't get a lot of news of people at home. They're no doubt too busy getting ready for the 2nd front to get themselves into domestic trouble.

I love all the titbits about David & Caroline – they do sound absolute poppets – the presentation must have been divine. I am longing to get the photographs of the house, it sounds so fascinating. I hope you are finding the finances all right, & aren't spending too much of your own money. I spent the whole of my month's allowance on my leave, so now I have to borrow from Bill. However he is always liberally supplied with every sort of thing & keeps us all well supplied with papers and magazines. Some more cigarettes arrived today, and I expect the tobacco will come soon; however David has given me a tin to go on with.

My darling, I will stop now. Once again I thank God for giving you to me, with all your love, and courage and help.

Bless you, my angels, with a million kisses your loving Tom

* * *

26 May 44

My Beloved One,

Since I last wrote we have been having lovely weather and quite a certain amount of gaiety. The real high-light of the week was our party last night. We took a lot of trouble to get the garden of our mess really tidy, & we were lucky in getting a lovely evening. Lashings of drink were procured & masses of goodies, like egg anchovies, strawberries and ice cream etc, etc. Added to that, we got a negro swing band, so you can imagine that the party was promising from the start. Masses of people came, including Lavinia Holland-Hibbert, whom I was delighted to see, looking very smart & well & in very good form.

Among those there were Johnny Drury-Lowe, Jack Profumo, Bernard Bruce who flew down to represent General Oliver. We

161

drank, talked & ate and danced unceasingly, & before long I displaced the pianist & had one or two really hot Blues, fairly getting a lift out of them. Dream-Man Steele is said to be arriving today: just think how jealous you would have been if he had been there too!

Another great day was that of the Coy's Sports and Smoker. We had 5 a side football, darts, slippery poles, duck apple & lastly obstacle race. The teams for that comprised 4 men: the first was blindfolded and had to run 100 yds to his partner, who was making an allotted noise – e.g. a woman singing God Save the King etc – on arrival No2 was given a vast sandwich to eat – full of beans, jam, raw meat and 1/4 inch of mustard – plus a pint of tea full of salt to wash it down! Having gorged these monstrosities they had to run to No3 who dressed backwards in full battle order – he then had to run to No4, who, in correct battle order had to take off every single garment except steel helmet and gym shoes – crawl under a tarpaulin beneath which was a mixture of oil, mud, anti-louse powder and thence to the winning post. I almost got cramp from laughing. Needless to say Tim & Tom & David had to do the last lap. The smoker was a great success, not too alcoholic. Tho' we put away 28 bottles of white wine & 50 gallons of red. Altogether a very good day. It is indeed wonderful news from the battlefront. Perhaps we are at last beginning to see the end of this Italian campaign.

Bless you, all my pretty Darlings, and a million kisses from
your ever adoring Tom

30 May 44
My beloved Maria

I got your letter of the 21st on the 28th, which was good; your party sounds the greatest fun. I very much sympathise with your feelings on the morning after, as I am at the moment suffering in the same way myself. Last night I went to see Bernard Bruce and Ian Calvocoressi who regaled me with delicious sherry and salted almonds etc, which we sampled, sitting peacefully in the evening shade. I saw General Oliver just before I left – in terrific form – and he gave me some parcels of comforts for the Coy. After that I went on to dine with Toby Lowe,* who is an old friend. He has been working desperately hard during the battle, but with brilliant success. Things do certainly seem to be going well, and with luck we may be able to put most of the Germans in the bag south of Rome; for that would mean we needn't go chasing after them all the way to N Italy. I am simply thrilled to hear about Lionel,† and I can't wait to hear that he really is back and that you have seen him. Do try to get him to stay, I feel sure that he could get a special exemption from the ban, and he would be the most delightful companion. I quite agree with you about Bartle‡ and Veronica – her sister married Billy Bull – so the families may be mutually attracted.

I never managed to get those little hats for David but I will try later on; you've never mentioned the word "sailor suits" – are they still too big for him?

There is terribly little to say my Darling, but I will write again soon. Bless you all, my Darlings, and a million kisses from your
ever adoring Tom

---

*   The future Lord Aldington.
†   A Canadian, son of Vincent Massey. He served in the King's Royal Rifle Corps, and was wounded in Greece and made a German POW.
‡   Bartle Bull.

Major TC Harvey
1st Bn Scots Guards
CMF
2 June 44

My Most Beloved Darling

Since I last wrote I have been the victim of diarrhoea, rather un-
comfortably, but am now quite better and by tomorrow I hope
to be able to eat, drink and be merry once again. I am so glad
that John was able to give you that message, as I well knew how
anxious you would be. But things are going wonderfully well
here, and having gained the initiative we have great advantages
in the fighting. I was pretty well confined to my bed yesterday
but the day before I went over to see Robin Muir – whom I
found very well, in spite of being very busy lately. He had 18
consecutive days in Cassino without once seeing the sun and has
been busy since – but he was in great form. I also saw Ashley
Ponsonby and Desmond Chichester and David Cuthbert. David
has been having his leg pulled unmercifully, because one night
he was listening in to Haw-Haw, and heard him announce the
Second Front. David was wildly excited, rang up his Commanding Officer who in turn spread the news through all the H.Q's
in the country. It subsequently transpired that in fact David had
been listening to a play, and not a news bulletin. I saw in the
paper that some more repatriated prisoners had arrived – and I
imagine Lionel is among them. I really can't write to him at the
moment but I will try as soon as I can: meanwhile do send him
many messages of Welcome Home from me, and tell him I hope
it won't be long before I see him again.

There is a man from the Coy who lost a leg and is on his way
home. Do you think you could, a little later on, get in touch
with his wife, through RHQ. His name is ROUGH – but I don't
know his address. There are often complications about payments,
pensions, treatment, etc and you may easily be able to help them.

I don't seem to have written to Mother for ages, but I know you give her what little news you get: I have been getting both your letters very regularly. What a time you all seem to be having with the Salute The Soldiers Weeks – it sounds a nightmare! As regards standing for Parliament, I have no objection to my name going forward though I think you would have to mention it to Archie Pearson first. I think it would be wrong for me to come home just yet, but it will be different once we have fixed up the Germans in Italy – and I hope that will be possible. I think it must be up to me (and my Commanding Officer) to say when I leave here. I feel also that I must have some other, part time, job which will bring in a little mon – but no doubt something will turn up. I must stop now.

Bless you all, my Darlings: you are all so close to me, and I know that you are walking beside me on my journey. A million blessings on you from your everloving Tom

* * *

Major TC Harvey
1st Bn Scots Guards
CMF
7 June 44

My Beloved Darling
Letters are I fear getting rather few and far between, but yours are still reaching me pretty well and I also had one from mother and one from Tom Dundas, with quite a lot of news in it. I only wish I could give you the story of our little party out here – most amusing and gentlemanly it has been, and long may it continue so. I visited Cassino one day, and it certainly is flattened – in fact it looks like part of the hill side. The country surrounding it is appalling for infantry, and I still gasp with admiration at the Poles and the French for overcoming it. There are increasing signs

165

of the haste with which the Germans are having to fall back: and they must be getting very disorganised by now, although they still no doubt will show a certain amount of fight. We were thrilled to hear of the successful offering of the landing in France, and coupled with the capture of Rome it has made a memorable week. I happened to be in Rome for the King's speech, which was really rather historic. The people appear to be pleased to us, but purely for what they hope to get out of us. I have very little patience with them – they start by trying to take our Empire, and end up by accepting our charity. Though it has been cooler today, the weather has been lovely – about 90° – and wonderful at night. The country and towns seem to improve greatly as one advances, and it is a pleasant change to see towns not destroyed – as the continuous succession of squalid, dusty, rubble gets rather monotonous. I can quite imagine T & E* getting in a terrific tee-wee over their journey – I trust they get given some extra coupons. I am delighted to hear that Simon has gone back to the Brewery: there appear to be terrific changes in the 2nd Bn, with Henry Clowes commanding and almost all the Company Commanders senior to him. I can't see what it is all about. I trust the nit-pots are in good order and behaving themselves properly. They must both be gigantic by now. It's a pity the Drysdales haven't children of David's age for him to knock about with, but after the war the brothers Clyde and Rupert Hambro will be able to be his sparring partners.

I will write again soon, my love. If we can really fix up these Germans who knows but that we'll all be back before long. What a wonderful thought.

A million blessings on you all, and lots and lots of kisses to the babies. From your ever loving and adoring Tom

* * *

---

*   Tommy and Eliza Clyde.

Major TC Harvey
1st Bn Scots Guards
CMF
12 June 44

My Beloved Maria

I have just got your letters dated 31 May and 1st or 2nd June, and am delighted to hear how well you all are. I too am "in the pink", the weather is still good, and so far we have little to complain of. I naturally can't tell you anything about what is going on: and I know you are being wonderfully cheerful and trying not to worry too much. There is no question but that we've got the upper hand here, but naturally the Germans still show a good deal of fight. Everyone is in good form. I have seen Andrew Cavendish and Ronnie several times. I am glad that our company got a good write up – that is the company with Robin Muir's battalion – commanded by David Cuthbert with Andrew Nielson – David was on leave during the battle, very wisely too! Mama tells me that Digby and Co are home from Canada – I wish you could get a chance to see them, but travelling is so impossible and they can't get to you. I am sure they'll make an exception for Lionel: I do hope the old boy isn't too groggy – I fear that he may be. I can't wait to hear about your speech in Norwich. I do so hope it went off alright. What a proud mother you will be at Dinah's party. That dreadful tank-busting child of hers must be kept in control or he will smother poor little Caroline. What a sweet she sounds: I do hope Susie is bearing up under the double strain!!

I do hope my last parcel arrives safely – it ought to be with you very soon, unless it has got lost, which would be tragic. Thank you so much for sending the hair oil – I badly need it. Could you possibly send a cheque for a £10 to Corby's wife – whose address (GDSM Corby No 2692855) RHQ will give you. I haven't been paying him here as he doesn't want it.

No more for now, sweetest heart. I am sure it won't be so very long now before we are together again, and our love can once again make a little home for ourselves. Bless you all my pretty ones, from your ever loving Tom

*　*　*

Major TC Harvey
1st Bn Scots Guards
CMF
15 June

My darlingest Maria,
As things are thought to be fairly quiet for 24 hours I have nipped away for a change and am writing this in General Oliver's Mess. I had a brainwave to invite myself for a couple of nights to stay with Bernard Bruce and here I am, in the lap of comfort. I arrived late last night, somewhat afraid that I was going to commit a fearful social blunder – but I was most kindly received, and shown to a luxurious caravan with a bed, sheets, running water and electric light. I rose this morning at a leisurely hour, had an excellent breakfast and have been pottering about ever since, talking to people and sipping lemon squash. John Tweedsmuir is here, with whom I have long talks – in fact it is a hot bed of Mrs Milburne's boys – General Oliver himself, David Butter and myself. I haven't yet been able to visit Rome a la touriste, but I hope to do so before very long. I might fly over it, if I can arrange it, but the real glamour of city life is forcibly denied for the time being. Your letters have been very good, two yesterday dated 4th and 6th – I imagine that the capture of Rome and the subsequent quick advance has cheered up everyone and started off the Second Front on the right leg. It will be a hell of a battle – but when Russia gets going I can't see the Germans lasting for very much longer. The nits sound in terrific form – I expect David's talking

is getting on fast now. I am delighted that Bartle took a fancy to Caroline. I would trust him with her now – but I would not be so sure in 18 years time: and you can tell him so! Your visit to Brancaster sounded most amusing. Montague I know well – he is the only local man who can sound the Last Post at British Legion rallies – but his teeth always fall out. By all means send my name into Harry Lance, to be considered – for it wouldn't matter a bit if I was defeated first time. Do tell Mother all my news. I will try hard to write to her soon but it isn't too easy at the moment. Meanwhile my love, a million blessings to you all.

From your ever loving Tom

* * *

Major TC Harvey
1st Bn Scots Guards
CMF
June 19th

My Belovedest Heart,

This is first and foremost an "anniversary" letter, which I hope will arrive more or less on the right day, bringing with it a special message of love and thankfulness for that wonderful day. I think you will agree that from that day began for us an altogether new and lovely life, enriching us both with deep happiness and a perfect sense of union and partnership. Added to this, if that were not enough, we have been blessed with two adorable children, pledges of our love, the consolation of our parting. To think it all began 4 years ago, and yet we are still young lovers, only achieving the fullness of our being when we are together, and as one. It is indeed an occasion for rejoicing, and I shall open a bottle of champagne and drink your health.

Not much more news since I last wrote. I thoroughly enjoyed

my sojourn at 8th Army and on the way back picked up David Henniker and Christopher Stone, who are snooping about doing various propaganda jobs. On Sunday I went to a short Thanksgiving service held in the cathedral at – it shall be nameless. Outside the church is pure Italian Gothic, with fine carving and gay mosaics. Inside it is vast and very impressive. High Normanesque columns, blue and white stripes rise up to a exquisitely carved hammer beam ceiling, and the great open space of the body of the church is filled with an enchanting softness of light, coming through the windows of transparent marble and alabaster. There are magnificent frescoes in one chapel, painted by Signorelli – the master of Michelangelo – while the ceiling, a striking contrast in style, being earlier and altogether more mystic, is the work of Fra Angelico.* The service was charming, a solemn Te Deum, with quite good choral singing, preceded by an address by the Bishop: it was all fairly informal and very pleasant to be in such peaceful surroundings. Col Guy has been to Rome for a few days – having a whale of a time, and met John Hope there, who seems very well: I hope perhaps to see him. Corby asked me what colour Caroline's hair was and was it curly? I couldn't answer – wasn't it awful – so you must send the latest bulletin. Bless you all, my loves, and a million kisses to you all.

From your ever devoted Tom

* * *

Major TC Harvey
1st Bn Scots Guards
CMF
25 June 44

My Beloved Maria
Last night a lovely bunch of letters arrived, dated 15, 16 and 18

---

*   Chapel of San Brizio, in the Duomo at Orvieto.

which was wonderfully quick. I think the idea of the Red House is a very good one, because as you say we can then afford to live in London as well, which we shall certainly have to do. Also the car – not that I like Austins – I suppose Tommy's car is not for sale too?! I am glad you have persuaded Susie to have a rest: and Mama will adore to help. What a handful the nits must be; David sounds a little devil, shaming you and insulting his hosts. I imagine that his energy is something terrifying. So the Russians have started; that ought to give the Germans an extra headache. Here their resistance is toughening considerably but they still lack any considerable reserve and can really only manage to delay – tho' the country is still very much on their side – the hills having started again. The weather is still on the whole quite good, but we get these torrential thunderstorms, which completely flood the ground and make things very tiresome. If the sun then comes out, it is not too bad – but things are not improved. I fear I am not the bronzed bombshell you picture – but I am doing my best, tho' I have to avoid the risk of excessive sunburn. But in time I may be able to realise your dusky dreams! I got a parcel from Mother – with Edith Sitwell's Anthology which looks fascinating. Will you thank her very much and send her lots of love, as I shan't be able to write to her for a bit. I am getting rather worried about the safety of my last parcel – it really ought to be with you soon: it will be an awful tragedy if it fails to appear, as there were some rather nice things inside. There's nothing one can do, alas: Dolly Petre's was sent off at the same time so you can ask her if she's had any better luck. I do hope you are not going to be bothered by the rocket bombs – as you say they are unlikely to wish to attack Fring, but I should be careful about going to London: but that I leave to your own judgement. I am sure the RAF party was a wizard prang, bags of booze and floosies! Roy Boy must be in his element. I feel terribly guilty at not having written either to your parents or to him but I just can't. I know you give them all my news – but I don't want them to think that I never think of them.

Poor old Ned and Edgar, the latter particularly, he is so nice.

Freddie Hesketh has just produced an excellent bottle of wine so I am sipping it, between sentences, (12.15pm). Darling I must stop now: as I am rather busy. Will write again soon as possible. Lots and lots of love to you all my Darlings,

From your ever devoted Tom

* * *

From the Official History

June 24

While they patrolled and reconnoitred, Brigadier Clive ordered the Scots Guards to send a mobile column round by the left, over the top of Point 846 to La Foce, a small village and road junction near the source of the Astrone, from where it should be possible to outflank the Germans opposing the Grenadiers.

The column, which was commanded by Major Harvey, consisted at first of about half Left Flank, together with carriers, the Battalion's Vickers machine-guns and four light Honey tanks of the Pretoria Regiment.

June 25

It set out at half-past nine and soon, about a mile south of the summit, enemy were encountered, which civilians variously reported as being in battalion or company strength. The column was reinforced by two troops of the heavier Sherman tanks, and with their aid the enemy were quickly driven back, retiring in the direction of 846. No further advance was made that day, and, reinforced by the remainder of Left Flank and half the mortar platoon, the column spent the night preparing to attack the heights next day.

June 26

At half-past six in the morning the force was on its way, followed closely by B Company. On and around Point 846 were dug in the best part of three German companies, which constituted an ample garrison for so formidable a position. But here it was that the perfect understanding and confidence between the tanks and the Guardsmen were born. The attack went swiftly and was directed with great skill from one of the tanks by Major Harvey. By ten o'clock the company was on the objective, having flushed the enemy from their trenches, killed many of them, and driven the survivors on to the next hill, with the tanks in pursuit doing great execution. The speed and accuracy with which the tanks had engaged the enemy's Spandau posts directly they had been pointed out by the infantry, gave the Guardsmen that fillip to morale which converts a steady assault into a storming. The enemy reacted strongly to this success, and besides having to beat off the routine counter-attacks the Companies had to deal with many isolated enemy posts which had been by-passed in the woods. Moreover, while Left Flank were consolidating their position on the plateau they were subjected to constant and heavy mortar fire, during which the Battalion suffered a grievous blow. The bombs killed the Commanding Officer, Lieutenant-Colonel Taylor, and Captain the Hon. W. H. Vestey, who was commanding Left Flank in the place of Major Harvey. In addition Lieutenant D. J. Forbes and sixteen men were wounded that day, and two Guardsmen killed. The Battalion was ordered to halt where it was, for until reorganisation and replenishment had been effected, there could be no further move towards La Foce. All the Companies now came up, and by six in the evening the whole Battalion was firmly established, having made contact with the French on its left, thus getting the first reliable news of their whereabouts for several days.

The death of Colonel Taylor was a sad event, more especially for those who had served under him in the Second Battalion and had come with him to the First. He had always been most careful of the lives and welfare of his men, and during that first Italian autumn, in a battalion which included many who had been away from home nearly five years, that care had been greatly admired and appreciated. He was succeeded in command by his second-in-command, Major R. D. Cardiff, who in his turn was succeeded by Major J. S. Sanderson.

* * *

Major TC Harvey
1ˢᵗ Bn Scots Guards
CHF
June 29ᵗʰ

My Beloved One,
This is I am afraid, a very sad moment, because as I expect you have heard, Col Guy and Bill have both been killed.[*] I should not be writing this yet, but I know I can trust you to say nothing, absolutely not a word to anyone, until the announcement is in the paper. But I know how very sad you will be, and how worried about me; so I hasten to reassure you on my behalf. You can imagine how miserable we all are, and what a terrible loss Bill is to me; even now I cannot realise that I shall never see him again. One realises, of course, that such tragedies are a daily part of war – but the shock of their reality is sudden and terrible and so final that one's thoughts are confused and one's feelings numbed. No one had finer prospects or showed higher promises.

---

[*]   TCH was called to attend a Company Commanders' meeting with Colonel Guy Taylor. In the general confusion he could not find the place and returned to his Company. A message was received clarifying where the meeting was. Bill Vestey said, 'Tom, you are exhausted' and so went in his place. TCH always deeply regretted that Bill Vestey was killed in those circumstances.

May God bless and comfort poor Pamela. I realise only too well what a hellish time you are going through – worsened I fear by the lack of news – tho' I have written often. But these many and great tribulations will pass away: already the night has passed, leaving but the morning mist in the valleys and on the hilltops. The sun is mounting, and soon the warming rays will chase away the loitering clouds to let us see the full and sunlit prospect outstretched before us. Let us hang on like grim death, to our Hope, for therein lies ones only comfort, our only sanity.

Luckily I have been much cheered by getting 2 more letters from you, one yesterday taking only 5 days. I am sorry about the Guards Chapel; what a merciful escape for Tommy. One's life nowadays depends entirely on sudden whims or chance decisions. I am sure our good Mamas have adored being nannies again – and Susie will be getting a lovely rest. After rather rotten weather, it is superb today – and as I sit on this hill shirtless, and look across at the valleys, at the forests clambering up the far off hills, the little farms, some nestling in fields below, others perched precariously on the slopes, it is hard to realise that 10 yards away is a slit trench and a sentry. Cups of tea circulate, at a rate the MU would never believe, but now it is 11am and most people are sleeping. The last week has been hard work, but we may get a rest soon. Casualties have not been heavy. You were wrong in your guess about where I am – if you want to see me; get out your walking shoes and climb the beautiful mountains.

Bless you, my heart's desire, and a million kisses to the babies,
from your ever devoted Tom

* * *

1 S.G.
2 July, 44.

I am so sorry that I have not written to you for so long but I have had an unpleasant week, and have been frantically busy. I expect you will have heard by now that poor Guy TAYLOR and Bill VESTEY were killed Monday. The Battalion were starting off on a long flanking movement by itself and in the first little battle Guy went forward to see the positions and while walking with Bill was killed by a mortar bomb. He was killed instantaneously and Bill was knocked unconscious and died about half an hour later. We were all terribly upset. I had to take over the Battalion and continue the battle. Tom Harvey, whose Company were involved, fortunately had the whole thing under control and did very well darting about and putting the fear of God into the Germans, and they killed a lot, after which they withdrew.

The next day we continued without much opposition except shelling and the next day we had a small battle and so it goes on; today should be quiet as we have joined the Brigade again and are in Reserve but one can never tell. I've stayed one night at a lovely house belonging to an English woman married to an Italian. The place had been fairly smashed up by the Germans and the owners evacuated, but we caught up with them and sent them back home again, and they were delighted to see us.

The weather is now boiling hot and one just stands and sweats all day; it is terrific but I think it is really better than the cold and wet as one can sleep in the open. I must end now and go to a Church Service at which I have to read the lesson.

* * *

CMF, July 2nd

My own Beloved Darling,

The memories of today four years ago are very vivid, as I sit here in this pine wood, leaning against a tree, writing on my knee and sipping a glass of wine given me by a nearby S.A. tank man. Our dinner "last night" when our family parties collided, the blur of the service, the reception at Aunt Marge's, the drive to the country, and those 3 blissful, shy-making heaven-making days. We'll have to have a proper honeymoon again when I get back! I am so glad the nightdress etc arrived safely – and was a success. I was getting rather worried about it. I haven't seen a shop for weeks but no doubt the time will come and I can get David some little goodies. I haven't yet been able to write to Pamela as I mustn't until I know that she knows. So perhaps you will let me know when the announcement appears. I feel his loss very much, a gap that can not be filled; I think Sacha is going to be my 2 I/C[*] it's a slow business plodding along here, demolitions and mines hold us up a good deal; but we plod steadily on, tho' somewhat at the expense of our sleep. I have recently been concerned with trying to help an English lady[†] who married a wop marquis: we found their house – which was superbly lovely tho' in an awful mess. They had left on foot for a village 7 miles away, under shell fire, flanked by mines and escorting 27 tiny children whom they have been looking after. Their adventures with the patriots and with escaped prisoners were thrilling. Now we have found them all ok and I dined with them, in the nursery, their first night home. It was a very pleasant interlude and I long to see the house again when it is cleaned up and repaired.

This pilotless bomb sounds perfectly bloody – I do pray you have no close contact with it. Possibly our successes in France will reduce its effect. I can't see how Germany can last much longer,

---

[*]   Second in command.
[†]   Iris Origo of La Foce.

but no doubt they have some more dirty tricks up their sleeve.

No more now, my angel.

Lots and lots of love to you all, from your ever adoring Tom

* * *

CMF
July 8th

My Beloved Angel
I have just got your letter dated 28th and am so worried about my letters taking so long. I fear when they do arrive they tell you nothing very amusing (in fact too often the contrary), but the mere fact of getting letters cheers one up. It isn't easy to write much now as we are in the thick of things – and they are rather thick just now – but I hope that by the time you get this we will perhaps be having a not undeserved rest. Some time later I will be able to tell you all about it: I think the Coy has done very well, and are in very good spirits: we are having a bit of a rest just now, and the Naafi ration of beer and chocolate has appeared to fortify us. I saw David Cuthbert the other day for a second – in excellent form and somewhat less podgy. His Brigade has been having quite a time; Dick Chaplin was wounded tho' not badly, and not a few other casualties. I also heard from John Hope but he is in Rome and I fear unlikely to find his way up here. It is perfectly lovely country here – the Chianti country – tho' not food for fighting. Where we are now, there are steep wooded slopes, with little winding roads running from one valley to the next. From 10am to 6pm it is about 90 degrees in the shade, but it is usually tactically difficult to find any shade, so one just sits in one's slit trench, or vehicle, and bakes and bakes. There appears to be no streams, so the heat and glare and dust do tend to get rather oppressive, and sap one's will to action.

By now you will have got my letter endorsing the Red House

suggestions – I quite agree. I am so glad you were able to cope alone with the nits – it must have been hard work and you must take it easy – Susie will be in terrific form by now. I haven't forgotten David's hat – and it will appear tho' not for a very long time, as I haven't even bought one yet. I have just seen a Tatler very old but I must say it makes me laugh with the ghastly photographs and still ghastlier remarks. I have read quite a lot of books lately, an odd assortment but most enjoyable. If you write to Anne do tell her I met a soldier called Summers (I think) who is now a Mess waiter with General Oliver and was in John's platoon in the Ranges – he sent many messages.

Will write again soon. Bless you all, my pretty Darlings, and oceans of love from your ever-loving Tom

* * *

Major TC Harvey
1st Bn Scots Guards
CMF, 12th July

My Darling Maria
Another letter this morning – and sweet and sympathetic one about Bill. I hope by now you have got my letter about it. The opening of the fete must have been an awful ordeal for you, but I am sure you swept your audience off their feet. I long to hear all about it. Your shopping expedition, must have been much more fun: did you get good prices for your sales? That sort of stuff does fetch quite good prices now. Dermot Daly arrived this afternoon, but so far I have only seen him for a second: I expect he'll have a lot of up-to-date gossip for us. I have been spending the afternoon with some gunners, taking advantage of a slight lull, and had a most pleasant time, in quite a nice house. There was a piano and one of the officers played beautifully, every sort of thing from Chopin to dance music. We had quite a good lunch

and altogether I thoroughly enjoyed myself. Though I haven't yet been able to get to Rome, Richard Coke spent a fortnight with the Marconis and had a whale of a time. I don't know what the family consists of or anything about them, but I gather they are all well, and help to make life gay. I seem to remember that one of the girls did some anti-British propaganda – but I can't remember which. I expect that she's changed her tune by now. They're having some very good concerts there Heifetz and others – which I would love to go and hear. The news continues to be very good, doesn't it, tho' things are stuck here for the time being. The Russians are fairly batting along, and they seem to be able to keep going in France. I must say the flying bombs do sound horrid, and I pray they don't reach Norfolk: I am sure they won't. What a bore the weather is being – preventing the nits from sunbathing and pottering about in the garden. I am longing for some new photographs of them. Out here cameras seem very rare, and I haven't yet succeeded in getting myself photographed but I shall try to get the Cecil Beaton of Rome to do a studio portrait of my profile against a background of ants' eggs and jellyfish.

Mother will no doubt have told you that poor faithful Corby died of wounds some days ago. I was not with him at the time, and was not able to see him before he died. I miss him very much, for he was a good friend to me, cheerful and willing and a great favourite with the others. I will be writing to his wife soon but if she writes to you first, explain why I have not yet written. Sacha is with me again – he is in very good heart and doing awfully well. I hear Eddie Moss and wife are "expecting" – otherwise no news of our friends in the G.A.D, tho' I have just written to John. What a dull letter: but there is no news. A million blessings, my beloved ones, from your ever adoring Tom

* * *

Major TC Harvey
1st Bn Scots Guards
CMF
14th July

My beloved Darling,

Another lovely letter from you last night, telling me all about your trip to Norwich. I do so congratulate you on such a successful debut at public speaking – you have beaten me to it, and I shall expect all sorts of hints and advice on how to face an audience! I have a little more news today, as last night Dermot and I went off to dine with Andrew Scott at his Bde HQ. They are very comfortably placed in a large house, with lots to drink and very good food. Jim Egan and Eric Penn are with him, and among those dining were Robert Elwes, whom I haven't seen for years, and also Dennis Singley. Robert is very well, and sends lots of love to all his friends; I believe Viv is at Congham now, so you might like to get hold of her. During dinner Andrew announced that one of the guests, a Subaltern in the Hampshire's had just been awarded the V.C. so there was great excitement. We duly set off to drive back in the dark, but soon got hopelessly lost and decided to stay in the first decent looking house. We found one, but couldn't get in, altho' a lot of Italians jabbered at us out of the window. This enraged us, both being in no mood for trifling and eventually we forced our way in, and spend a reasonably comfortable night till 7.30 when we left with 4 eggs for our breakfast. Our housebreaking was killing, and put the Wops into a frightful tee-wee. I simply can't understand what is happening to my letters – I have been able to write about 2 a week always. I fear they must have been sunk. From what I gather others are rather the same – but it is sickening.

I am so glad that David and Caroline are in such good form; they must be a blessing to you in these times. I am sure your Papa will love staying with you – try and get him to dine with the

Ingleby's, he'll love the good talk and good wine. Mind you keep Lionel* up to the mark about visiting you; and if David Robarts comes to Norfolk make him visit his goddaughter! No more now, my angel.

A million blessings on you all. From your ever loving Tom

* * *

Major TC Harvey
1st Bn Scots Guards
CMF
July 19th

My Beloved Darling
Your letter dated 11th arrived yesterday – why o why are mine taking so hideously long. Though I fear they are very dull when they do arrive, yet at least they got a little news. Bless you, a million times for being so brave and cheerful – it is a tremendous comfort and help to me. The war news fluctuates a good deal, and personally I have found the last ten days rather depressing – but today again it seems to be better. We are gradually pushing him off the high ground S of Florence, but it is hard slogging work. However I think the end of that phase is approaching, which leaves the Gothic line to be dealt with, not I trust by yours truly. Our activities recently have centred round a huge fortress-like castle, owned and inhabited by a Baron – King of the Chianti world.† He was not best pleased at the attentions paid to his home before our arrival, but we bought a lot of his wine which may have soothed him a little. His wife was charming, young looking and very handsome with 3 equally handsome daughters, none of whom, I may add, did I set eyes on. We would have had quite a peaceful time had it not been for the flies, which attack one

---

*   Lionel, Vincent Massey's son.
†   Baron Ricasoli, living at Castello di Brolio.

in strength all day, covering everything with filth, and contaminating every mouthful of food. The dust though is something appalling – so that what would be a lovely drive with superb views, is like a white pea-soup fog, covering ones face, eyes with a thick mask of powder.

I had my first bath since Capri yesterday. Lovely and hot, a real treat. Mind you I wasn't as dirty as all that – but the water was I must confess, fairly fruity by the time I had washed my hair. The heat continues to be terrific, but no real opportunity to enjoy it as there is no water anywhere. What ghastly weather you seem to be having in the Channel too. Sickening for the nits who will miss all the summer fun. Give them both lots of hugs and kisses from their Poppa and to you, my Darling, a million tender blessings and adorations.

From your ever very devoted Tom

* * *

Major TC Harvey
1st Bn Scots Guards
CMF
26th July

My Most Beloved Darling
Once again I put pencil to paper, tho' I fear after rather a gap, for the usual reasons. Those same reasons tend to limit my being able to give you much news – the same old wearing grind goes on, with its usual ups and downs, and inevitable tedium and worse. So I won't weary you with further vague allusions – but will wait until I am allowed to say what has been happening. The highlight of the week was the arrival of the photographs which I adore – David looks an absolute poppet in that ridiculous hat, and the one of him sitting between the old ladies is a real study of self-assurance – not, I suspect, without a touch of self-

satisfaction! I must say the house looks most attractive and must be lovely if you get decent weather, which by now I trust you do. I can picture you having children's picnics on the beach with Anne's family – I trust they get on well together, and do not show the usual cousinly antipathies. I am sure David will benefit by being knocked about a bit, as so far he has been blissfully used to having his own way. It will make him irritable for a little, but he will be all the better for it. Your Papa's visit must have done him a lot of good tho' as you say, it was a pity he didn't stay longer. You never mention Eliza these days. Do give the old girl lots of love from me, and tell her that I do so hope all is going well and that her saintly burden isn't lapping up all the gin.

I don't know what to make of the news – it makes one's mouth water and one's mind reel. Is the war really going to end soon? I really believe so, tho' "soon" might mean anything. Mama continues to write cheerfully, and full of tit bits. It is lovely for her to have all her grandchildren so much around her, and I feel sure Florrie is hopping about from dawn till dusk, with not a minute for a morsel of food, not a second for a sip of tea, added to that, the torment of a thousand heterogeneous and unprintable diseases. I am glad about the car – except that I HATE Austins and will change it as soon as I get back. But I'm sure it will be a great success and very suitable.

No more for now, my honey bee, but a million blessings on all my Darlings three from your devoted and loving Tom

* * *

Major TC Harvey
1st Bn Scots Guards
CMF
31st July

My own beloved Darling,

Am writing this very tired and dirty for our rest has not yet come and we're in a rather inaccessible place. However I was much delighted to get your letter dated 23rd last night, with all its news. How very disappointing for Tommy and Eliza – yet I am glad she is alright, and now I feel there'll be no stopping them. I can't understand the muddle of Australia – surely they must have known beforehand how big the house was – it sounds a most skimpy little villa. I am also delighted about the nomination – Lt Col. was here yesterday, but unfortunately I did not know when I saw him, and now he has gone away. However when things settle down here and I know more details I can find out what the form is. I imagine you will decide to stay on at Peddars Way for the time being, now that the Red House is off – I feel you might do a lot worse, particularly if you can get old doodle-bug refugees to come and stay with you. I heard from John by the same post – very cheerful and busy tho' finding things naturally thoroughly nasty. He tells me that Rex Whistler has been killed – I am so very sorry – if anyone could have got a cushy job he could have. Poor old Sacha has been wounded again – just after becoming a Captain and my 2 i/c – a nasty cut in the leg, but not serious. Tom Bland and Jack Baxter also, tho' neither serious – so Tim[*] and I are left holding the fort. Gussie Cunningham and Neil Douglas have come to me now, but we will have to wait until we get our relief before I can really get things straightened out. It will be a deliriously lovely change to have a civilised life again. But in spite of everything I am keeping extremely well – which is maddening! How charming of the people at Ringstead to think of sending something to Mrs Corby, so like them to do that. I had a charming letter from Lady Vestey but haven't heard from Pam[†] yet – poor Darlings, it has robbed them of all they cherished. I didn't get a chance to see HM which was a great pity as I wanted to test his Boogie-Woogie memory. No more for now,

---

[*]   Lieutenant Tim Mostyn.
[†]   Pam Vestey, Bill's widow.

sweetest heart, except thank you, or someone, for some lovely books which have brought me great comfort. A million blessings to you all, and many tender kisses.

From your ever loving and adoring Tom

* * *

Major TC Harvey
1st Bn Scots Guards
CMF
August 5th

My Beloved Heart

Have just got your letter dated 29th and am so very delighted with all your cheerful news. I really think that we have at last reached the end of our journey, and my next letter will I hope come to you from a rest area. Even now I am more comfortable than I have been for many weeks, and I am writing this one at the dinner table, at which I eat my meals with my elderly Italian host. He feeds me very well, and I have a nice bedroom with sheets – but there are still apt to be nightly alarms and excursions. So that one doesn't get a perfect night. In addition, I had the most tremendous dog-fights with mosquitoes, and came off very definitely 2nd best – with a large bite in the eye. But it subsided very quickly and is quite alright now. How well the war seems to be going in France and Russia: it really looks as tho' we may win soon. Here the defence has been very stubborn, possibly partly for political reasons and it will not be any easier north of Florence. I have heard from both Sacha and Tom, and they are getting on well, tho' I don't quite know how long they will be. Anyhow they both sound very cheerful, tho' they are as yet in different hospitals. I miss them both terribly. I can't imagine what Col Derrick must have written, for I can assure you that I have been guilty of no acts of gallantry – far from it indeed. We have, it is true, had some must successful little actions, in which I have commanded a composite force of infantry, guns and tanks, usually from the bowels of a tank, and someone else has been left to do the dirty work. But on the whole the results have been successful, thanks more to the good work of the various units than to the somewhat facile command of your Plaza-Toro husband.* However, I can tell you all about that later.

The babies sound in terrific form, and getting on very well with their cousins: tell Anne I had a very cheerful letter from John a few days ago: very busy and in the thick of things, I gathered. They certainly seem to have had a real victory all along the line.

I saw Bernard Bruce and Ulick Verney again the other day, and they brought us some Kimmel and Havana Cigars, which I just got my hands onto. We have accumulated quite a little drink during the past weeks, and so I hope to get down to some serious drinking in the near future.

No more for now, Angel Heart, a million blessings on you all and many many kisses.

From your ever loving and adoring Tom

* * *

Major TC Harvey
1st Bn Scots Guards
CMF
9th August

My Most Beloved Darling
Well, as I prophesied in my last letter, here I am in a "Rest Area" – to be precise the Eden Hotel at Rome! You can imagine what it feels like, after ten solid weeks without a rest, to be living in luxury in the loveliest city of the world, bathed in hot sun, and lulled to

---

*   Plaza-Toro, from Gilbert & Sullivan's *The Gondoliers*: meaning 'not very brave'!

sleep by the gentle lullaby of ice tinkling in a glass. George Ramsay and I motored here, virtually non-stop from Florence. I fear that so far we have done little proper sightseeing concentrating rather on getting clean and tidy. My first morning I visited the hotel barber, who performed the most dynamic execution. Suffering, I diagnose, from a repressed urge to conduct a symphony orchestra, he brandished his scissors like a baton, round my head, and at wild irregular intervals plunged them fiercely into my hair, snipped frenziedly here, sliced off great hunks there, as tho' he wanted the brass to play fortissimo. This tempestuous passage would then sink into a quiet andante movement of the clippers, flare up a moment later into the rapier-like thrusts of an agitato, which in turn yielded to a delicate pizzicato, when he would lift up the great mass of my hair and snip little bits from below with the tip of his, by now, white hot scissors. In vain did I protest – non troppo – I wailed but mad with power he just frowned devilishly and pointed to the wall saying "Diploma" – for there, true enough was hanging his illuminated Tonsorial Commission, dated 1934. Eventually it was over. The orchestra, and the audience alike exhausted, the conductor bathed in sweat, proud, happy and triumphant. After that ordeal George and I continued to potter, getting extra clothes, arranging to fly to Naples tomorrow to visit the hospitals, an excellent lunch with Bobby and Johnny Drury-Lowe, 2 hours siesta and then dinner with Jim Egan, a bottle of Kesselring's Champagne, and later with Jim to see some Principessa who wanted news of Florence. A most delightful woman, very chic and amusing, and so we sat talking and laughing until midnight. Today Tommy Bulkeley and his wife come for drinks at 12, Lavinia Holland-Hibbert dines with me tonight, and with the others we are giving a bottle party, with swing band etc – nothing is arranged so far, so that I can see today is going to be pretty hectic. Oh my darling, how I wish you were here to enjoy all this fun with me, and thereby to double it. I feel that only half of me is really here!

We tried last night to see St Peters but it closes at 6pm – but the day after tomorrow we can go to a Papal Audience and see St Peter and the Sistine Chapel first. I am trying to get hold of the Marconi's, but have lost your letter and can't get straight what is a Marconi and what a Marignoli. However I hope to find them soon. Boogie's brother is here too and is lunching with me, but Boogie is I believe still in Capri.

I am very thrilled about what you say of the Conservative Committee, and also the Staff College, though I doubt my being selected for either. The difficulties of getting to England are enormous and I am doubtful of being successful but it is at any rate worth trying. If I am allowed back for a brief fleeting visit I shall probably appear before you know anything about it – but as I say the chances are exceedingly small. I have of course said that I will return here when my business is done, but naturally if RHQ post me elsewhere that is a different matter. I can't really see why they should send me to the S.C. In fact I don't believe they will accept one as an instructor unless one has first been a student. The battle in France must have swelled to a vast size now, and certainly seems to be going superbly well. I feel that the Germans may have some devilish weapon up their sleeve and the Nazis want to hang until they're ready to use it: whereas many of the Army, knowing that no weapon can avail them, want to stop. He's well on the run now and I feel that the next 3 months may see him beaten. My love, another letter from the Great Roman Scandal will appear with you very soon.

Until then, herewith all my most fervent love to you and a mass of kisses to the nit pots from your ever adoring Tom

* * *

189

Major TC Harvey
1ˢᵗ Bn Scots Guards
CMF
11 August

My beloved Heart,

Our party was a great success the other night, in spite of the whirlwind preparations required. We had a large dinner party to start with, to which I took Lavinia H-H, at a restaurant in the Borghese Gardens. Thence on to our flat, which was by then well organised with lots of flowers and drink, and a reasonably good Italian band. There was unfortunately no electric light at the time, but it was no hardship to dance by candlelight and as it was a fine evening, we were able to get out on the balcony. There were many exquisite young ladies about, but as they were each being tailed by at least 3 officers and one Italian, I took no part. However at about 3 o'clock George and I thought we'd go, as we had to be at the airport at 7.45 next morning. Feeling not quite our best, we duly arrived there and had a pleasant uneventful flight to Naples – but once there our troubles began, as we had no transport and didn't look like being able to get any. However by a stroke of luck we found a strange officer who had a spare jeep, so into that we piled and drove like the wind down the Autostrada to Pompeii where we found Sacha in hospital and about a dozen of the company. I think they were a little surprised to see us. Sister gave us lunch, so we were able to have a good gossip – Sacha is very well, in very good spirits and mending fast. We became airborne again at 3.45 and got back here at about 4.45. A hurried bath, change and cocktail, and then to the opera with Johnny Drury Lowe. Rigoletto – it was superb. The Opera House is the loveliest I have seen. The gallery consists of nothing but little boxes, lined with red velvet, a complete semi-circle of little windows like those of the Doge's palace. On either side of every box hangs a pair of exquisite glass chandeliers, so that the general effect of row after row and tier after tier of these is very handsome. The production and whole performance was superb, in particular Rigoletto himself and the orchestra. We just wallowed in the fun of it all. After that we had a superb dinner, starting with iced melon and ham, a delicious mixture. You can imagine that on top of all our other activities a large well "watered" dinner made one frightfully sleepy, and by the time we got to bed at 11.15 I was just about unconscious. But I feel terrific this morning and George and I are now off to see St Peters, the Vatican and I hope the Pope. I have found Gioia Marconi or I think it is her, and had a delightful tea with her. Lord Gort had just been staying with her. She is perfectly sweet, and simply thirsty for news of you all which I was able to give her. I hope to see her again today or tomorrow. I have done no shopping yet but I must try – though there is not a great deal in the shops, and what there is very expensive. I went to see John Dalrymple for a moment to give him all our news, but naturally being away I have had no letters from home for some time. However I know there are lots waiting for me, and it will be a consolation for returning back from leave. We go back on 13th via 8th Army where I hope to put in a little useful work.

Very short letter this time, I fear: but time is dashing on and I will be writing again before I leave. Bless you all, my loves, and many kisses to you all.

From your ever adoring Tom

* * *

Major TC Harvey
1st Bn Scots Guards
CMF
Aug 16th

My most beloved Darling,
My visit to Rome didn't quite finish in the blaze of glory it should

have done, as I became the victim of an ignominious bilious attack, and spent the whole of my last day in bed, retching and generally having hell. I was better next day, but it was time to leave, so we started back after lunch stopping at Lake Bolsena on the way for a bathe. It was superb, but I lost my wallet with all my money and treasures – so that was a second disaster. We got back here in time for dinner to find the Bn fairly comfortably placed, round a big house – all under canvas, but plenty of shade and a swimming pool. We mess in the house but sleep outside. The views all around are superb, the heat quite tropical, in fact it's lovely provided one doesn't have to do anything – which fortunately we don't at the moment. I pop about seeing people a bit, but it's really too hot to move, and today I think I shall just get basked. What little sunburn I had has almost gone, so I must try to get a little back. I quite sympathise with your decision to return to Holkham, tho' I do hope you're not convincing yourself that I am coming home at any minute, let alone for good: admittedly one can never tell what is happening, but one mustn't be too optimistic. Most of the people out here have better reasons for going home than I have. But the news is thrilling and I really feel the war may end at any second of the day or night. What fun your parties sound – yes do rope in Anne, and cheer her up because she would so love it once you got her going, and it would be a most christian kindness even if things were a little sticky to start with. And in any case I am sure she'd rather be shocked than lonely.

I got on very well with Bea Marignoli and Gioia Marconi finding them both delightful – also Denia, but I did not meet Giulio.* Lord Gort had been with them and had given them a lot of the gossip. Gioia is great fun, the image of Bridget A. and has a great success with the boys. 4 of us took out 4 of them to dinner and I bought them all orchids which was a great success! What

* Gioia, Denia and Giulio Marconi, all children of the famous radio pioneer with his first wife (vaguely related to Mary).

your reactions will be, who have never got so much as a nettle from me, I dare not think.

I am so glad the nittle-pots are so well and happy: how stinky of the weather to stay so foul. I hope that by now you have had some sailing. I must stop now and settle orders.

Bless you all, my Darlings and many loving and devoted kisses from your Tom

* * *

Major TC Harvey
1st Bn Scots Guards
CMF
August 17th
My beloved Darling,
Nothing of very much interest to tell you since I last wrote – I was delighted to get two more letters from you dated 3 and 6, to hear of all the fun and news. What a nightmare time you must have had with the photographers and all the simultaneous calamities. I trust that everything has calmed down now, and can hardly wait to see news: I find myself very antipathetic to writing at the moment. I can't think why. But I know you keep her up to date and give her my love.

So glad the weather is better and the poplets can sunbathe. Here it is too hot really and our swimming pool too dirty. Bless you all my precious loves, from your adoring Tom

* * *

Major TC Harvey
1st Bn Scots Guards
CMF
August 20

My Beloved Darling

No news from you very lately, but a letter from Mama today, telling me of the wonderful birthday present to me. Have you got the car yet? She also told me of the photographing – poor David to be stung on the BTM and again on the tummy – it must have been agony, and I can't believe he settled down very placidly. I am sure you all looked too heavenly. Just like a goddess and her nymphs, surprised, playing together in a fairy woodland.

Very little news from here: I took part, with some others, in a Brains Trust at which the star was Eric Linklater who has been here for a couple of days. The questions were quite good – far better than the answers – and I heard myself being thoroughly long-winded, confused and dull. The future of Germany after the war, Demobilisation, looking into the Future and other similar problems were all discussed and on the whole I think the men enjoyed listening. I took a substantial whack of money off the little man at poker, but lost it all and more last night with the Coldstream. As I am living on credit, having lost my wallet, that is altogether rather sad. However, what the hell. The war seems to be going better and better every day, and the latest landing appears to have met with virtually no opposition – but out here its extraordinarily difficult to get news, up to date at any rate. The Yanks have indeed done well, and perhaps, as I write, are in Paris. It will be an undying tragedy if Florence is going to be badly damaged, but nowadays it's no good expecting anything. I am most grateful for the Spectator and New Statesman which arrive regularly now: I forgot to thank Mama for some Penguins, will you tell her. Books make the whole difference out here, and I read the whole time (or as often as I can) when in the line. Out of it I don't so much: there are other distractions like bridge, the piano, visiting friends and dining out, which while they last make a pleasant change.

I fear my application has got stuck in some pigeon-hole or other – though I still live in vague hopes. It is almost impossible to get home at all, on any pretext, for any length of time, the only hope is to be posted back to England by the War Office. Still things are going so well now, that one might, I feel, wake up any day and find that it is all over. Not that I should be surprised if a certain number of fanatical soldiers went on of their own accord for as long as they could. After all, in their place, with the Russians loose at home, we would probably do the same.

I saw Andrew Scott, Jim Egan and Malcolm Erskine for a second the other day and Andrew said he had heard from Simon. I saw Rex Whitworth who told me that Lionel had gone off to the country "with some girl" – so I feel it's as well to let him get that over before meeting you!!

Tim is on leave in Rome at the moment, but will be back any day now: I hope he was able to see Tom in hospital, as I couldn't manage to. Just in case I manage to get back, could you collect for me the various reports issued by the Tory Reform Committee, there are a number of them. I don't want them sent out here, but would like them as it were, in readiness.

My Darlings, I find it so hard to say how much I love you and long to be with you again. The time is rushing on, though God knows it seems to take long enough. God bless you my love and the babies. From your ever adoring Tom

* * *

Major TC Harvey
1st Bn Scots Guards
CMF
Aug 24th

My Beloved Heart,
There is very little news of interest since I last wrote: but what
more exciting can one expect, than the tremendous surge forward
of the armies in France. Just think what the French people must
feel at Paris being free again – Paris which to any Frenchman
anywhere means the very life-blood of France itself. They must be
beside themselves with excitement and joy. The other landing too
seems to be developing fantastically well: whether the Germans
in Italy are going to be affected by all these things remains to
be seen. They are a bone-headed, fanatical lot, and will certainly
stay put if they are ordered to. At the same time, if a real threat
to their homes develops I should imagine they would become
restless and anxious to defend them.

The heat has, in American jargon, reached a new high, and we
have been sweltering for days on end. It is now 9.45 and already
very hot – even at night it's terrific, and with one blanket and no
pyjamas one just drips with sweat. Naturally every bit of metal
gets frightfully hot, and it is quite common for the bedding rolls
strapped on the sides of tanks and carriers to burst into flames.
Many people swear that it's hotter than the desert, and certainly I
have never experienced anything like it. On the whole, although
one doesn't feel like doing anything, and although it's really too
hot to eat or sleep much, still it is preferable to the wet, which
disturbs and upsets things far more.

I have just heard I'm sad to say, that the authorities won't play
over my application to return to England for an interview: they
say that they would let me go if I was adopted as candidate –
but they naturally don't say how one can manage to be adopted
without first being interviewed. In other words, no young man

can hope to be adopted unless he happens to be in England, which seems to be me all wrong. However you might talk to Maurice Fermoy about it. Of course, if RHQ post me back to England, I can then go ahead – but that is most unlikely. If by some extraordinary chance the Committee do decide to adopt me, tell them to let me know at once, and get Maurice to get in touch with the War Office, to find out the correct procedure. Even then, I believe the authorities would only let one go if a by-election were actually about to take place. However there it is, and there is little one can do about it, except finish the war off, and then we can all come home!

I am so glad the babies are flourishing and at last getting some decent weather. It must have been a poisonous summer with you. Caroline is sure to have a rotten time with her teeth, poor sweet, but I am sure that the combined attentions of yourself, Susie, Billy, David and Kuniang will do much to alleviate her distress. Give Billy my love, and tell her that whenever I see a beautiful Signorina, I think of her, and instantly regain my self-control!

I expect by now you have heard some news from the Lt Col – I was filthy dirty when I saw him, not having washed or shaved for several days – however that has its advantages, for I don't think he would recognise me again.

No more for now, my Darling, I fear like me that you will be very disappointed by the rejection of my application, but it can't be helped. Things are moving so fast now, that anything may happen.

God bless you all, and oceans of love and kisses from your ever
adoring Tom

* * *

Major TC Harvey
1ˢᵗ Bn Scots Guards
CMF
August 27

My Beloved Angel,
Two more lovely letters yesterday, dated 17 and 20. So glad you
are all flourishing, and naturally thrilled by the news, just as we
are. All the Balkan rats seem to be pretty sure that their German
ship is sinking. I haven't heard any news from John lately, but I
imagine that he is too busy to write. How extraordinary it is of
Anne to feel that way about us – poor girl, she does seem to make
heavy weather of life, and anyone less jealous than John is hard
to imagine. I think that I am the cause of the trouble, as she has
always thought that Mama spoiled me, at John's expense – but
now she seems to have turned against us all. There's nothing to do
about it, except ignore it, or laugh at it. What annoys me is that it
must be making Darling Mother's life such a hell, and no one on
this earth has a greater right to happiness and consideration than
her. She hasn't mentioned anything to me about it, apart from a
terse account of Anne's refusal to take any part in the Ringstead
School "Speech Day" – but I too was afraid that things were not
going too well. Personally I've always found Anne extremely difficult and I always will.

I've been reading quite a lot lately, some good and some bad,
but anything helps to pass the time. Tell Tommy that he can
come and command Left Flank if he likes, and I'll go on Alex's
staff for a change! I see Alice G has produced a boy – why couldn't
it have been the other way round, with Eliza? Do tell Lionel to
write to me some time, and let me hear all his news: I wonder if
he is thinking of going back to Canada. Hart I imagine is bearing
the full weight of the entire invasion on his shoulders, and is
quite ungettatable. The M's long-awaited visit to Holkham is, I
take it, quite out of the question for the time being. By the way, I

am glad that your Papa is making an effort to be a good LL. I am certain that the highlight of the news for you has been the arrival of Bing* in England: all the terrors of the doodle-bug will vanish at the thought of him. I must say I wish he'd come out here and sing to me.

Rather a poky letter today – but there isn't much news. Life is on the whole very peaceful and will stay so for some time I trust. Give the babies lots and lots of love from me: I don't know when I'll get a chance to buy them birthday presents – but to be on the safe side you must get them something from me.

Bless you, honey pot, and a million kisses to you all and Susie Q. from your ever loving Tom

* * *

Major TC Harvey
1st Bn Scots Guards
CMF
September 3

My Beloved Darling
In great haste, a rather scrawly letter to catch this evening's post. Have just got your letter dated 27 Aug, and am so glad to hear you are all in good order, and having nice days on the beach. Mama has told me of her decision to leave Ringstead after the war, and I must say I think she is wise, as it will give her more money to spend on herself and give herself a few of her well-deserved treats. Ringstead has unfortunately become a bone of contention with Anne – tho' she made no reference to that and I don't think there has been any further quarrel. What a blow about the income tax – that's what comes of increasing one's petty little income. I think we'll have to get in the habit of putting cash aside £10 a month into a separate account, in order to be able to pay it without

---

*   Bing Crosby.

too much of a shock. Child's would arrange it for us, I am so distressed about poor old Jocelyn,* tho' relieved to hear that he is alright. Would you send him and Silvia a very special message from me. Do continue sending me news of people in France: depressing tho' it is, it is preferable to not knowing how anybody is.

Life here goes along pretty well, and we are lucky in having a quiet and reasonably comfortable time. I have been lucky in getting a series of really quite nice houses, and we can complain of nothing. Events move so fast nowadays, and on such a gargantuan scale, that one can only hold one's breath, and hope. One's wildest dreams have been made to look silly by reality. Your plea for silk stockings won't go unheeded, I promise, but they are very scarce and not very good. I'll have a chance to do some shopping some time, I trust, but not probably for some little time. Well my beloved, I must stop now. I expect you have, too been thinking of all that has happened in the past five years: it is indeed difficult to assess one's own wonderful happiness in the midst of such widespread suffering. It is a typical paradox of this crazy, unhappy world.

Lots and lots of love and kisses to the babies, Susie and your Pa and Ma from your ever adoring Tom

* * *

Major TC Harvey
1st Bn Scots Guards
CMF
9 September

My Beloved Darling,
The light is not very good so I am writing rather big, but as there is no news, it doesn't much matter. We are all very well and life has been quiet and comfortable. I am writing this in a most

---

*   Jocelyn Hambro, who lost a leg in Normandy in August 1944.

comfortable and well appointed little house, high up on the side of a hill, with a superb view of valleys, either side. I expect we will soon be moving on again, but I hope to find another "casa" as nice. No letters have arrived from you lately, but I expect you have been up to your neck in "flitting". By now I trust you are settled and rested: David and Caroline will be very happy and I hope were able to have really happy birthdays. What thrilling news about the Gads entry into Brussels. John must have done superbly well to cope with such a terrific supply problem. I feel the next few weeks are going to be rather tantalising and even exasperating – enemy resistance may well continue for some time and there may be some fierce fighting as at Rimini. However it will all come right, tho' we may need all our patience. Equally well it may end before you get this. Sorry for such a foul letter.

Masses and masses of love, my Beloved, and hearty kisses to the nits. From your ever adoring Tom

* * *

Major TC Harvey
1st Bn Scots Guards
CMF
18 September

My Beloved Darling
I fear it is rather a long time since I last wrote, chiefly because there is so very little to say, and party because I have been waiting to hear your latest news. I got your 1st letter from Holkham yesterday and was very pleased to hear that the move had gone off alright and that you were all happily settled. Give all my love to all at "The Hall" and tell them to keep some pheasants, and some cartridges for me – tho' whether I am back or not depends more on these damned Germans than on me. If you happen to see a newsreel of activities out here, keep a sharp lookout for

me and the Company as we have been exclusively photographed today. Your friends in London will no doubt tell you if they see me, binoculars in hand, surveying the scenery!! The only other item of excitement was that I visited the dentist the other day – which gave me two nights "off duty". The first evening I spent at a party given by the Greens, with their Regt. Band. They are in a very pleasant hotel, frequented in peace time by sufferers from rheumatics etc for in the town are the most superb natural Turkish Baths. Dermot has been to them once or twice but I find my pores get quite enough exercise from my journeys up and down the hills. I got two long letters from Boo and Digby a few days ago – and will write to them when I can. I am longing for the books – can you also send me Ned Grigg's "British Foreign Policy". I am longing to hear of Darling David's birthday festivities, and shall be thinking very specially of Caroline on Thursday – I am sending her a sweet little bonnet, to be worn a l'hollandaise – given me by a dear lady with whom I was billeted. Her husband was a partisan leader some 20 miles away, and before I left, she had word that he was wounded and missing. I have left her note in the box, so think of her when you open it.

No more now, my most Beloved Darlings. Give the babies specially big kisses from me, and tell David not to be too naughty or he won't enjoy my return!! Ever your loving and devoted Tom

* * *

Major TC Harvey
1st Bn Scots Guards
CMF
22 September

My Beloved Angel
Yesterday I got your letter describing David's birthday and am so glad he had a happy day. Bless him. I hope the glamour of the

whistle wears off before the house becomes too like No 10 platform at Paddington. I am so glad the weather has been better. What wonderful war news still – tho' much heavy fighting, particularly on the East Coast here – tho' now it's beginning to look as tho' they have got through at Rimini. I am very well, tho' heartily sick of the war. Tim has left me to go as a Captain/Instructor at the IRTD. I am delighted for his sake but will miss him sorely. Sacha and Tom are getting on well, but I am hoping the war may be over before they're ready to come back. It seems impossible to tell how long the Germans are going on for – it is clearly hopeless for them now, but they hardly act like normal human beings. Even those who would like to stop, are too frightened of being shot by their own side to do anything about it. We have just been having a bit of a rest and clean up for 48 hours and I went to quite a good little concert party show – also I had a drink with Dick Westmacott who is at Bde HQ – he tells me that Gerry Pilkington is being or has been repatriated which I pray is true. It would be such a comfort to poor Ruth. What cheek of Gwyneth Cook – I fail to see how you could refuse, but it is a doubtful privilege. No news from John for ages – I can't wait to hear how he is, and Tom and Alastair and Co – they must be frantically busy. Mama must be relieved that Anne has gone – it is sufficiently hard work keeping the house going, without having squabbles all the time. I fear I sent Caroline's little bonnet to Fring, but I expect they'll send it on. Anyhow it is sure to take ages to arrive. I am so glad you have written to some of the casualties' next of kin – but I haven't got a Lawson except one who was very slightly wounded and was not ever evacuated. You should get very nice letters from the Watsons – they are most devout R.C's.

I feel more and more relieved at not becoming MP just yet, as I do feel horribly inexperienced, and would like to get down to some jobs for a year or two, and find my feet in it. I notch 56 points on the Demob Scheme, so with any luck I shan't be kept hanging about too long!! The only thing I insist on is getting a job with at least as much pay as I get now. You might write to Child's and ask them to check my pay and prove that I really am getting every penny I'm entitled to!

No more now, my Beloved. But a million kisses to you all and so much, oh, so much love. From your ever adoring Tom

* * *

Major TC Harvey
1st Bn Scots Guards
CMF, 27 September

My Beloved Darling
Once again, pen to paper, again with very little news to be passed on – life being generally tedious and unsatisfactory. Not that we can complain at the moment, for we are comfortably ensconced in a large Franciscan monastery: there are 14 monks here, a lot of school children, and an undivulged number of refugee civilians, all in considerable disrepair, mental, moral and physical. The brothers are very friendly, and pad about in their sandals, while the children can't disguise their pleasure at our presence, since it means for them a prolonged holiday from lessons, their dormitories and classrooms having been yielded up to the soldiers. Naturally there are too, all the attendant excitements of military apparatus – petrol cookers, roaring busily in the twilight, vast shadows of cooks and messmen tossing titbits into the pot, trying to look nonchalant and unself-conscious – dark groups of monks, chattering busily over the scene, their white girdles swinging in the light of the flames. Some children find a football, and kick it about uproariously to the terror of the older brothers, who duck stiffly as it flies towards their tonsured pates. Others clamber over the jeeps, tooting the horn, heaving at the levers, with the smallest child of all wedged down by a vast steel helmet, and half-suffocated by a gigantic pair of goggles. It is all very

friendly and incongruous. Alas, we only arrived last night and are off again at cockcrow tomorrow. One never seems to stay in the same place for 2 minutes.

I haven't heard from Tim since he left, because he immediately collapsed with jaundice – for which he must have been sickening for a long time. Anyhow he'll be able to have a good rest and change and it will do him all the good in the world. I haven't seen Andrew since Billy's death* but I gather he has won the M.C. which is splendid. It hasn't however been officially granted by H.M yet. I have got some photographs of the Company of which you can order copies from London if you like – there's only one of me, and you can't see my face which is hardly a disadvantage. They're not particularly thrilling but you can order some if you feel like it. I have just been told the man with the photos is away, so I will have to send you the number in my next letter. I expect your canteen work will be quite fun, tho' the ambulance car may be less so – particularly for the patient, if the car, not to mention the driving, are as I remember them!! I am so glad that the atmosphere at H. is so much easier – long may it continue. That old rascal Thomas, certainly seems to have found a profitable niche. What depths of scandal you must have plumbed with Lilah† – who is no person to cast the first stone herself. The exquisite Lt Col Geary will have to look out for his inheritance. I would love to see Bill Urmiston, tho' I fear he will be moving in higher circles than mine – not that he would try to contact me if he could. I adored hearing about David pottering about with Hassell‡ – I believe you're all beastly to the wretched man and David's the only person he can fall back on! I have heard from Digby twice now, so I must stop and write to her. It was very pleasant to see that a grateful Govt. are going to give me an extra 35/- a week for

---

*   Brothers Andrew and Billy Cavendish; because of Billy's death, Andrew would become the Duke of Devonshire.

†   Lilah Morrison-Bell.

‡   Dr Hassel, Librarian at Holkham.

the rest of the war – they must think the end is very near – Pray God it is, tho' the Germans haven't apparently had their bellyful yet.

   Give the babies lots and lots of love and many kisses to all my Darlings. From your ever loving and adoring, Tom

* * *

Major TC Harvey
1ˢᵗ Bn Scots Guards
CMF
3 October 44

My Beloved Darling
The chief topic of interest in this letter is that I have been very slightly 'nicked' in the back of my leg, and so am wandering about with a couple of stitches in it. So you can see that it is very slight, but has the advantage of excusing me from duty for at least a week! And I am planning to go off to Florence if I can and enjoy myself. The most painful part of all was having the stitches in, a couple of hours ago, but the sting will soon wear off. Things were pretty hot and bloody at the time, and so I have good cause for being thankful.

   I got two very good letters from you the other day and also one from Veronica Gilliat who was very touched by your letter and asked me to tell you how much she appreciated it. Otherwise there is very little news from this part of the world – the weather has become really foul, drenching rain, and very cold, so that one is grateful for Battle Dress and its attendant Winter Woolies. Bad weather is a tremendous help to the Germans, and coupled with the appalling terrain, enables them to make good use of their forces. I have heard no news from France etc lately, but things are going hard there, in I suppose, a frantic effort by the Germans to keep us from getting deep into the Fatherland. I wish I could get a letter from John telling me all about his doings, but he is obviously terribly busy. I am sure the children are blissfully happy at Holkham – but do promise me that you won't let David get spoilt or too much attention from his doting grand-parents. He might so easily become self-centred and also too dependent on others for his amusement. Baby tears now will save so many bigger and painful tears later on. They sound to be the most divine pair, and I long so much to be with them again soon. Perhaps by now the little bonnet for Caroline has arrived – she should look a picture in it.

If I can manage to get to Florence I will try and do some shopping again – I have neglected that badly of late – tho' not entirely on purpose. This time I will try and get you something you can show off to your friends without danger of indecent exposure or improper suggestion. I'm told that there are quite nice things there. Well my Darling, no more for now: don't worry about my leg, as it is really slight, and a good excuse for a rest and a change. I fear those photographs I mentioned have disappeared, for the time being at any rate.

All my love, my Beloved Ones
from Tom

* * *

September 30

The two assaulting companies set off at three o'clock with Major Harvey in the lead. He took them through the woods on the eastern slope of the ridge, getting quite close to the summit before being detected, and thereby avoiding most of the defensive artillery fire which fell close behind. By half-past five Lord Hesketh had C Company firmly established in the woods on the eastern shoulder of 707, and half an hour later Left Flank, which had met stiffer opposition, had reached a track which ran along the north-western end of the wood immediately south of the summit. The SS men withdrew before the advancing Guardsmen, moving with a casualness and deliberation which, for several, can only be described as suicidal; the Machine Gun Platoon saw to that. The lack of caution displayed by the enemy throughout the action was exceptional, being one of the main reasons for their heavy casualties, and, it must be conceded, for their success. Beyond the woods lay open, harvested fields. The summit itself was rounded and coverless, save for heaps of stones which the peasants had removed from the fields and piled up in the manner of rough walls. In these walls and in a sunken track the SS Spandau gunners had entrenched themselves; on the reverse slope others could with ease make the bare summit untenable. Nevertheless Major Harvey led a bayonet charge which reached the crest, putting the enemy on it to flight but to hold it in face of the fresh fire of the Germans beyond was, in the conventional if officially deprecated infantryman's phrase, "not on". Left Flank withdrew to the wood south of the summit. But some progress was maintained beyond the wood, for a platoon under Captain R. T. Hunter charged across a hundred yards of open ground to capture a small house to the west and immediately below the top. This proved to be the limit of the advance. Good intentions of continuing the attack at first light next day were frustrated by the counter-attacks of the coming night. Henceforth the battle was one of defence.

Left Flank were not left in peace for long. Shortly after dark the enemy started his attempts to infiltrate into the position. By midnight several counter-attacks had been launched at the platoon in the isolated house, but all had been beaten off. In addition there were diversionary movements round the rear of the Company which boded ill for the future.

October 1

At midnight the platoon in the house had to be withdrawn into the wood, and for the next two hours there was some diminution in the cascade of rifle grenades and mortar bombs which had been falling among the trees. During this lull some much needed ammunition was brought forward, an undertaking of great difficulty and hazard. Its arrival was timely, for at two in the morning a more deliberate attack was launched from two directions; from the house recently vacated and from the cover of a wood to the south-west. This fell upon the left-hand platoon, which was forced to give ground further into the wood, joining up with the remainder of the Company in the southern part. The enemy now penetrated to another house between the two Flank Companies, from which they could be most troublesome. When at first light they attacked in force from the west and south-west, they had the advantage of covering fire both from this house and from the north. This was the most formidable attack of all, and it called on all the fighting qualities of the depleted company to repel it. Major Harvey, by now wounded in the thigh, inspired his men to beat back the two companies which beset them: his example was taken up by many. For instance Lance-Sergeant C. H. Starkey from a shallow slit which afforded him but little protection passed back most valuable information which enabled the Newfoundland gunners to plaster the attackers with the greatest accuracy, even to within twenty yards of our men; and Guardsman W. G. Cocker, one of the platoon runners, performed prodigies of valour with a Bren gun he had acquired; when the Bren was destroyed by shelling he was equally untiring with rifle and grenade. In the end the early morning attack was halted, that from the west by the gunners, whose whole Regiment was now in action, and that from the south-west by the small arms fire of the Company. But the position was now precarious in the extreme for the Germans were established between the Flank Companies in greater strength than before and were beginning to infiltrate between Left Flank and C Company. To complicate things still further both Left Flank's and the Gunners' wirelesses were now put out of action, whereby communications with the Commanding Officer and the Field Regiment were severed.

Though there could be no speech with Major Harvey, it was clear that his situation was desperate. B Company was ordered up to support him and, if necessary, to relieve him. Major Hague led it forward, but soon after starting it was caught by heavy defensive fire, causing casualties and disorganisation. It could not reach Left Flank, and instead joined C Company in its wood and there dug in. At half-past ten Major Harvey ordered Left Flank to withdraw, for the steadily mounting toll from sniping and mortaring had reduced the Company to but forty-five men, and he considered that the enemy penetration could be held no longer. He brought back all the survivors, and only when he was satisfied that all were accounted for did he have his wound dressed. For his gallantry on Monte Catarelto Major Harvey was awarded the Distinguished Service Order.

* * *

From National Archives, reference WO 373/9/237

On 28th September 1944 at Castiglione, contact having been lost with the enemy, Major Harvey's company was ordered to advance in a "dense mist" and occupy a prominent feature covering the Div axis, 4,000 yards to the North, Major Harvey completed this advance with great skill and at dawn the following morning he found the Germans were occupying posns on both his flanks. He immediately proceeded to liquidate the enemy posts, thus enabling the remainder of the Battalion to be moved forward without interference. There is no doubt that by the speed of his advance he forestalled the Germans on an excellent delaying posn.

On 30 Sept 44, 1. SG were ordered to attack Monte Catarelto – a formidable feature 1,000 yards away which completely dominated the Div axis. The Germans had fully appreciated its importance and to its defence had committed an entire SS. Battalion subsequently reinforced by yet another coy. Under extremely heavy shelling and mortar fire, he led the two assaulting coys forward till he was confronted with a bare precipitous slope of 200 yards, swept from the the front and both flanks by Spandau fire at close range. Fixing bayonets he at once charged the German posns and carried the crest. The Germans fled in confusion from their slit trenches and the artillery were then able to take a heavy toll. Owing to the great numbers of enemy on the reverse slope, the bare summit was completely untenable and Major Harvey proceeded to consolidate some 200 yards below the summit, under violent Mortar and S.A. fire. Although wounded in the thigh he remained in Command while his coy repulsed a determined counter-attack at dusk and another in the moonlight.

At dawn on Oct 1 44, the Germans counter-attacked a third time, with two coys supported by heavy arty fire and eventually succeeded in infiltrating behind the coy. Despite heavy casualties the coy defended its posn, all day fighting at point blank range, till ordered to withdraw at dusk. Casualties on both sides were very heavy and all movement in the coy position drew fire from enemy snipers, who had worked round the flanks in the closely wooded slopes. Wherever fighting was thickest, Major Harvey was to be found inspiring his men. Only when he had insured that the last of his surviving men had been withdrawn, did he leave himself to have his wound dressed.

By sheer personality accompanied by utter disregard for his own safety, Major Harvey dominated the battlefield. It was entirely due to his magnificent leadership, cheerfulness and endurance under the most arduous conditions that his coy held their posn against greatly superior numbers and inflicted such heavy casualties on the enemy that they were forced to withdraw sooner than they had intended.

* * *

From Tom Harvey's comrade-in-arms

BRITISH CONSULATE GENERAL, NAPLES
20th June, 1947

Sir,
I trust you will excuse me writing this letter, but as one guards-man to another after seeing the enclosed cutting in a copy of the Union Jack I could not resist the temptation.

I often enquired and wondered, Sir, how you and the rest of the old officers and boys had fared in the latter days of the campaign, but news in Naples, where I was eventually posted, was very scarce.

Well, Sir, please allow me to congratulate you upon receiving your award from the hands of H.M. the King, an honour which I know you will treasure and look upon as one of the proudest moments of your life, an honour you truly fought for and deserved.

When I look back upon them days, I cannot help but marvel at the courage and determination of the Brigade of Guards and I am very proud to be able to cherish the thought that I fought and marched with the Scots Guards.

After I had recovered from my wounds I was regraded on account of my ears and eventually posted to "Lammie Camp" which was situated just outside Naples and where I stayed until I had finished my service.

I did Mess Room Sgt., than Provost Sgt., and finally concluded my time as a W/C. Q. M. 8.

In the meantime I applied for a position in the British Consulate at Naples, my application was successful and here I am trying to make a success of it.

My position is not a very exalted one, I am a Chancery Guard, but I hope to secure employment more beneficial later on, if possible.

Well, Sir, if you will forgive me for recalling that day upon the mountain, there is two things what stand out clearly in my mind, the main one being how you "stuck out" to the last minute before giving your order to retire, in spite of our heavy casualties, because I frankly admit to you now that I thought we'd all "had it".

The other thing was when I was going to retrieve my pouches you said "never mind them B.....y things you'll get some more."

I would like to congratulate you, Sir, also upon the position of trust you now hold, a position I know you will administrat in the best tradition of the Brigade.

The citation you forwarded to higher authorities concerning myself and my award, I appreciated very much and from the bottom of my heart, I thank you.

Upon my return to civilian life one thing was very noticeable the lack of comradeship and "mucking in" spirit one finds in the army, it "stuck out" a mile and it was quite some time before I finally settled down, and even now the memories return at times and deep down in my heart I yearn for the old times, and the thrill of a night patrol or a good "Brew up" and the "Patter" of the boys.

Well, Sir, I will now conclude my letter to you on the same lines as I started and that as one Guardsman to another I wish you the very best of luck and every success for the future, and should you care to forward me a few lines, I assure you that they will be highly appreciated.

I am, Sir,
Yours faithfully,
G. Starkey

P.S. There is one point I forgot to mention and that is do you know what happened to my old Platoon Commander Mr. Douglas, I would very much like to know.

* * *

Major TC Harvey
1st Bn Scots Guards
CMF, 6 October

My Beloved Angel

Well here I am in Florence, having a lovely quiet time, pottering about the shops, and trying to do my Xmas shopping. My leg is getting along fine, and although I still have to walk slowly and delicately I shall soon be having the stitches out, and that should make it more comfortable. I believe the BBC broadcast the story of our battle, but I didn't hear it – in any case I imagine it was a quite untrue account! I have been to the cinema twice, and yesterday I went to hear the Florence Symphony Orchestra, conducted by Igor Markevitch: they played the Siegfried Idyll, which I love, and finished up with Beethoven's Seventh, which was conducted and played splendidly. He is a good conductor to watch, and the orchestra responded very well. The concert hall was the big 16th century hall in the Palazzo Vecchio, but unfortunately the authorities had failed to stop the traffic outside, and there were some hideous interruptions from horns and trit-trotting horses. I found Ian Skimping, Ashley Ponsonby and Jamie Leveson there, and dined with them afterwards at the Excelsior. Somehow they got hold of some French wine which was delicious. I was going to dine with them again tonight, but Col Derrick will be here, and so I am going off to beard the local aristocracy and try and arrange a "soirée" for him. I also saw Lavinia H-H again, in there for a second to shop: but otherwise I've seen no friends. I have had no letters from you, because I'm away, but I shall send a truck over to collect them when I can. I find it very hard to know what to try and get you all for Christmas: a toy for David seems out of the question but Caroline is easier. There are some quite nice things in the shops but very difficult to choose, I haven't found any silk stockings yet but I will have another try: I'm told their quality has gone off a bit.

As for sight seeing, I haven't really begun yet; outwardly the town is not as lovely a picture as Rome, tho' there are some magnificent houses. I hope that my entry into society will open up some more treasures. I think most of the pictures are hidden away. Its possible that Bernard Bruce may be coming to England, in which case Tommy will possibly see him. I am trying to contact him before he goes, but I'm rather afraid I shan't be able to. Winter has set in with a vengeance, heavy rain and cold wind, making life in the hills v. rotten. I trust that before it gets really bad we shall be in the plain, but its slow hard going with everything on the side of the defence. Our hopes of an early finish seem to have been a little premature, but there are still a lot of experts who think that the end can't now be far off. Let's hope they're right.

A million blessings on you all, my Darlings, and many kisses from your ever loving and devoted Tom

Major TC Harvey
1st Bn Scots Guards
CMF, 8 October

My Beloved Maria

As I told you in my last letter I was about to plunge into Florentine Society, and accordingly I beetled off to the Palazzo Corsini with a letter of introduction to the Nobile Signorina Andreda and her sister. It is a vast, gaunt, Victorian palace lived in only by the old Prince, but now full of various branches of the family. I found my lady to be an ugly little thing of about 30, but amusing and very kind, and she duly promised me to introduce me to her friends – Derek Cardiff is there with me, and Richard Coke appeared for the day – in very good form – and so we all got together. The "set" seems to consist of the 2 Corsinis, a nice very pretty girl called Donina Gucchi, who is about to produce her first born, another girl called Maddalena something or other, whose husband has been a prisoner for 3 years, and who is being pursued very heavily by one of the most fantastic figures I have ever met. This is Issy (to my pals, old boy) in other words Prince Ismael of Afghanistan or somewhere, who dresses fantastically (eg camel hair Norfolk jackets as uniform), talks in a very common and hearty way, is very amusing and completely untouchable and too "precious" to be allowed near the front. When I get bored with this lot, I have other letters of introduction up my sleeve. I had my stitches out yesterday, and am nearly walking alright now, tho' in no hurry to go back. I have done a little more shopping, but nothing very exciting. I am trying to get myself some shoes, for mine are in a dreadful state. I am going to another concert this afternoon, but I haven't seen the programme yet – I know it includes the Grieg Piano Concerto in A (flat?) played by a Yank called Rock Ferrio – also some Mozart, Verdi and Beethoven. Last night I went with Derrick to see Andrew Cavendish at the Keppels' villa – the most lovely home with a perfectly superb view. They have got it as an officers' rest house, and very nice too. I went to the English Church this morning, and will be busy writing letters until lunch time. The "gang" are all saying they want to go to the concert, but I am not encouraging it very much. I'm sure they'll gabber away all the time.

I have sent back to the Bn for my mail, and so I trust I will be getting your news soon: one other party was fun, with a man called Carini, who has a fine house in Fiesole. He had had a terrific time dodging the Germans, and eventually finished up with the Vatican minister; they were shelled from every side, and had to spend 14 days in the W.C., the only safe place. Another of the inmates was Berenson, the art critic. To illustrate the German mentality: a German Engineer Officer, having just blown up all the bridges and many houses, came to say goodbye to Carini and said I am in love with Florence and hope to return after the war. He was amazed when Carini expostulated that his love took a peculiar form and just said "War is War" and went away. What hopeless people they are!

No more news now, my Darling. A million kisses and blessings on you all. From your ever loving and devoted Tom

Major TC Harvey
1st Bn Scots Guards
CMF Albergho Helvetia Firenze, October 9

My Angel

Tim Nugent has very kindly promised to deliver this, plus a mouldy little parcel of presents, originally intended for Christmas. There is a bag, a brooch and 2 pairs of stockings for you, a spectacle case for Nanny, and 2 for Mother, a frock for Caroline, and 2 horrid little toys for David, who is the most difficult person to find anything for! I will try and find some other tit-bits, but Tim can only take a small parcel. I am very much better now, but am giving myself another 10 days leave!! It is lovely to think that you will get these things so quickly: how I wish I could tie myself into a tiny parcel and come back to you. I find this town great fun on the whole – there are my normal letters on their way to you, with all the gossip. I haven't yet been able to get hold of my mail from the Bn, so I have had no news of you for ages. Various friends appear here, and I am taking off Andrew Cavendish to meet some of my exquisite Italian lady-friends!! I feel it safer to have an escort, even as mercurial a one as Andrew. I am dining with Tim tonight and he will be able to tell you all about me. Dereck has been here with me, but left today. However he has given me his Staff car to dash about in, so I am really living in great luxury. Unlike in Rome, there are no restaurants to which one can take one's girls, so a good deal of money is saved thereby. But there are a lot of private parties, if one can collect a few rations for them. If you hear of anyone flying out, try and smuggle a note telling me if there is anything you would particularly like me to buy, as I find it terribly hard to choose things for you.

However these little things bring with them all, all my love to my precious Darlings, at home, and many kisses and blessings.

From your ever adoring Tom

Major TC Harvey
1st Bn Scots Guards
CMF
Oct 11

My Beloved One

I have done a little more shopping today not terribly exciting, I fear. I do so hope you are not bored at getting clothes – but there isn't anything else much here, which you can't get, and better, in England. I am still enjoying myself here very much and am already feeling better; I hope to be here for another week. It poured with rain all yesterday, so I didn't do much in the morning – but there is a daily Rendez Vous at a bar called Lilda's, where we all fore-gather to make plans for the evening. I had my usual snooze in the afternoon, and then found that Dereck had returned, so we went off to see the Corsinis: every branch of the family have all repaired to this one house, and it is great fun seeing them all there together – the young children are perfectly sweet, most amusing, and naturally talk English perfectly. All the Corsinis are very amusing, and most of them were imprisoned and/or condemned to death by the Germans. Their loveliest Palazzo has been pretty badly knocked about – I am going over it this afternoon, after looking in at the Thé Dansant!! I have been summoned there by the Capponis, who are very grand, and I believe very nice – but luckily all my acquaintances are in the same lot, so that there are no risks of social friction!

I dined with Tim Nugent and General Budget one night, I hope by now the parcel I sent back with them has arrived. If you ring up Tim at London District he will give you all the gossip. Andrew Cavendish has been here and asked me to stay at the Coldstream Villa – Mrs George Keppel's – which is lovely. I haven't quite made up my mind whether to go up there or not: but I think I shall, as it means I can have breakfast in bed!! Here they make one get up, and the breakfast is disgusting at the end of it. I don't believe I've written since the 2nd concert I went to, with Serafin conducting quite superbly.

They started with the Overture to Figaro, then Rock Ferrio played the Grieg Piano Concerto, rather indifferently – and then we had 2 lovely overtures, Leonora No III and Tristan and Isolde (Prelude): both exquisite. Oddly enough they ended up with Verdi's La Forza Del Destino, rather tin-pot and an anti-climax. Serafin was most impressive to hear and tho' nothing to watch: very much a la Toscanini. Tomorrow they are playing the New World: so I hope to go again.

My leg is practically alright now – but I pretend it still has a long way to go. Things have been quiet since I left, so that I have no conscience about staying away for a bit. I will write again soon, my Angel.

Meanwhile, a million blessings on you all. From your ever loving and adoring Tom

* * *

Major TC Harvey
1st Bn Scots Guards
CMF
13 October

My Darling Maria
Yesterday I got the most wonderful batch of letters from you, and also, joy of joys the two divine photographs, which I have been longing for. I was so thrilled to get all your news, and much amused by your rows with the airmen! I thoroughly sympathise with you: make them apologise! What a terrible shock Caroline must have given you – I think I can guess where she gets her appetite from! The last two days have been particularly nice here, partly because of improved weather, and partly because I have

done some lovely sight seeing. Yesterday a.m. young Franco,* our late interpreter and an art student in Florence, took me off to see the Church and Convent of Santa Croce. The church, which is Franciscan Gothic, with a decorated exterior added later, stands in a medieval square, of typically Florentine tradition, plain, simple houses, with pillared balconies, covered with sloping red-tiled roofs. The church is very fine inside, simple, strong, thin Gothic pillars, and an austere beamed roof. Most of the treasures are removed or bricked in, which is very sad; the cloisters, double deckers, as so often in Florence, with the same sloping tiled roof, and slim, yellow pillars, were very peaceful and we wandered round, with Franco explaining to me, very well and most inter-estingly, all the history of the Florentine Renaissance. There, in the cloisters, is the little chapel of the Pazzi family, the first of Brunelleschi's genius to be finished: he was the first of the new school, and in this little place one can see the Birth of the ideas which, 300 years later, enabled Holkham to be built. At 5pm I went again to a concert, again very good, with the Overture to the Meistersingers, the New World, and Finlandia as the best.

This morning I have been out with Franco again, and found two even more wonderful places. First we went to the Church of San Lorenzo, which Brunelleschi was commissioned to build for the Medicis. It is superb: alas, the pulpits, statues and crucifixes by Donatello and Cellini are hidden away, but the main glory of the architecture is there: there are two rows of grey stone pillars, supporting Romanesque arches, exquisitely carved – while the roof, carved and gilded, and quite flat, shows the crest of the Medici. Over the high altar, is a dome, painted with mosaics – while over the main door is the Balcony of Michelangelo – 3 little marble doors and a balcony – but unforgettably lovely. The Michelangelo Chapel, again could not be entered. Thence on to San Marco, not a nice church, but a wonderful monastery, where Savonarola taught, and Fra Angelico painted. All the great

---

*   Franco Zeffirelli.

paintings are hidden, but in this very cell, painted on the wall, is a little masterpiece by Fra Angelico. Franco has it all taped, and fascinates me with all his tit-bits of information.

No more now, angel heart.

But a million blessings on all your fair beauty. From your ever loving Tom

* * *

Major TC Harvey
1st Bn Scots Guards
CMF
15 Oct

My Beloved Sweetheart

I have moved house again, and am now in residence, and great comfort at the Villa Ondrellino, the home of the George Keppels. It is the most lovely place, superbly situated, high above Florence, where domes and towers peep through the early morning mist, as it rises from the river below. It was a lovely morning today, when I went off to church, and the sun is still shining. One of the chief joys of this house are the photograph books and the social memoirs – wonderful "snaps" of the house parties – precariously crowned heads, distinguished men of letters, heavenly women in perfect 1929 hats – and a lot of friends. Joe and Bridget,* Barbara Astor and Mary Pratt (fat and adolescent), Margot Leslie, John Fox-S and many others. It must have been a staggering place – more formal than Court itself, and everyone a Lion. I moved up here yesterday when Dereck went back. I was delighted to find Basil Eugster, who has just landed, on his way to a staff job. A little more sightseeing yesterday: two very fine churches S. Miniato and S.Somebody else at al Monte – both on the s. side

---
*   Joe and Bridget Airlie.

222

of the river high up with a glorious view of the city, and the river and the mountains beyond. I had tea with the Capponis and the old English mother, Mrs Arbuthnot who has lived in Florence for 54 years. She is a real grande dame – very correct and punctilious, but rather sweet. I met some quite amusing people there, including a heavenly elderly body called Torrezani – an American – who doesn't care a hoot what she says. "My butler can only make 2 cocktails now – one a White Lady and the other is very strong – he calls it Between The Sheets" was one of her cracks – and she proceeded to explain why she thought the name was appropriate!

Donald Deane is also in Florence, recovering from a poisoned hand incurred when slipping out of "the bag", and we are all going to another Symphony concert this afternoon. My tiny wound is recovering fast, but so far not too fast, and I am making the most of it. I expect I shall be wending my way back in a week or so, but I am going to find it an awful wrench to tear myself away from the delights of comfort and civilisation. Ronnie Jenkinson is in hospital with jaundice so I am now dashing off to see him.

Will write again soon. Bless you all, my Darlings, and all my most devoted love from your ever adoring Tom

* * *

Major TC Harvey
1st Bn Scots Guards
CMF
Oct 19

My Beloved Darling
I don't seem to have written to you for days – which is very naughty of me, as I have got lots to tell you. As you know, I have moved up to Villa Keppel, and we suddenly decided to give a little dance the following night. Naturally it meant a frantic rush,

getting food, the band, candles, etc and I had to go off into the country to buy wine. We got hold of the most terrific swing band – Italian – really good players individually, tho' of course they suffer a little from lack of music and practice. However everyone enjoyed themselves enormously: I am still not dancing yet, but pottered about, looking after people. The Coldstream officers who are here have rather picked up with a "set" of girls whom many friends rather pooh-pooh – quite rightly too. So we have great laughs at our own superiority!! But, believe it or not, this dance has now become a nightly affair – but I don't ask my girls anymore: I hope, later, to have another one for them. I have, in spite of the sound of things, been having a pretty quiet time, as I stay in bed till about 10.30 every morning, and then write letters. Jack Sanderson has appeared here now, and we are going off to some Yank Ensa show this p.m, and then we are picking the famous Titina and taking her and some others to a cocktail party. Titina is fantastic – she went to Paris to be gingered up, and tries to look 20 instead of 45 – the people of Florence tell me that her bosoms are artificial and worked by a pressure gauge and pump – which occasionally go wrong and produce a lop-sided effect. She is frightfully fluttery-wuttery, and a real scream!

The concert the other day was lovely, particularly the Beethoven No 2 – I think the second movement is one of the loveliest I have ever heard. They also played a very attractive thing by Borodin, "In Central Asia", which I liked. Quite a party of us went, including Tom Egerton.

Billy Steale, your great love, has been here for the last few days and asked tenderly after you. He was looking awfully well. I am hoping that perhaps Andrew Scott may appear here before I go – I got a 6 day extension, till the 23rd – as my wound is still open, but I expect (and fear) that it won't be very much longer now. I have tasted the wines of civilisation too much to relish a return to the hills. I must stop now, as time is short, and I must write a birthday letter to Mother. It's terribly difficult to get hold of my mail, but I am hoping for some soon.

Bless you all, my honey darlings, and oceans of love from your every adoring Tom

* * *

Major TC Harvey
1ˢᵗ Bn Scots Guards
CMF
22 Oct

My Beloved and Sweetest Heart

Still no mail has arrived from the Bn, which is maddening – but I am hoping for a lot anytime now. However, a wonderful parcel of books was brought to me yesterday, so do thank whoever got them. Life goes on here just the same: I do so wish you were here to enjoy the fun, because the gossip exceeds by a thousandfold the worst limits of "The Terrace" and since I am by now an old inhabitant of the place, I get the low-down on everyone from everyone else, and then repeat it. My latest self-appointed protectress, is a great blonde Duchess who is the world's snob of snobs, and will only allow me to meet the most select people, as she says, only they will be nice for my wife to meet after the war! I hear all the scandal from everyone – and consequently have a high old time. The last few days I have been to bridge parties for tea: the Italian play bridge at about 90 m.p.h; they call their hands quite differently, and rather wildly, but play the cards quite well. I find it an amusing way of filling in the time. Tomorrow there is a private showing of the Great Dictator, which should provide some entertainment. Added to that, the Doctor yesterday told me that I must stay here for at least another week – so that was a piece of good news. My leg is perfectly comfortable now, but it naturally takes a little time to heal up completely. Before I forget, could you try and send me out some more hair oil? My anything but tame Duchess took me out shopping the other day, as she does with all her innocent protegés – and was furious when I refused to buy you a lambs' wool coat for £50 – however she selected a most attractive and unusual necklace for you, which will I trust arrive in due course. Naturally the shops haven't nowadays got a very good selection of such things. I am so glad David has started his ABC – and I do hope that you are really keeping up his Italian – it is astonishing out here to see the way that all the children are taught and brought up in at least 3 languages – and there is no difficulty for them in learning at that age. Do encourage Susie to keep it up: tho' it will be a little embarrassing when you and I have to ask him to translate!!

I saw a certain amount of Nick Villiers last week, who seemed in very good form, tho' a little depressed because he had no definite job. I also saw Bill Birkbeck for a second: he had apparently been in hospital after some motor-bike spill, and was on his way back. My cousin Douglas Leslie also appeared, but he never turned up for our dinner on Friday, so I don't know what has happened to him. Otherwise I haven't seen anyone very startling – Edward Astely was sitting behind me at a concert, but I stifled the inclination to embrace him. I hear that Michael Hawkins is going with the Hardcastles. He is charming and did all in his power to get me home for that interview – so if you can get to thank him, it is no more than he deserves. A nicer person you couldn't find. He has lost an arm. Bless you all my pretty Darlings, and a million kisses upon you all. From your ever adoring, Tom

* * *

226

Major TC Harvey
1st Bn Scots Guards
CMF
25 October

My Darling Love,
Since I last wrote nothing very exciting has happened, and lack-
a-day no mail has arrived: so I am feeling horribly out of touch.
I think I shall be driven to returning to the Bn, in order to get
your letters! As it is, my leg is almost alright now, and so I shall
probably be going back at the end of the week anyhow. Last
night I went alone to one of the hotels to have dinner, and sat
down with a strange officer in the RF's. We started talking, he
mentioned that he was an artist, I, that I lived in Norfolk, and
suddenly it dawned on me that it must be Edward Seago – and of
course it was. He is a charming person, and we found a lot to talk
about, including Norfolk stories. He told me that he is looking
for a house, in the Holkham area, and would be most grateful if
you could make enquiries of your Father. His ideal is a nice house
of 8 bedrooms and 3 sitting rooms (approx) and if possible one or
two hundred acres, tho' he would take less if necessary. I feel that
he would be a great addition to the neighbourhood, and it would
be nice if you could find something for him tho' he doesn't want
it till after the war. Margot and Doris Jamieson know him very
well. In any case I made him promise to ring you up when he gets
back (in about 6 weeks) and you might be able to get him over
for a weekend. I have only just finished reading his book: wasn't
it odd meeting him like that?
  We had another little dance here the other night, but it wasn't
really a great success – we got the most superb American band,
some of whom had played with Artie Shaw and Hal Kemp – but
they had had such a day of it with concerts and broadcasts and
their attendant rehearsals, that by 12.30 they were finished. So it
meant that I had to bang away for an hour or so, to everybody's

intense boredom. Still, all the girls seemed to enjoy it, tho' the house is rather cold unless one is sitting round a fire.

"The Great Dictator" is showing here now, and it was quite amusing to go to it with the Florentines, and hear their comments. It seems to have amused them very much but it is too long, and drags in places. There have been no very tempting concerts this week, but I believe there's a good one on Sunday, and also the Opera is starting again, with "Boheme". The weather is being pretty raw and beastly, but here one hardly notices it: it is horrible, tho' in the hills. Still the news of the Russian advances is really terrific and perhaps by the time you get this, it may be even better. I feel they may easily be forced to leave Italy entirely, if they are not careful. What a day that would be!!

I wish I had more news of you, how you are and what you are doing: I am doing all I can to collect the mail, but so far without luck.

However, my Darlings, this brings a million blessings to you all. Tell David to be a good boy, and give him and Caroline a big kiss from Daddy. Bless you, Angel Heart, from your ever adoring Tom

* * *

Major TC Harvey
1st Bn Scots Guards
CMF
Oct 28

My Beloved Angel
I am almost desperate for lack of mail, and am making frantic efforts to get hold of it from the Bn, but so far without success. However, I shall be going back on Tuesday, and so will have a lovely bundle waiting for me. Since I last wrote I have had some delightful times: one day I went out into the country, with a

young married couple, Lally and Terry Carnivari, both charming, with 2 divine children, both a little younger than David and Caroline. We met out there a wonderful little boy aged 7, whose mother deserted him and his dying 3 month old sister to go and live with a Siamese who gives her drugs. Not content with this she wrote awful accusations against her husband who has been locked up. So the poor little boy was left alone, with 4 nuns. He was the greatest fun, and we had tremendous romps: I hope he is going to be adopted by some friends, but they don't want the Mother to hear, or she will claim him as a hostage against the father. A tragic story.

There have been more dances at the Villa, but I only went to one, which was great fun. I took Kenneth Crawley and Douglas Leslie to it: I felt dreadful next morning and stayed in bed till lunch-time. Yesterday I went to 4 parties between 4 and 8 pm – the first a children's birthday party, with candles and cakes and whistles etc, and then an 18 year old's birthday, very correct and dull, and finally 2 cocktail parties!! But I insisted on an early night and felt all the better for it. I have really met a lot of very charming Italians here, who have loaded me with invitations to bring you to stay after the war – it would be fun, with a car, to motor through France to San Remiggio, then to the Carnavaris at Florence, the Origos at La Foce, the Passarinis at Siena, the Marconis at Rome, finishing up with the Riassio's [?] at Naples and then home by sea. We give these Italians frightful stick about their doing nothing and being idle, and not altogether without reason. They will undoubtedly suffer for it if they do not take a more active part in public life, even now they are waiting to see what the various parties are going to do, instead of forming a policy of their own.

The war seems to be creaking on slowly and painfully, but at the same time inexorably. I feel the Russians are going to do a good deal before they're finished. How nice it would be if the Germans were compelled to leave Italy altogether!

I do trust you are all very flourishing. I imagine you must be very busy with the children and all the various domestic and social chores. By the way – Edward Seago's address is Brooke Lodge, Nr Norwich. He said he'd give us a picture if we found him a house!! I fear he hasn't had good weather for painting.

I will write to you once more before I leave this glorious place. I have asked for a Despatch Rider to bring down my mail tomorrow, but who knows?

Bless you, sweetest heart, and a million kisses to you all from your very lovesick Tom

* * *

Major TC Harvey
1st Bn Scots Guards
CMF
October 31

My Beloved Maria

At last the mail has come, a wonderful batch of letters full of good and cheerful news. I was so glad to hear about your visit to London and Janet and Co. I trust you gave them all terrific messages from me. What fun you must have had, seeing them all again. I can imagine the giggles you and Janet and Eliza had together – as for the shopping, it must have been a seventh heaven. I am afraid my parcels were rather dull, but at any rate I am glad they've arrived alright. I was due to go back today, but the night before last I got a message telling me to remain here on duty, to deal with courts-martial – so that was a lovely surprise. I don't know how long it will take, but a week at least. We had the best party yet, on Sunday evening, a dance in a tiny flat: the band was so good, played so well and so quietly that we went on until 4am!! Very good food and enough to drink, all my friends there – in fact a perfect evening. I felt very well next morning, which was just as well as I had to get up fairly early.

You would adore to meet the Corsinis, they are quite raving: one of them found a baby tortoise in the garden, and taking pity on it for its frailty and cold, popped it down her bosom, where it has remained ever since, even at dances.

The shooting parties must have been great fun, and you will be having more of them: isn't Norah Lindsay killing, she used to entertain us when we were at Oxford. Tommy seems to have picked up a plum again – but if he tries to fly home for shooting too often, I expect he will be in danger of losing it again. I did get a letter from John, but it was very old and said nothing. I hear Jocelyn has got an M.C. – I am simply delighted. I knew you would fall for Vonnie – or had you met him before? He is the most delightful person – poor old Temple, collapsing like that. It will be a great loss, I feel, as he was beginning to win back, for the Church, the confidence of the people. Perhaps Garbett will carry it on: how paradoxical to think that a Christian Bishop increases the size and confidence of his flock by flying to see a nation (Russia) that is officially Anti-Christ. What a world! The opera has begun here now, but so far I haven't been: I may go tomorrow – all Italian of course. Down at the Villa at the moment are Henry Green, John Pope, Bob Herschell and Tom Egerton, the latter just the same as ever, very quiet and dreamy and nice. Tony Harbord-Hamond and Bill Birkbeck I have also seen.

Must stop now, Beloved, a very poor letter, I fear. Tell David I promise to come home as soon as I can, and that I expect him to look after you and Caroline very well while I'm away.

Bless you, my lovely ones, from your ever adoring, Tom

* * *

Major TC Harvey
1st Bn Scots Guards
CMF
November 4

My Beloved Maria

It seems a long time since I last wrote to you, and I am terribly behind hand in writing to Mother – however here goes, tho' there hasn't been much news lately. I am still in Florence, doing these Courts-martial, which is very nice tho' I shall be going back any day now. As a result I have been pretty busy lately, and have avoided the social round as much as possible. I went to Rigoletto 3 days ago and to Boheme yesterday, both of which I enjoyed enormously, tho' Boheme was far better sung. I also went to a music-hall, which was a typical old London show, and as such great fun. Early to bed the last two nights, having dined with Robin May-Smith and last night with John Nelson. There was the usual dance at the Villa the other night, again a good party, tho' a dreadful night. The weather in fact, has been appalling the last few days – torrential cloudbursts. Today is however lovely. I am writing this, with a foul pen, in the foyer of a hotel. I have been working at the C-M's all morning, lunched with Dermot Daly and am off again in about ¼ hr. Bernard Bruce has appeared here and I am dining with him tonight, after having my hot bath!! He is on his way home, and I shall give him a little parcel for you – a Florentine necklace, not v exciting. Robert Elwes is also staying here, but I haven't seen him yet. He should have some fairly up-to-date local gossip, which I want from him.

I have had a letter from Vonnie, also Boo and Digby, both of whom write ceaselessly, Digby always sending me old books she comes across – so you can see I have got a good deal of writing to do soon. This I fear is almost illegible by now! Richard Coke has been at the Villa for two days, in very good form – he will be coming back to us soon, and will be a great addition.

I must rush off now and defend this criminal. Whenever I defend anyone he always gets the maximum sentence!!

All my love, Darlings, will write a proper letter soon! A million blessings and kisses from your ever adoring Tom

* * *

Major TC Harvey
1st Bn Scots Guards
CMF
Nov 9

My Darling and Sweetest Heart

Well, here I am back at duty, but duty of an easy kind, as we are having just a few days leave and rest. So I am able to break myself in by degrees. It is very easy to get back into Florence and I occasionally revisit the old haunts. I went to a very good dance last night, charming people, good food, drink and music. I persuaded Dereck to go and landed him with the blonde Duchess, which caused him a good deal of amusement. We went on and on dancing and I only got back at 20 to 4 this morning, so I feel a little part-worn at the moment. My departure from Florence didn't take place in the blaze of publicity, which you might have expected, nor has the general gaiety of the city noticeably saddened. But there are many kind people who have asked me back, and I shall genuinely look forward to seeing them again. The other night, for an hour after dinner, I went round to romp with the young Corsini children, and soon found myself dancing Boomps-a-daisy with Andreola's mother, a very good-looking, highly strung lady with great dignity and blue hair – the Blue Marquesa we call her. After a good deal of this nonsense, she sat down at the piano and proceeded to play the Schumann Piano Concerto and a host of other lovely music – they are astonishing people – all the children knew all the melodies and the words of every opera – they really have got astounding culture: admittedly, they have nothing else to do, but cultivate the glories of the arts.

I think the Shooting Box sounds very promising, and I expect you will get a lot of fun out of making plans and thinking out alterations. I had forgotten that you'd asked Seago to paint David; do try again and make him stay for a weekend. He'll be home fairly soon. I am so glad the nits are well – give them enormous hugs and kisses from me; I long for the photograph to arrive. What a cow that woman is to publish the worst one. I heard from Robert and he says he told you to ask for your money back. Had a good and quick letter from John the other day – he seems to be very well. No more now, angel heart.

Oceans and oceans of love to you all. Pray Heaven we shall soon be together again.

A million blessings, from your ever adoring Tom

* * *

Major TC Harvey
1st Bn Scots Guards
CMF
Nov 12

My Darling Maria

Have just got your letter of November 3, telling me all about the horrors of looking after the children: what a time you must be having. Still Susie is having a lovely rest, and I am sure you are blissfully happy doing it, in spite of all the alarums and excitements. It must be fun having Jack to stay because he always has plenty of good, if quite untrue, stories about people. I have been given the D.S.O., but as the formal consent of HM hasn't come through yet, one isn't supposed to say much about it, tho' I am wearing the ribbon. Funnily enough Robin May-Smith met me on November 1st and told me that I was officially approved, but word only came to the Bn on Nov 8ᵗʰ – it so happened that Dereck and Jack were away, and I was taking Commanding Officers Orders – so I had to present myself with the thing – which caused a good deal of ribald comment. I feel genuinely unworthy of it, but it is a great tribute to the Company. I had been recommended for a periodical DSO for the advance to Florence, but after the battle the other day, no doubt as a consolation prize, they changed it to an immediate. In any case it looks thoroughly unsuitable, and I shall continue to duck as fast and as low as ever. Don't, I beseech you, advertise the fact until HM has approved, as if he got to hear of it he might be cross. I am still in touch with Florence, but say my good byes to her today: however I shall get back whenever I can. I haven't been to any more parties since I last wrote, but have had one or two rather alcoholic evenings. I was feeling rather cheap during the last week or so, but am now quite alright again, except for a slight sniff, which worries others more than me. The weather is very fine now, but v cold, real siren suit stuff – it would be lovely if Poulsen could make me some shoes – warm and comfy, crepe soles if possible, if not send out my old brown nail-less shoes. Also I could do with another pair of marching boots, as one of mine has gone missing. Do try and get some little round torch batteries for my magnifying glass torch: the number is 8.

V.2 sounds a brute, and I pray leaves you all severely alone. It won't be easy to finish the war this winter, but I do feel it might happen. Everyone has been wrong about everything so far. Will you find out the name of the Medici bride whose husband was given The Book of Hours – I feel it may have been Corsini – in which case I would like to tell my friends, the present Corsinis.

   Bless you all, my pretty Darlings, and lots and lots of love

         from your ever adoring Tom

* * *

Major TC Harvey
1st Bn Scots Guards
CMF
Nov 18

My Beloved Darling
I got your letter dated Nov 8th very quickly and am so glad that all is well with you. We only get our mail every 48 hours now so that I shall not get another batch until tomorrow. However I got a wonderfully kind cable from Clynick, which touched me deeply, and for which I would like you to thank him, until such time as I can write him a letter.

I also got a note from John Marriott. Susie's Italian epistle filled me with admiration and also grave discomfiture at my own short-comings. I was able however, to understand it pretty easily, but took the precaution of getting an Italian friend to translate it. The fluency of style was much admired, and I am so grateful to Susie. Your beloved Billy Steele paid a call on my little home this morning. He is now commanding instead of George Burns, who has gone home. You'd better dig Hersey out and marry them off quick. I am sure that you and Mama were able to pack in a tremendous amount of fun into your two days, and I trust that none of the V.2's came anywhere near you. I hope that John bought some of the trains he played with: which reminds me that I never congratulated you on your cleverness in getting David a Hornby train for Christmas. The famous Tatler has arrived in the Bn but I haven't seen it yet. I am longing to see the children and am very sad it isn't good of you. However my memory hasn't entirely failed me!! There have been the usual jokes at the expense of Va-lerian's and Gerard's outfit* – that in 4 or 5 years they had so little fighting and so few casualties that, whereas most regiments have no one left they had to send the whole lot back. However, good luck to 'em! I see William Douglas-Home has got into trouble

---

*   Valerian Wellesley and Gerald, his father, the Duke of Wellington.

– just like him, he never had the slightest control either of his tongue or his temper.

Mercifully the weather the last few days has been lovely and tho' it is naturally chilly, the sun shines all day, and the country looks lovely. Long may it last for when the trees lose their leaves and the rain pours down and the nights are 13 hours long, time drags heavily. But now that it is fine, and thanks to all my books, the hours soon pass. I am delighted that they have at last started home leave – it has cheered everybody up, altho' before I'm due for it, I trust the war will be over! Once she's settled in, I don't believe Mother will find the little house too bad, and she is quite right to make the break quickly. I am sure she will make it very sweet. No more for now, my Darling one.

But many many kisses to the babies and even more for your lovely self. From your ever adoring Tom

* * *

Major TC Harvey
1st Bn Scots Guards
CMF
Nov 23

My Beloved Darling
Your lovely letters of congratulations have been arriving these last few days, and have quite overwhelmed me. All the nice things you say make me realise even more than I did before, how undeserved my medal is. I too have yet to see the citation, but I have a feeling it must be a tissue of lies! From your last letter which arrived this morning I gather you had great fun in London, and I am delighted that you picked up with Old Brygski, who I'm sure loved taking you out. I am simply thrilled about the shoes, as you will have seen from one of my letters, how much I wanted a nice

pair. I can't wait for them to arrive. I am very glad, too, that you have pinned Lionel down to a definite date for going to Holkham – he will love it so. What tremendous form the children seem to be showing – and Caroline walking too – it just shows what she'll be up to whenever you turn your back for a second. Tommy seems to be enjoying himself a good deal in France. I expect he's got all the latest news about everyone. I am much more cheerful again about the war, but one usually is by fits and starts. Perhaps now that Mr Seago has seen David and approved of him, he'll persuade Edward to paint him. There's very little news from this way, except that the weather has been better lately, which is such a joy. Derek Cardiff is on a course at the moment, so Jack is in charge with Dermot to help him. I wonder if Bernard Bruce is home yet – he said he would be going down to Walsingham and has got that necklace for you – a necklace sounds rather terrific – matched emeralds and diamonds – but I fear its nothing like that – just rather unusual! Will you thank Silvia and Simon very very much for their charming letter – they told me not to answer, and as I have so many letters to write I will take them at their word. But I am most grateful and send them both lots of love. Simon told me that Leila has got a home nearby – that will send the local scandal by 100%.

I hear from my spies that Jakie's[*] marriage was not popular in the family – I can quite imagine that – but they'll probably get on frightfully well – and anyhow make a fantastic pair. I can't think of anything else to say, and as I've got so many other letters to write I feel I ought to stop and get on with them. Once again, my Darling, I thank you from my heart for your joy and pride in my award: if I had won it ten times over, it would still be only a small part of what I owe you for your love and devotion.

Bless you, all my pretty ones, and many kisses from your ever
adoring Tom

---

[*]   Jakie Astor.

Major TC Harvey
1st Bn Scots Guards
CMF
Nov 27

My Beloved Darling

There's really no news since I last wrote except that I have at last seen the photograph in the Tatler: and although I agree with you that it isn't perfect of you, I was nevertheless thrilled to see it, and amazed to see how much the children have changed since I left. I've never seen anyone look less camera-shy than David – in fact if anything he looked faintly bored and condescending about the whole thing! Caroline has got a definite "look" now – even if at present it's rather reminiscent of your grandfather!! But they both look absolute darlings and you must quite rightly feel a very proud and successful mother! I wrote quite a lot of letters when I was last "down the hill", including one to the Warden of Radley, about a brother officer who would like to teach there after the war – but I mentioned that I would like to put David's name down, as there is no harm in so doing, even if we change our minds later. I think I told you that I had a very sweet letter from Anne. I am very sorry that John hasn't become a A-Q now that Walter Sale has gone – but with regular soldiers about, its almost impossible to get those jobs, tho' I feel he has deserved it. Still, Humphrey Prideaux is very nice. I gather that Ruth and Gerry are down at Apple Tree, and I so hope benefiting by the rest and change: I hear his stammer was very bad, naturally enough, when he got home. It is pouring with rain, but luckily my dug out is pretty water proof, tho' the mud outside is a bore. I turned on the wireless as I ate my breakfast, and heard Dohnanyi's Variation being played – which I haven't heard since last Xmas at Holkham – little did I know where or when I would hear them again!

I am getting v absent-minded and can't remember whether I have written to Vonnie or not, so I am going to now, just in case.

So, for the present, my Angel, herewith a whole host of kisses for you all, and very much devoted love. From your ever adoring Tom

* * *

Major TC Harvey
1st Bn Scots Guards
CMF
Dec 2nd

My Beloved Darling

This appalling green ink is all I can find – I'm sorry but there it is. After rather a long gap, I got a lovely bunch of letters the other day full of all your gossip and news. We are snatching a few days' rest, and I have been able to get to Florence again. Last night there was quite an amusing dance given by the Town Mayor, to which I went. I saw most of my friends again and enjoyed myself. Today I am taking it easy but will go in after tea and come out soon after dinner. I suppose that soon I shall have to start writing my Christmas letter to you but I will hold it for a little, and try to time it as close as possible. I am delighted about the shoes, batteries etc. thank you so much – also I have just got a lovely parcel of books – both War and Peace and also the Culberston, Cheyney lot: you have chosen just the sort of stuff I want, and I am longing to get down to them. As usual there is very little news – Freddie Hesketh broke his leg last night, falling over a half-open coal-hole, so he is off the active list for some time. I am glad Gerry is in better form, and I am sure his trip to Norfolk did him a lot of good. I see also that Susan Maxwell has married again – an American sailor – I am so glad for her sake, but I'm sorry she couldn't find an Englishman to suit her. Charmian will certainly be a rather hot guest to handle, but Eliza is very good at coping with difficult cases: I only hope you don't lose all social caste as a result. There was a picture of Hazel Cook being christened, but no mention, I'm glad to say, of her six godparents. I trust you are fully aware of your duties, and eager to discharge them conscientiously!

I have had some charming letters, including from Mrs Bland (Tom's mother) and Alastair Ritchie. John of course, wrote me a lovely one. The Lord Lloyd is now his Staff Captain – so it is quite a family affair.

Give Darling David and Caroline a big kiss each from me, and keep many for your self. Bless you, my Darling, from your ever adoring Tom

* * *

Major TC Harvey
1st Bn Scots Guards
CMF
Dec 7

My Beloved Darling
What a melancholy tale you had to tell about your dinner party for Ken and Rory – I gather that the bickering is less than it was, and I suppose it's too much to hope that it would ever stop altogether. Anyhow I imagine that when you get this you will still be at the Red House, sheltering from the shooting party. I hope all goes well, as it will put everyone in a good temper. I am writing this in a little room of the house in which I have my HQ and another platoon. The padre has produced a wireless, which is turned on at 7am and goes on till 10 – I woke this morning to Bob Hope, followed by Mozart's 7th violin concerto played by Yehudi Menuhin. We are now having a selection of Welsh folk-tunes. I am well started in War and Peace, and know that I shall enjoy it enormously. I have seen all the Tatlers now with the plethora of family portraits in them, the Coke and Harvey

families being rather over exposed I think: however, it was lovely seeing them, tho' I should also have enjoyed to see one of Simon reclining on a mossy bank, dangling a daffodil from his shapely wrist. Do keep up the idea of having David painted by Edward Seago – in fact he promised us a picture if we could find him a house at Holkham or thereabouts – why not try Ringstead – he wants a fairly big house and could use the squash court as a studio!! What a fool I am not to have thought it before. (The wireless is now playing an eightsome, and as you may imagine, it is being very well received).

Christmas will indeed seem strange, without you and away from the children, but we will be very close in our hearts and in our prayers to one another. We will make ours as gay as we can, and all being well, that should be very gay.

Have just been "blown for" by a Big Shot so must fly.

Will write again soon. A million blessings, Angel One from your ever adoring Tom

* * *

Major TC Harvey
1ˢᵗ Bn Scots Guards
CMF
Dec 11

My Beloved Darling

This is my Christmas letter to you, bringing for you all a very special message of love and hope. I feel that Hope is, more than anything, the thing we all of us need at this time, the great "booster" which will drive us over these last testing miles – and what better message of hope than the message of Christmas. I badly need, and I expect you do too, to have a long, refreshing draught at that fountain, to get, as it were, a second wind for the final lap. Christmas can mean a great deal to us if we keep it in that spirit, and we will be able to take fresh comfort from thinking about it in that way. I know that you pray daily for me, as I do for you, Christmas will bring us even closer together, and our united prayers will give us even greater strength.

Things go on here much as ever: I have been feeling, and still am, rather seedy but hope to shake it off, otherwise I shall have to go to bed. It is getting fairly chilly now, but no snow as yet. You'd hardly believe it, but Sacha's been wounded again – a stray shell as usual – not badly, a little bit in the cheek – but it means he has had to go away for the time being, so I am without his help, and worse still without his company.

We played bridge last night for the first time for ages – if we play cards at all we play a rather childish with a rude name, which is fairly entertaining. Henry Green and Ronnie Strutt are coming to dine tonight, but I have no idea how we shall pass the evening.

War and Peace continues to enthral me, but I ration myself carefully, so as to preserve the pleasure. It's an amazing book.

No more for now, my Darling: your letters are taking longer again now, so I am not quite up to date.

A very very Happy Christmas and a Happy Reuniting New Year to all my pretty Darlings from your devoted and adoring
Tom

* * *

Major TC Harvey
1st Bn Scots Guards
CMF
Dec 16

My Angel Heart
The last letter I have got is yours of the 6th – I am sorry mine are taking so long – I hope to get another from you today with luck. I gather from Mother that Silvia's car did turn up again next day –

I must say you chose some rather testing dance partners – they'll be whipping off your jewellery before you know. Yes, Europe is a difficult child to handle, and without the full facts it is hard to make up one's own mind: if only we could finish the war off soon, how much simpler everything else would be. I have been playing a little poker recently to pass the time, and with great success being about £14 up at the moment. By the way, while I think of it, could you get Child's to send me a cheque-book, as I lost mine some time ago – you might tell them that mine was lost, in case some rogue tries to make use of it!!

I went back to dine with Dermot one evening, and with Ronnie Strutt and Dick Westmacott, and we played Slippery Sam – Dermot failed altogether to understand it, and lost more and more money – luckily the stakes were very low. He has gone off to Florence again, and will I hope make contact with Sacha, whose whereabouts are again a mystery. If you can by any chance get me some more new books from Hatchard's, I should love them: not too many at a time, say two a month. I am well stocked at the moment – but I would love the poems of Keats and also of Wordsworth: not too good editions, as they're bound to be knocked about a bit.

Joy of Joys, the photograph arrived the day before yesterday, and I am not about it! I stared at it for ages, and think David is the most divine thing I've ever seen: a really saucy little face too. What fun they will get out of Christmas. He should be old enough now to be told a baby version of the story of Christmas: also do encourage him to be generous with his toys, as it makes such a good start. He could perhaps be asked to give one of his toys to the children's hospital – and I'm sure would do so, even if he hadn't the faintest idea what it is all about!!

The thing which I shall have to do first after the war is to buy about six suits of clothes – and it might be advisable to buy some cloth here – can you find out from Leslie and Robert what the position is as regards coupons for someone returning from overseas, and also if there will be rationing for a long time. Otherwise I can see myself going about in rags, or having to stay in the Army!!

No more for now, my Darling, Many kisses and hugs to David and Caroline, and all my love to you from your ever adoring
Tom

* * *

Major TC Harvey
1st Bn Scots Guards
CMF
Dec 17

DAVID'S PAGE
DARLING DAVID, HERE'S A LETTER
FROM YOUR DADDY FAR AWAY
HOPING THAT YOU'LL REALLY GET A
VERY HAPPY CHRISTMAS DAY

REMEMBER MOMMY ISN'T MOCKING
WHEN SHE TALKS OF SANTA CLAUS
SO EXTRACT THE BIGGEST STOCKING
OUT OF GRAND-PA'S CHEST OF DRAWERS

WHEN YOU SIT DOWN AT THE TABLE
MUCH YOUR APPETITE WILL WHET
EAT NOT MORE THAN YOU ARE ABLE
TO ABSORB WITHOUT REGRET

I'M SO SORRY I'M NOT BY YOU
AT THIS HAPPY CHRISTMAS TIDE
BUT MY LOVE WILL SWIFTLY FLY TO
SETTLE BY MY DAVID'S SIDE

CAROLINE'S PAGE
DARLING CAROLINE, YOU'RE SO SMALL
YOU'LL HARDLY UNDERSTAND AT ALL
WHAT'S GOING ON – BUT YOU SOON
    WILL
SO ENJOY YOURSELF, AND EAT YOUR FILL

WALKING EVERYWHERE, WHAT A GIRL
YOUR'RE BECOMING – BUT WHERE'S
    THAT CURL?
DU YU GROW STRAIGHT – AS NORFOLK
    SAYS
I WILL HIDE YOUR HEAD IN A TURKISH
    FEZ

AS YOU'RE TINIER THAN YOUR BRO
THIS IS AS FAR AS I SHALL GO
THREE VERSES WILL SUFFICE TO BLESS
MY CAROLINE WITH HAPPINESS

* * *

Major TC Harvey
1st Bn Scots Guards
CMF
Dec 17

My Beloved Darling

I fear those blots may occur more than once. Have just got two very good letters dated 11 and 13, in which you describe an unparalleled variety of gay companions, varying from J.S. to H.M. and I bet I know which was the more entertaining. He certainly sounds what I am now pleased to call "molto simpatico" and old Chamber Potts seems to get along alright too. I can see Eliza

246

being offered a million-dollar 7 year contract with MGM! I am afraid I get angry when you tell me that Tommy is bored with his office job: surely he must realise how lucky he is. I know that people in the line always tirade against people who aren't but I do feel that for a professing regular officer in the Regiment Tommy is a damn sight too fastidious – though I love him dearly. What a funny old person Bernard is, with his humming and he-ing and slow hesitant speech, lit up at sudden intervals with a charming smile. I am so glad you like the necklace, and I look forward to seeing it round your lovely neck. I have got my eye on another one (necklace not neck), but cannot do anything about it at the moment. I haven't heard from Lionel yet in reply to my letter, but I lose all account of when I write, and so he may only have just got it. I got the Tatler today but I had already seen it, if you haven't already sent them, don't bother about the November ones as I have seen those too. They are fun to read and I enjoy seeing them. The news of the German attack on the US 1st Army was quite a surprise, tho' very much in keeping with their theories of defence and delay – by the time you get this we will know more about how it has fared. It seems quite clear that the authorities have decided to fight to the bitter end, tho' how this will last when the Russians get going in E. Prussia it is impossible to say. The weather is a tricky friend in these days. I am sure Frank Cringle was in his element during the shoot, and looked more like a goose than ever. I hope he's keeping a few geese for me, not that I imagine I should hit anything. Henry Green in the Coldstream is a very keen and knowledgeable swing drummer and he and Jack and I have got permission to broadcast on the Wop Radio for quarter of an hour as often as we like – nothing like rubbing in defeat!! Of course we shall have to practise madly and I shall have to contrive to be inaudible, but it is fun thinking about it even if it never takes place! We shall have to find some solo melody instrument to make up the Four!

There for the moment I will stop.

Thank you a million times for your wonderful Christmas message which went straight to my heart, and lies there, nestling close to it.

Blessings upon you all, my Darlings from your ever adoring
Tom

* * *

Major TC Harvey
1st Bn Scots Guards
CMF
Dec 27

My Beloved Darling

I am feeling very guilty at not having written before – I think it's the longest gap I've ever allowed to occur. But I trust my letters have been arriving in fairly regular intervals, and that you haven't been worrying about me. Christmas is over, but we were not able to observe it and are going to try to today. Certainly the countryside looks very lovely in the snow, but it is bitterly cold. I was able to get to Church however, and a very nice Carol Service at which we yelled our heads off and then HC afterwards. Your last two letters were full of gossip and I was so glad to hear you are all flourishing. Now I can't wait to hear your account of the Christmas festivities – I pictured you all round the tree in the Manuscript Library, with shrieks and yells of excitement and kisses of gratitude and general enjoyment. What fun it must have been for David – I'm sure Reynold's present was as usual the piece de resistance. I also had an airgraph from Margot and one from Ruth: also sea letters from Archie and Ken Davison: I liked his poem very much, and will be replying to him later on when I can. From here there is no news whatever: we have been playing bridge and poker to pass the time and I have been consistently successful so far, so you need have no fears yet of your allowance being stopped or of the children to go to a state home!! I have at last finished War and Peace, much to my regret, but it has made many weary hours pass quickly and happily. I also had a charming letter from Robert, who was comparing his present situation with mine last year: I had already gathered as much and written to him accordingly – but our letters must have crossed each other. The Christmas rush seems to have slowed down the normal flow of mail, but that is I imagine inevitable: tho' most of the Christmas parcels arrived if anything too early. I saw a very glamorous picture of Jakie's wife in the Tatler: a super pin-up type, and I should have thought very unsuitable. I see Bill Vestey left £645 000. Have you heard anything of Pamela lately? Did the god-parents do well by their protégées or were they neglectful. I'm sure John Hope was bad: let me know and I'll write him a raspberry. I gather he is still at the Staff College. I can't make out what is happening in France – as the news is very late and anyway I haven't heard it for some time. The most serious item is that Captain Glenn Miller* is missing! I think the best thing to do is to take a long sleeping draught and wake up when everything's over!! It's no good pretending that 1944 has been the happiest year we have known: many good friends have gone with it, and we have been far apart from each other. But a merciful Providence has been looking after us all, and we have a great debt of gratitude. I fear this New Year's Message will be late my Darling – but you know what that message is – that 1945 bring us a quick victory and that reunion which is the thought always uppermost in our minds.

God bless you all my Darlings from your ever adoring Tom

* * *

---

*   Glenn Miller, the famous band leader.

Major TC Harvey
1st Bn Scots Guards
CMF Dec 29

Beloved One

Christmas dinner really went off very well, and were enjoyed by everyone. The day before yesterday the Company had theirs; in a big barn belonging to the farm in which we are billeted. When cleared of all the primitive Italian farm carts, and with the floor clean, and the tables loaded with bottles of beer, nuts and oranges, it really looked quite gay. They managed to collect a lot of greenery, with which they decked the roof, liberally sprinkling it with cotton wool and red berries. "Balloons" painted blue, hung from the ceiling, and I need hardly tell you the nature of their more usual employment. The food was delicious, and with plenty of brandy to round it off, everyone got in very good form. The Sgts had their meal in the evening, and I joined them. Things got pretty rough as usual, and being myself very sober, I went off to bed fairly early. Last night we had our dinner, also excellent: but the activities of the previous night had left their mark and the evening was very subdued. The snow is going fairly fast, but it is still very cold, and very slippery.

Tubby and old Tom Lattley [?] have sent me their Christmas wishes and the hair oil from Thomases has arrived: so the post hasn't been too bad – I hope to get some more letters today. I keep having to move my chair, as I am sitting right on top of the fire which is blazing. Naturally the rest of the room is arctic. I have given up listening to the news as it all seems bad – but once we start fixing up the German counter-offensive I shall take an interest again. I think I'll stop now, as I must write some more and there is no news. If I get a letter from you tonight I will try and answer it tomorrow again.

Bless you all, my loves and lots of hugs and kisses to the nits.

From your ever adoring Tom

Major TC Harvey
1st Bn Scots Guards
CMF
Jan 1

My Beloved Darling
Though this letter won't go till tomorrow, I cannot start 1945 without writing to you – and tho' we are far away from each other now, and were together last year, I can't help feeling that this New Year's Day is a brighter one for us, and opens a happier prospect – at least we can look forward to a reunion, when last year it was a parting! So Roll on 1945 say I! The mail must have met with disaster as I have had nothing from you since Dec 19. However the shoes have arrived from Poulsen but I'm afraid they're not really what I wanted. I think I shall send them back and get something else instead. The boots shall be here soon too, and will be most useful, as the snow and ice are rather hard on my one pair. Luckily we are in buildings and really very comfortable – I even have a spring bed, so hope to stay here unmolested for some time – I may slip away on leave for a few days when Sacha gets back. I had a letter from Isabel Dundas in very good form: she said that her "spooks" had whooping cough.

We cannot wander about by day so I sit indoors and read or write or possibly sit in the O.P. After dark the business of visiting the platoons begins, the mules bring up the rations, visitors arrive and so on, all gliding about like ghosts in their white cloaks with the full moon shedding down its baleful glare. I then stay up till about 2am, writing as I am now, with my signallers playing cards on an upturned log, and the firelight adding a friendly tho' irregular glow to the efforts of the hurricane lamp. At first there are many noises off, but they gradually subside, the Italians next door stop teaching their children to count, and the only sounds are those of the half whispering card players, or the click-clocking mutters of the reliving sentry, or the sudden shrill call of the telephone. Soon it is time to start dozing, and finally at 2am, to wake the CSM and wander into bed, to be called at 9am with breakfast and to lie there, drowsily till about 11. Not a bad life, when the alternatives are so much more uncomfortable!!

Bless you, all my Darlings, and an extra special if rather belated kiss for each of you for 1945 from your ever adoring Tom

* * *

Major TC Harvey
1st Bn Scots Guards
CMF, Jan 4

My Angel Heart
3 lovely letters arrived last night, dated 18, 22 and 23, full of news and fun. Christmas seemed to get under way very well and smoothly. And I'm sure the nits tummies have been in a state of exalted distension ever since. And the train! How kind of Grandpa to produce such a wonderful present. Your more humble contribution will be relegated to the goods yard. John wrote to me once that he had found some Hornby trains in Brussels, so I daresay he has sent Jonathan* one. I wonder where it is laid out – the Statue gallery† would be a good place if not too cold. I was delighted also to hear about the local child artist – get one done of both the children and I will give you them for a birthday present – expense no object!! Do do that – if only for my sake!! The Concert too sounds first class. How enterprising Norfolk is becoming. I listen to the wireless a bit, and occasionally hear good things, of different sorts. I am hoping to hear Irma?? again soon, but as I have not the faintest idea what day of the week it is, I don't know how long I shall have to wait.

---

*   Jonathan Harvey, eldest son of his brother John.
†   Statue Gallery is at Holkham.

I shall write to John Hope a long letter after this, upbraiding him for neglecting his godson. He is the only one left, and must be all the more attentive to his duties. I am so glad you are keeping Roger up to the mark in gaiety and social frolics: he does so enjoy them. I wonder who'll get Ramsay's job. I expect both Turtle and Cis's brother will be promoted. Country Lifes and Tatlers arrive non-stop and are most welcome: thank you very much for them. I think one could write a very cruel skit about some of the stock Tatler people, called "They started with Oysters". Get Susie to make David play trains in Italian – I am determined he should be bilingual!

Bless you my Angels three, and a million hugs and kisses.
From your ever adoring Tom

* * *

Major TC Harvey
1ˢᵗ Bn Scots Guards
CMF
Jan 6

My Beloved Darling
Your descriptions of Christmas arrived yesterday, and I was delighted to hear that the festivities had passed off smoothly and were enjoyed so much. But how wretched to have colds – the brutes never leave one alone – I pray you are all well again now and none the worse for it. Tell Susie that I'm ashamed of her getting so tipsy – even I was sober, admittedly of necessity. We too are in the grip of winter, with quite deep snow, and more to come: luckily we are in houses for the time being so not too uncomfortable. Every five minutes the old girl in the house comes in and laments about the villainies of the Germans, "Tanti Tribulazioni!!" I have heard some good jazz on the wireless lately,

some on records and some by the USAEF band. The American arrangements put us to shame – there was a brilliant arrangement of the Volga Boatmen, with trumpet and trombone counterpoint duet.

No I fear you must not jump to conclusions because I order civvy suits – I was just for once trying to be practical and look ahead. I have no coupons whatever – so it may be better to buy the cloth here: there is still some quite good stuff here. No more for now, honey pot. Of course I admire my daughter – how dare you suggest anything else – but she has to get to look a good deal more like her Mother before she reaches my required standard of beauty. Bless you, darlings three, from your ever adoring Tom

* * *

Major TC Harvey
1st Bn Scots Guards
CMF
Jan 9

My Darling Maria
Your letter of the 29th came to me two days ago, which is very quick considering the weather conditions! But in spite of the lurid accounts of the snow which you will have read, I am managing to keep out the cold, with my many excellent winter garments, and by dint of moving from the fireside as little as is consistent with the reasonable discharge of my duty! It is now 3am and I am writing this beside a very cosy fire – we have just discovered an electric light bulb in the house and by connecting it to a wireless battery have got a good light – a nice change from candle or hurricane lamp. It is the first time we have found an electric light bulb. So glad to hear that your colds are better – you will be having great fun on the lake if it is still freezing. I had two very good letters from Mike Furse and David Robarts: also an Income

Tax Assessment, addressed to Major Harvey referring inside to Captain Harvey and enclosing a post war credit in favour of 2/ Lt Harvey. It didn't inspire me with confidence in its accuracy, so I am writing to the Army Pay Office to query it. I have just read and delighted in the Diary of a Nobody, which your Father has often recommended, but which I've never got hold of before – I thought it magnificent, and certainly had just that touch of tragedy which great comedy always has. Exactly the same thing goes on today, though more often I fear the respectability is more sordid. Sacha and Co have been down in Florence, staying at the Medici Villa, which the Bn now runs as 6 day leave camp for officers – and Sacha is convinced that it is haunted and has seen a ghostly couple walking about in and out of keyholes. It sounds very weird and he denies the impact of alcohol as the "fons et origo" – (Origo being the name of the owners who have lent us the villa, that, as Mr Pooter would say, is rather a good joke!).

I wonder if George Burns and Hersy have picked up with one another again – I do hope so. I look to you to get that organised properly. A diary arrived from Mrs M with a pursuing letter – I wrote and thanked her and all but said how Eastlea always reminded me of Scotland.

Give the tiny wees lots and lots of love and for yourself a million blessings. From your ever adoring Tom

* * *

Major TC Harvey
1st Bn Scots Guards
CMF
Jan 10

My Beloved
You will be surprised to get another letter so soon, but I think you will be pleased to hear that my name has been put in for

the S. African Staff College, so I shall be getting a lovely rest and change. Camberley of course would have been too good to be true: but this is a wonderful break as it is. I have no details yet about dates, but I gather it will be a matter of some weeks before I go. I don't yet know how long it lasts as I was only told about it this evening. Army plans as you know are notoriously unreliable and you have suffered often enough to know not to believe anything until it happens – so don't be too sure about it and keep your fingers crossed!

What happens afterwards I know not, but my place in the Bn is filled when I go so I don't know what I will do – it rather depends on how I manage to cope with the problems of the Staff – but that is a long way off and much may happen. It has been a tiring year and I feel I need a rest, though I don't like leaving the Company many of whom have been at it as long or even longer than I. However I have thought it over carefully and have made up my mind. What an anti-climax it will be if it doesn't come off after all. However, in case it does, I feel I should like to have my Service Dress with me – if you can possibly manage to give it to an officer who is coming out soon – if not wait and I will give you an address. There may be time for it to get to me by post but I will have to let you know. Anyhow you might get it out and see that it is fairly respectable.

I must say. I am very excited at the prospect and can hardly wait to hear if it is definite, and if so when. But we must possess ourselves in patience. No post today, but tomorrow I hope.

Bless you my Darlings – give David and Caroline big, romping kisses from their Daddy and give Susie a kiss for the gin bottle. Ever your adoring Tom

* * *

Major TC Harvey
1st Bn Scots Guards
CMF
Jan 14

My Darling Love

Not much news since I last wrote, and have heard nothing more about my proposed journey. However I have been inoculated in case and consequently my arm is fairly sore today. However I have handed over to Sacha for a day or two and am sitting beside the fire listening to Nat Gonella. The news seems to be better now, and perhaps by the time you get this we shall be getting great news of the Russians. Here it is snowing harder than ever.

With regard to the house, first there doesn't seem to be much likelihood of my getting home, and secondly I quite agree with you about the desirability of moving, so that the children can lead a more normal and steadier life. But equally well it is better not to move house too often, which you are in danger of doing. If you do move, I should do so with the intention of staying put for as long as possible. What a pity you can't make a nursery out of the downstairs bedroom – it's so important for children to have a day nursery to have their meals in!! If it's going to be another case of moving back again at once, then I think the children getting spoilt is the lesser of two evils. This, I fear, is very unhelpful – the only definite things I can say are, one don't count on my coming home and two, cut down house moving as much as possible. I had a long letter from Bernard Bruce describing his visit to you, which was very nice of him, as he told me all sorts of tit-bits. Fancy Caroline making such a hit with the artist – I'm sure she's going to be a beauty. Does David talk any better now? And if so how many words can he string together? To think that we embarked a year yesterday – and what a year it has been. I view this one with great hope. I am sorry my letters have been so slow

– perhaps this one will be quicker. By the time you get it I hope to be on leave.

Much love and many kisses to you all, my Darlings, from your ever adoring Tom

* * *

Major TC Harvey
1st Bn Scots Guards
CMF
Jan 17

My Beloved Darling
No mail has arrived very recently since I last wrote in fact but I am hoping for some tonight. However I have to write this now, otherwise it won't get the post – as it is, the mail takes quite a bit of time to get under way. Have heard nothing more yet about the Staff College. Dinner just arrived, must stop. Well, that's over – we usually "dine" at about 5pm, have a cup of tea, and some toast about 8.30pm and as I sit up at night the signaller and I brew up at about 2.30am. Then breakfast 8.15, bed till 3pm and so on. Very boring but quite tolerable. I had an awfully sweet letter from Aunt Marge and one from an old Radley school master, which I must answer some time – I haven't yet replied to Ken Davison but I must feel in the mood before I try!!

The tempo of the war has again increased suddenly and I must say I await the news with great excitement though I am not allowing myself to get too carried away. I expect that by now the thrills of Christmas have worn off: has David shown any signs of an urge to be musical – you want to buy him a baby violin and then get his grandfather to play to him, and get him to imitate the sweep of the bow. He would look so divine and might catch on to the idea. I can see the next stage is going to be a tiny pony – actually I think the keeping of pets is one of the best things for

258

children – but when they are a little older – it teaches them to take trouble and usually at some inconvenience to themselves. Not a squeak from Lionel M yet – has he proposed himself to Holkham yet. I'm glad you heard from John Hope – I wrote and hope he will answer.

All my love, my Darlings, from your ever adoring Tom

* * *

Major TC Harvey
1st Bn Scots Guards
CMF
Jan 24

My Beloved

Two lovely letters here just arrived, dated 15 and 17 which were very quick. I was tickled to death by your account of the Club at Norwich – nothing breathes decay more heavily than a County Club. I am so glad Mama's trouble was easily diagnosed – I have respected your wishes and not mentioned it to her – but in return, you will have to be very firm with her yourself – and I'm sure you are. It must have been a great joy for her to see John, tho' that going up to London for the day is a wicked journey. I had a long letter from Allan Jacobs the Conservative Agent at Sedgeford – very interesting. I had written saying that I hoped to take some part in local govt. when I got home. He deplores the lack of Conservatives who take an interest in local war-time and other committees – with the result that the whole trend of policy and influence of thought is left wing.

I adore your tales of the children, for it is the little details of their daily chores which help to build the picture – or rather to animate the photographs. They sound such a sweet and happy pair. With the war developing as it is, I cannot feel that we shall have very much longer to wait – tho' there will no doubt be more delays and disappointments. I suppose gas will be the next delight – in any case I should make certain that your masks are serviceable. Not that I have the slightest shred of evidence to say so, but it is always as well to be prepared.

Various forms of reading material have arrived recently – Tatler, Men Only and Also the Hills a delightful novel from Mother. I'm still getting a lot of opportunity for reading, tho' recently I haven't had anything to absorb me quite so thoroughly: it doesn't look as tho' I shall get leave before I go (if I go) to South Africa – have heard nothing definite yet. But life is very reasonable as we now are, and it is no hardship to wait a little longer.

I am determined (well may you shudder) to find my way to Cairo for at least a week, and get a little of my own back on you for those riotous weeks which you have ever since flung in my teeth!! So, hold your hat on sister!!

Well, angel blossom, I must stop and catch "the post" – which is a moth-eaten mule!! My thoughts are ever with you all, and as I look as I often do, at my photograph of you, I feel I am beside you all, sharing your joys and hearing your voices and your laughter echoing through the English air.

A million blessings on you all, from your ever loving Tom Richard Coke has got a D.S.O.!!

* * *

Major Harvey
Scots Gds
CMF

My beloved darling
You will be excited to hear that I have left the Bn and am now in Rome waiting to fly to Cairo and thence to Pretoria where I attend the Staff College from March to July. As always, these things happen in a terrific rush. I was sitting in my HQ at

10.30pm with six visiting Americans all talking their heads off, when the message came to go at once. I got back to BnHQ at about 2am, left next morning for Florence and then on to Rome. Here I am hanging about rather bored but hope to leave the day after tomorrow. The only snag will be that I shall get no mail from you, but it might be worth your while writing once to Shepheard's in case it gets there in time for me. Otherwise my address had better be c/o HQ British Military Mission, Pretoria, S.A. I am immensely looking forward to it; it will be hard work but the hospitality is terrific and the weather wonderfully almost too hot. I was very sorry to leave so many old friends, but otherwise I have no regrets. David Cuthbert is here in very good form, as you can imagine, but just as vague as ever. I was going to play bridge with him last night but he never turned up: I am afraid Gioia Marconi is no longer in Rome but I shall try to find her this afternoon. Not having a car makes it rather difficult to get around. There is a Beethoven concert I want to go to tomorrow, but the tickets for these things get booked up very early. The war news really is wonderful and I must say I shall be disappointed if the war is not over by July. Naturally I have no idea what will happen to me if it is, but I shall strain every nerve to get home, as soon as I can. I am toying with the idea of applying to go to General Smuts staff, as I can think of no one it would be more interesting or instructive to serve than him during the early post war period. However that is all a long way off, and I expect it is quite out of the question. The problem of clothes is rather acute as I can only take 40 lbs of luggage. But I shall be able to get quite a lot of stuff out there and am rather looking forward to spending some money again. I should have a nice fat balance, if you haven't been at it!! I shall open a bank account in Pretoria, and it might be a good thing if you wrote to Childs and asked them to fix it up; then it will be ready by the time I get there. They are sure to know what bank to contact.

It seems very strange to be out of the Battalion and to have no worries and no responsibilities, after so long – but I'm feeling quite a child again. You ask me have I changed. No, not much. On my left cheek I have a hard red wart from which 3 red hairs spring out: on my right cheek I have a soft great wart covered with a thin film of green hair: my lips are thick and drooling, once nostril is closed completely and from my eyes there seeps a continuous trickle of gum and pus. Both my teeth are now black, and whenever I wash my ears my boots fill with sand. Would you like a photograph?

Bless you, angels three, from your adoring Tom

Staff College, South Africa 1945

Major TC Harvey
HQ Brit Mil Mission
Pretoria
South Africa
February 3rd

My Beloved Darling,

I am writing this in the plane on my way to Cairo: it is dark and I can't even see the wing of the aircraft, but soon the moon will be up and we should be able to see something of the desert below us. We were kept hanging about in Rome rather longer than we hoped, and only left this morning. We had various false starts and so we were never really able to do much about booking for the Opera etc. However, I had some pleasant moments. One day I lunched with David Cuthbert at the house of Harold McMillan where I met John Windham, Tony Nutting and Dan Ranfurly. Another day, David and I lunched alone and the bill came to £8-10. My last night but one, I dined with Bobby Petre, Christopher Beckett, a Polish Prince called Dom Radziwill, and four very charming Russian girls!! We danced until about 1am, lubricated by proper Gordon's Gin which I produced. I did a little more sightseeing, but as I was without transport I did not venture very far afield. I went to tea with Bea Marignoli too – Gioia is nursing at Caserta – I fear they are rather under the weather, with little available money and rocketing inflation. Altogether the financial situation in Italy is appalling and something will soon have to be done by the authorities. The Black Market is universal – but since the poor supply it and the rich patronise it, both are satisfied: in fact, it is physically impossible for any civilian (in a town) not to make use of it as far as he can afford to.

Already the weather is getting warmer and at Pretoria will be tropical – I may stay in Cairo tho', for a few days. I'm longing to get "stuck into" the good food of the Mission, for my stomach has been a little unsatisfactory during the last few months and

266

now I've really got a chance to get it right. I'm so hoping I will get some news of you when I am at Stephiardi if not I shall have to wait even longer. But that is the trouble with any travelling.

Give the children lots of big kisses from their flying father and also many devoted blessings on your own lovely head, my darling.

From your adoring
Tom

* * *

Major Harvey
S.A.M.C.
February 12th

My Beloved Darling,

I have so much news to tell you that I hardly know where to begin. As you will see I have arrived safely after a very good air journey from Cairo. I got rather bored in Cairo, but met a few friends including Guy Jamieson as I told you. The flight over the desert was not very interesting, but once we got over the veld, I was fascinated. The country, to my surprise, is amazingly flat and open, not at all what I imagined. One could see for miles from about 13,000 feet and of course in the north there seems to be little sign of life. It was like flying over a vast park, miles and miles of grassland, with single tall trees scattered alone at intervals of 100 – 200 yards. After skirting the edge of Lake Victoria we came down to about 200 feet and looked at the game. The whole ground below was alive with it. Elephant, bucks, wildebeest, rhino, and best of all, giraffes, who at the sight and sound of the plane, galloped away, apparently in slow motion, with long slow rhythmic bounds, their long necks swaying forwards and backwards. All that was tremendous fun and gradually we knocked off the miles and finally landed at 3pm on Saturday. The country is pure heaven, with a hospitality beyond belief – and we are looked after incredibly well. Luckily, George Mann and a small leave party are here too so that is grand.

There's a few signs of war here – such a profusion of milk, eggs, chocolate, chicken, fruit, flowers and heat as is too good (pencil fails) to be true. Fleets of vast shiny cars sweep along the broad streets and at night, so warm and still, blue street lights mingle with the more garish reds and whites of the advertisements and hotels signs.

My Darling even in this heavenly country I only feel half alive without you – but our time is coming and then nothing will mar our joy together. Give the nit pots lots and lots of love from their Daddy and do pass on all the tidbits to Mother as I won't be writing to her for a bit. I got you some goodies (not to eat) in the bazaar – a bracelet, some gold silk and little Chanel No.5. I hope they'll get to you ok. My guide was Ali Baba No. 5 [?], a great pal of Tommy's and used to go shooting with him!!

A million blessings
from your ever adoring Tom

* * *

Major Harvey
S.A.M.C.
Pretoria
February 23rd

My Beloved Darling,
The course starts on March 1st, and ends some time in July, so it is quite a long one. I am going over to spend a day with the General before he goes back, and I shall take the opportunity of finding out what he thinks of the possibilities out here. They badly want people to come to this country – in fact they could, over say 25 – 50 years, easily absorb 15-20 millions, and develop the country accordingly, at the same time improving the status

of the native and giving him increased purchasing power. There is, as you know, a very bitter nationalistic element in S.A. political life, who are distinctly anti-British, to the point of violence, and they are always doing this to arouse bad feeling. But they are a minority, & given time I hope it will be possible to get a strong and united policy which alone could settle the tremendous problems which exist out here.

Give the picaroos lots and lots of love and let me know if there's anything they'd like.

A million blessings, Darling One
from your ever loving & devoted
Tom

* * *

Major Harvey
S.A. Mil. Col.
Pretoria
March 9th [?]

My Beloved Darling,
I do so hope you had a happy birthday, and were able to celebrate fairly reasonably. Now of course we are tremendously busy; we work from 8am to 1pm & 2pm to 4:30pm – and then we really begin, well into the night. However, it is great fun and v interesting, tho' naturally hard work. Two other British Officers are on the course, a charming pair: Mike Hardbottle and John Glanville. Both of the Ox & Bucks. Whenever the General and Commandant address the College, they make long and glowing references to the great honour of having Imperial Officers on the course & welcome us on behalf of the whole country – so you can imagine we blush to the roots and get our legs pulled mercilessly.

Meanwhile, I am meeting all the people I can and finding out as much as possible about everything. There is no doubt that unless very drastic changes are made out here, there will be trouble and the potential wealth of the country will be wasted. The salient problem is that of the native and until that is tackled bravely, on a long term basis, the native will turn nasty and then the whole set-up will go to pieces.

However, I can't give too much thought to all this, as it's going to take me all my time to pass this course.

I will be writing to John Marriott soon so perhaps he will let me know some news. How wonderfully well the war seems to be going – even in Italy they've advanced a little!!

A million blessings and a big hug for David and Car-Car from
your loving and adoring Tom

* * *

Major Harvey
S.A. Mil. Col.
Pretoria
March 24th

My Beloved Maria,

I write this on Saturday am, just before going off to play golf at the Pretoria Country Club. It is a lovely day and we should have rather fun. There's been a good deal of work this week, but last night became very hilarious. Mike Hardbottle produced an awful game called "Do you know the Muffin Man?", which involves people in turn being asked and singing back the answers, all to the tune of Jingle Bells, and the rule is that you must, when you answer, put a full pint of beer on one's head and keep it there till everyone else has finished. This began some nights ago, and last night we fairly beat the place up, till the mess looked like a beer garden. I slipped off to bed, but after an hour or so, I was forcibly seized and made to rejoin the party in my pyjamas. It transpired that Mike had formed a Muffin Club, with ridiculous rules, a fantastic membership, and ritual – and I was summoned to become Grand Musician Extraordinaire!! Further processions ensued, with disastrous consequences for the glasses – in fact we have had to turn to pewter!

Millions of blessings, my Beloved Darlings
from your ever adoring
Tom

* * *

Major Harvey
S.A. Mil Col
Pretoria
Good Friday

Beloved and Darling Heart
How I loved the photograph – thank you so much. They look adorable, the children, and vast – Caroline in particular as chubby as a cheese. I'm so pleased with them – and I know it's due to you and Susie's unsparing devotion. Bless you, and many, many thanks.

It's fantastic to think that the war is really nearly over and by the time you get this, even greater things may have taken place. The crossing of the Rhine has really been magnificent. I do pray that the price was not too heavy – I'm sadly grieved about dear Edward, as he was one of the finest and most delightful people I have known.

Do you realise that I am three times as far from you as Moscow is!! Isn't it a dreadful thought.

Bless you angel heart, and kisses to the nitpots
from your loving Tom

* * *

Major Harvey
S.A. Mil. Col.
Pretoria
4 [?]

My Beloved Darling,

I was going to wait to describe my weekend until a letter arrived which I could answer at the same time, but the mail has been a little delayed, so here goes. The weather was lovely over Easter & I played four rounds of golf, on the whole very well. We danced one night at a divine place called the Roof Garden right at the top of a high building. All the walls are plate glass & you can see the lights of the city all round & far below. There's a very good band and the most delicious food: we didn't stay very late, I'm glad to say. Apart from my host and hostess, the party consisted of a British officer called Guy Barber, a rather dashing blonde as my partner, and Eddie's sister a fantastic jewess of 40, who hasn't been to bed for about 20 years before 5am, drinks like a fish, swears like trooper & a filthy mind. Her name is Moose! I went to her house, which is quite lovely – but I must say a little of her goes a long way! I met almost entirely Jews, some very nice, others beyond description. Jo'burg is fantastically dissolute and one comes across some pretty unattractive specimens. I went to a very nice little church on Easter morning and later played some golf. In the evening I was asked if I would like a small game of mixed poker – but was a little dismayed when given 50 guineas worth of chips. However, I hid away the big ones, lost steadily at first, then gradually got it all back until I finished just 2 pounds down! But I had my nasty moments. Your cable arrived yesterday; with its Easter message & news of money. Thank you so much my Darling, I do so hope you had a happy time yourself, and that the weather was nice for you. This will seem a funny letter if the war is over by the time you get this. I'm told this course is going on till July just the same, but I feel, as far as I can tell, that I should be able to get home after that. Archer Clive was up here for two days & I dined with him last night – in very good form – but I wasn't able to discover what my future movements are likely to be. With David Dickson in the Mission, I have a very strong ally in the 'camp' and feel I ought to be able to get my own way. The women's course which has been going on here, ended with a farewell party last night, cocktails & then a dance. I arrived rather well oiled at about 10:30pm and proceeded to pull everyone's noses, I can't think why. But everyone was very cheerful and nobody seemed to mind except one poor little chap whose nose bled for two hours when he got to bed!! Most of the students are consequently feeling a little delicate this morning and are talking in hushed voices. Being Wednesday we get a 1/2 holiday and I'm going off to play golf, & I believe on Sunday David Dickson and I are going to play in some competition; but I fear with disastrous consequences. We are not expecting to be on speaking terms even at lunchtime.

I am longing to hear the latest news of you all, as my latest letter was the one from Buster;* with any luck there may be some in this afternoon. There's such a big time lag that it's virtually useless to answer things in each other's letters. How I wish I could telephone and hear your voice again.

A million blessings on you all and much love to the nitpots from your ever adoring

Tom

* * *

---

*   Buster Hughes-Young.

Major Harvey
S.A.M.C.
Pretoria
April 13th

My Beloved Maria,

All very sad today at the death of FDR* – which shows how great his work has been, and how appreciated & admired by everyone. I fear all our leaders are getting old and tired; but I trust all the others will survive to the end. Nothing very much has happened since I last wrote, but I have got 3 lovely letters from you, all in a bunch, dated 22, 26 & 29. So glad you are all flourishing, and at last having some decent weather. I'm sorry tho' about the incipient domestic crisis: I think it's a very good idea to take a cottage for a bit, & if I manage to get back in July, all the better, because we can be alone with the children which would be so much nicer – and yet near enough to be able to see our friends. I heard yesterday from Archie saying that he had instructed the Vickers agent to get in touch with me, so perhaps something is brewing in that direction after all.

As we approach our week's leave on the 28th the pace of the course is quickening a bit – also they find we become so riotous if we're not given enough to do, that they have to keep us reasonably busy. However, we have great fun pulling each other's legs, & one chap, who tries very hard, I made a point of tying to his chair during lectures, so that when he gets up, his desk and papers are scattered to the four winds!

The news is still wonderfully good, tho' by no means a walkover; I imagine they are deliberately taking things fairly easy in order to avoid casualties. I do so hope we don't go and give ourselves a bloody nose in Italy at this stage – tho' it is a vitally important campaign against the best organised German armies left. By the time you get this we will be more in the picture.

---

*   F. D. Roosevelt.

I must fly now and post this before our 2pm lecture.

My Darling, I am missing you so very much – let's shut our eyes and go to sleep until, suddenly, we wake up and find ourselves together – for ever.

Bless you all, my honey bees and all my love and devotion from Tom

* * *

Major Harvey
S.A. Mil. Col.
Pretoria
April 16th

My Angel One,

We have a very busy week ahead of us, but interesting and quite a lot out of door work. It was with very mixed feelings that we heard of the spring offensive in Italy – but I feared it was inevitable as it is still a vitally and perhaps decisively important campaign. I pray that it will not be too hard a struggle, but I fear the Germans won't budge an inch until they're killed. They seem to be having a final fling just at the moment, but it won't do them anything but harm.

One sometimes gets angry with the British politicians, but compared with the majority out here, they are perfect angels. There are more exhibitions of ignorance, prejudice, bad taste and incompetence than one could imagine and I fear it will go on like that for many years. The only thing which worries me about coming here is that there may be real trouble one day: it largely depends on how quickly & smoothly they get over their demobilisation problems. At the moment most of the govt officials are too incompetent to do anything.

No more for now, my Darling, but a million blessings on you and the babes! How naughty David is to shoot a line to Mr

Austin; I'm so thrilled about the pictures.

Your ever loving and adoring Tom

* * *

Major Harvey
S.A. Mil. Col.
Pretoria
April 19th

My Beloved Darling,
Not very much news since I last wrote, as I have been very busy
all week with a big scheme we have been doing. It has been great
fun, and luckily our instructor, Eric Jarvis, is one of the nicest
people of all times, so that has made things all the easier. I was a
little dismayed to hear of the attack in Italy, & it is now revealed
that the Springboks attacked the self same mountains Sole and
Cafrara, which we were all teed up to attack during December.
We never knew from day to the next whether it was coming off
or not, & about every 3 days for a month we got all set up to go,
till, at the last minute, it was put off. Finally on Christmas Eve
they said, Today it is definitely on – get ready at once – but again
it was postponed – we knew it would be a tough and grim affair,
so you can imagine that it was a pretty good nervous strain, that
month of December. But now the S. Africans, in true style, have
fixed it up & with many less casualties than we feared inevitable.
No news recently from 1SG, who are all busy too. I do hope all
goes well.

I do hope you were able to go to Debo's[*] party; you ought
to have taken James Stewart[†] and made a real splash!! I gather

---

[*]   Debo Cavendish.

[†]   James Stewart the actor, stationed at Lakenheath, who became a friend
of Mary.

Andrew's* succession is assured which is such an excellent thing. He'll have lots to tell you about Italy if you manage to see him.

Beloveds, a million blessings on your fairy heads from your ever adoring Tom

* * *

Major Harvey
S.A. Mil.Col.
Pretoria, May 4th

My Beloved Maria,

The news from Italy has sent me almost delirious and I am particularly glad that those two armies should be the first to triumph, after so many months of bitter and often disappointing fighting. I feel things really are being wrapped up now, and I can't really see how Japan will be able to keep going once we get going. Mind you, this will take quite a bit of time: but if they've got any sense they should pack it in now.

I wonder now what will happen to all the chaps, & how many will get home & how soon. It must be quite a business tidying things up & rounding the Germans into camps: but they must all be very much on top of their form. I fear the next two months here will drag very heavily unless one exerts a good deal of self-control and application. At the moment I feel I never want to see a uniform again.

I think it's so funny about Goering being condemned to death by Hitler – most of those rats seemed to have been killed or captured by now – & I hope they'll all be bumped on the head without being too much bother and palaver.

As for the news, it is barely credible – if the war isn't over by the time you get this, I don't know what will happen.

In any case, my Darling, my first thought on V-Day will be of

* Andrew Cavendish, to become Duke of Devonshire.

those dear people whose sacrifice has made it possible – then I shall offer up a word of thanks for the vast help and comfort that you have given me throughout the 5 1/2 years. The job of being a wife and mother in war time is grim and difficult and straining. But so well and so cheerfully have you done it, that you have made my own work immensely easier.

For that, Bless you and all my thanks and love
from your ever adoring Tom

* * *

Major T.C. Harvey
SA Mil Col
Pretoria
June 2

My Beloved Darling,
I have been awfully naughty about writing this week, and there is so much to tell you that I hardly know where to begin.

I was put in a most difficult position the other day when I was asked if I would like to stay on here till next May and instruct on the next course. First I said that I must have you and the children out here if I did, & Archer Clive thought he would be able to fix that. Secondly I said that I must get home in July to fix everything up & I think that should be alright too. The trouble is that nothing is definite yet, & it was very difficult to make up my mind. I am not likely to be demobilised for a year, & I might easily be sent to Europe where you couldn't be with me. I think it would be worth bringing the children for 6 months – tho' heaven knows whether we will get a house or not – I have already begun to make enquiries. I don't feel we can really fix this up without my getting home, because there will be so much to discuss, including whether we are to bring out a nursery maid – which I am in favour of, tho' it would be better not to have one too young.

In any case I shall go mad if I can't get back in July for a month or so, as I miss you more & more every minute, & so long for you to be here & share the fun. And there has been a lot of fun too.

We spent the day in the country, which was looking lovely – round the Magaliesberg Hills and by the side of the Hartebeespoort Dam – rather like motoring from Sorrento to Positano – winding roads cut in the cliff, and the water below one on the other side, with little yachts bobbing about on the waves. But even with a few miles out of Pretoria one is completely in the blue, odd scruffy little 'dorfs' or villages with very disreputable looking inhabitants – the squalid ramshackle kaffir huts and an occasional little farm house. The farming is appalling – entirely ignorant, idle and inefficient, with good land wasted and the wrong crops sown. It is one of the many virtually insoluble problems that face this country.

I expect feeling is already beginning to run high at home over the Election – what a to do it is going to be. I'm sure your Father must be wallowing in the blackest pessimism. How jolly for you, my poor Darling! I feel Winston may get in again, with a vastly reduced majority – which wouldn't be a bad thing. What a lot of dirt will be slung about!!

No more for now.

Lots of love and kisses to David and Caroline and to you my beloved from your ever adoring Tom

* * *

Major Harvey
SA Mil Col
Pretoria
July 2

My Most Darling Maria
With so many wonderfully happy memories revived and animated
on this great day, I long more than ever, if that were possible, to
be at home with you again, and resume those gloriously happy
chapters which began this day 5 years ago.

But alas, I still have not got the vaguest idea of what may happen
to me, and am waiting impatiently for the course to end and the
War Office to give their decision.

Our trip down to Badplaats, to play soldiers, was a pretty
dismal affair, v. cold & uncomfortable, & a lot of work to do with
quite inadequate facilities for doing it. Being GSO I was pretty
busy, but we all worked hard & our lords and masters seemed v.
pleased. We had a chaotic journey there – 180 miles, with all the
trucks breaking down, & all the stones getting scattered far and
wide.

I can't see myself back before August at this rate.

Lots and lots of love to David and Caroline, & to your own
beloved self

from your ever adoring Tom

Norway and Dover Castle
August–January
1945–1946

HQ 50 Div
Aug 19

My Beloved Maria

You can imagine what a shock it was to me to hear that I am off to Norway on Tuesday, after all the confidence we had both had about the immediate future. I suppose it is the price we must both pay for having come thru' the war so safely – & looked on in that light it is easier to bear, tho' nonetheless bitter a blow. It is, of course, easier for me to talk glibly about 'seeing it through' & stuff like that, but with all my colleagues on this staff being people who have hardly seen England at all in this war, I could hardly feel proud of myself or of you, if I were to apply to be left at home. I am, too, glad in many ways that we didn't know beforehand, as it might have spoilt the last few days of our leave.

I had a detestable journey, leaving Fakenham 1/2 hour late, & not making it up on the way. There was a large reception committee of senior officers to greet me, but I never turned up!! However, I telephoned from Doncaster & all was well. Last night saw the last of a series of farewell parties, but I was too late for it. You can't conceive how charming my "hosts" have made themselves, nor how attentive. I hardly know another from which yet, but I'm sure we'll hit it off alright.

The form is that this HQ is going to Norway for a few months (till December) to take command of all Brit troops there, & to settle things up for good. Nobody yet knows what the details of it will be, but I imagine that much of it rests with ourselves. We live in great state at Oslo, & have been told to take plain clothes etc. So I will be taking all my stuff; we motor to Liverpool & embark there. I am on the advanced party with a number of others.

How wonderful our leave has been, my Darling, you've no idea how proud & thankful I was to see you & the children not only live up to the idealised picture my mind had of you all, but to excel it even. We are indeed a blissfully happy family, and when, in 1946, we can really begin to make our own life, it will be a joy given to few people. Not many husbands are able to come home & settle in as happily as I did, and it is entirely due to you, & the great love you have shown me & the children, that it was possible. This last separation is therefore both harder & yet easier to bear – and it is as you know in the "continuing right unto the end" that lieth the true glory.

Bless you all, my pretty Darlings: hold your breath, keep your fingers crossed, & the time will fly past till once again I am back on the doorstep & you are in my arms.

From your ever loving & devoted Tom

* * *

HQ Brit Land Forces
Norway
Aug 26

My Angel One,
Well, here we are, safely arrived after a very pleasant and uneventful journey. There was a composite Guards battalion on board, including James Bowes-Lyon, but few others I knew. Anyhow the time passed quite quickly & we were v comfortable (on the Stratheden). We came sailing grandly up the fjord & up to the quayside, but the Captain then decided that there wasn't room to berth, so we backed out again, to the dismay of our reception committee. It then started raining & we waited dismally for a tender – & after some hours they cleared another quay, & in we went. I must say, it is hard to believe that we have fallen on our feet quite so well – there is everything here, fleets of cars to oneself, a superb hotel, each room plus bathroom & often sitting room, limitless French and German wine – Pol Roger '28 by the tens of thousands!! & so far lovely weather – also I am told that the girls are quite lovely, but as you know, that means nothing

to me!! Most of the Airborne boys are so exhausted after three months of Oslo that they can scarcely speak. I fear we may all be in the same position before long. Today we are going racing, which I think should be amusing, tho' very 3rd class – to show the form, 5 ex Derby winners are running!! (some of them must be about 30 years old).

As far as we can tell we shall be home at the beginning of December, but there will be quite a lot of work until then, and I am still out of my depth, tho' in many ways my job will be much easier than if I was with a proper Division – for here we have none of our brigades.

Could you send me 200 players a week & also get Siesner (is that the hairdressers) to send some more setting lotion – I hope v soon my service dress will appear. The General & G1 go off on a tour on Tuesday so I shall be able to settle down a little better, & write a longer letter. I do so hope you are flourishing and that the babies are well. Give them big hugs and kisses from me & keep a lot for yourself.

Bless you my Darling, from Tom

HQ British Land Forces
Norway, Aug 29

My beloved Darling
A lovely letter arrived from you today dated 22 Aug – & I think they will normally take even less time.

Here we are settling down well, & as I said before life is extremely comfortable and agreeable – with not very good food, but quite a lot of really good wine. I had a 'holiday' yesterday pm & went with Michael Henderson, the ADC, to play golf on the local course, as we have got a game v the Norwegians on Saturday. It is only a nine hole course, & rather difficult to find – so we jumped about in a wheat field for some time, before deciding that we had gone the wrong way. When we did find it, it was charming, with a well equipped club-house. They provided us with clubs, (mine have still to arrive) and off we went. The view is as only Norway can produce fir covered hills, green, sweeping fairways, & a vast lake, along the shores of which many of the holes run. The sun was hot & a soft cool breeze drifted off the hills. Afterwards I dined with Mike in the General's mess – perched on a headland, overlooking the bay – & beyond it the powder blue hills. Lots of little yachts flecked the blue water on three sides, & the setting sun lit them up in gold. It really is a paradise of a country. So far my civilian contacts remain very slight, but I hope to improve them. Two nights ago I motored for 35 miles to dine in a little restaurant stuck on an island in the middle of a lake – very pretty but horrid food. I was with Bill Gordon, who is my opposite number in Airborne Div – a charming person who married Margot Lumb. Otherwise there have been no v exciting events. The racing on Sundays is great fun & informal, but alas the best of the weather is over.

How I laughed at QM's[*] arrival in the cloudburst – I'm sure she steamed through it as proudly as her namesake – I'm sure the

---

*   Queen Mary.

children looked sweet, but I don't believe she is mad about any children.

People are all v happy here – but do no work: the Quisling trial might as well be a knitting competition in Brisbane as far as we are concerned – & none of the Norges seem to bother much about it – but I think they do really. The chief division is between those who stayed & those who left (to go to England etc) & both are bitter & ever eager to absolve their own consciences. Food is undoubtedly short – but they all look v well and still seem to be glad that we are still with them. I haven't so much as looked at a shop – but I'm told there is nothing to buy. Sweden is different – but I fear I won't get a chance to go there.

No more for now – Angel heart: much love to all (!) the nits many blessings on your fair head

from your ever loving Tom

* * *

The ship!
HQ British Land Forces, Norway, Sep 1

My beloved Maria
Two letters arrived today, dated 24 & 27 – I was sorry that none of my letters had arrived by then, but it seems to take 5-6 days. So glad the weather is a little better – it must have been ghastly.

Here it is still superb – not unbearably hot but very warm. I had a frantic night playing poker the other day – I must say I enjoyed it enormously, but the stakes were madly high & I lost far more that I should ever dream of – however the fellow who won insisted on halving the sum, which was very nice of him. Needless to say, we were all a bit ginned up, to play for so high, but I really adored it. However, I am not playing anymore!! I had rather you didn't tell our families about it – but as you know, I have no secrets from you!

Our 'main body' has arrived here now, and my guns & golf clubs are safely in my room. I move to a better room tomorrow, with a proper bath & a sitting room – so I shall be comfortable in the extreme, not that I have anything to complain about here.

I don't feel that my demobilisation will be so horribly delayed in spite of all they say. I don't honestly feel that it will be worth your while coming out here for so short a time, divine tho' it would be. I'm sure as one can be of anything that we shall be back in the first half of December – but there is a fantastic amount to be done in that time, with so many Germans in the country. The Boshes are all behaving well, & give no trouble – it's just a question of shipping them back to G. but that takes time.

Give the honey bees big hugs and kisses from their Daddy, & also to all the families.

To you my lovely Darling a million blessings & all my most devoted love

from your ever adoring Tom

* * *

HQ BLFN
Sep 14

My Beloved Maria
Just as I finished my last letter to you I was whisked away on another tour, and only got back last night – it was v pleasant, tho' fairly hard work, as I was with the General.

We are having a great struggle to get our jobs going really well & there are many difficulties – however we hope to break the back of them soon. Unfortunately the Norwegians are hopeless when it comes to doing anything, tho' they are delightful at dancing all night.

Bless you my darling and lots of love to the nits from your ever adoring Tom

HQ BLFN
17 Sep

My Beloved Maria

The RAF dance for the Battle of Britain was a very good party, on a lavish scale, with limitless champagne, superb food & two excellent bands. There is a chance of my going over to Bergen for a couple of days, to have a party with Tony Trilborne – they are going to a dance, in fancy dress & everyone to go as children, which might be fantastically funny. I shall go as a baby girl, complete with pram & gob-stopper – I dread to think what Tony will go as, or look like. I hope to get James Bowes Lyon to go with me, & possibly Iain Macleod too.

By some miracle the weather remains good, tho' there is quite a nip at night now.

I expect you have seen in the papers all sorts of dates about our leaving here, but I imagine that I shall be here most of December, & possibly all of it – not that any of us want to stay particularly, nor do the Norgies want us; but so vast are the problems of getting rid of the Germans & their stores and ammunition that there would be a disaster if we were to leave. As far as I can tell, there is no question of our being here after 31 Dec, & with luck some of us may get back before. There are great rumours that the 'Appletons'* may be coming out here – in which case you had better attach yourself to them as temporary acting unpaid woman of the bedchamber – but no doubt the rumours are quite false.

I heard from Sasha the other day – he is having a cure for his stammer at the moment, and sounded a little miserable –, he thought I was at Pirbright, so I must write and tell him my news.

I haven't had your descriptions yet of the birthday party, but I

---

* The 'Appletons' are the Norwegian Royals, in exile in Appleton House in Norfolk (who befriended the Leicesters at Holkham).

hope it will be at the hotel when I get back for lunch: I'm a little worried about my last letters I wrote, as I think they may have been delayed – I do hope not, as it will have meant a horribly long gap with nothing.

Your trip to London must have been great fun – but I fear the combined gaieties of Johannesburg & Oslo make London seem a little dowdy – particularly with the cost of things as they are.

You'll soon be back at Brancaster, which will be lovely for you – I do hope the house will be warm enough: I hope you try the arrangement of the day nursery for the nits as I think they will benefit from it. How naughty David is to cut his hair off – I shall have to fly over to England & talk to him – would that I could!

Bless you, my Darlings, & lots & lots of hugs & kisses
from your ever adoring Tom

* * *

HQ BLFN
Sep 20

My Beloved Maria,
I'm so glad the birthday was a success – a real elephant surpasses one's wildest dreams, & must have been a great triumph – and also the catapult. At this rate, he'll be having an atom bomb in his stocking for Christmas! And tomorrow (as I write) another feast. Once again I hope my cable will arrive in time.

We are doing a lot of hard work as well, & if we can only have our way, we may squeak home a bit before we are due to – but I fear that is a lot to hope for. I heard from John who hopes to fly here next week, which will be great fun – he is borrowing Monty's* aircraft – so like him!!

What ghastly reading the papers make with Belsen & the Japs

---
*   John Harvey was on his staff.

& starving Russia – what a world it is: let's hope it's a little better before the nits get much older. Do find out about the Appleton's in case anything can be worked.

Millions of blessings, honeybee, will write again from Bergen on Sunday.

Lots of love to David, Caroline, & Susie from your ever adoring Tom

* * *

HQ BLFN
24 Sep

My Beloved Maria
I have just got back from Bergen after a most amusing weekend. I got there at lunch time on Saturday, feeling a little weak after our American dance on Friday. The General gave a small dinner party first (a thing unheard of for him), and I took my "popsie", Astrid Freider. We had a very good dinner & within 2 shakes the General had added Astrid to the races on Sunday; again, unheard of for him (something awful has happened to my pen!) It was a grand dance, superb American band & the usual lavish food & drink. But we left about 2.30 as I had to catch the early plane.

Well, as I say, we got to Bergen for lunch, the passengers consisting of an ENSA party, some Americans, a Swedish mission, the Norwegian Prime Minister & myself!! Nigel Nelson & Tony Tichborne met me, & after lunch, I snatched some sleep. Ink all gone! I had nothing to wear for the party except riding breeches, so I went as a stable boy – George Pereira was the fairy Queen, Tony a little boy in velveteen slacks with cross braces, in fact everyone entered into the spirit. We all behaved like children, screaming, crying, playing with toys, pulling our tongues out, & swanking about our ages! You can't imagine what fun it was. We had a deaf & dumb conjuror!! Sunday included a little card game (not altogether to my advantage) & the ENSA show in the evening, which was seriously good, considering how deadly the artists were off the stage.

I got back to hear that my car has been piled up in my absence – but luckily I am getting some over from Bergen this week, so I shall be alright. There were two lovely letters from you, dated 18 & 19; so glad you are all flourishing – I will see about the shoes, but I fear things are still rationed.

I hope John may get over this week with luck, which could be grand – what a mess the Conference has been – I am quite out of touch with the news, but what little I hear sounds ghastly. Still, we may as well have a good row now & clear the air, rather than suffer a Damoclean sword dangling above our heads, as it did before the War.

Millions of blessings, all my pretty Darlings & all my love
your ever adoring Tom
P.S Miss v H – rang up – I am to 'drop in'!

* * *

HQ BLFN
Sep 27

My Darling Maria,
Not much news since I last wrote: except that I tried to go and see Miss von Hannow yesterday, but having invited myself, she failed, or rather the Equerry failed to confirm it, so I never went. Last night I went to hear the broadcast of a Mendelssohn symphony, which was beautifully played. The Oslo Broadcasting House is very magnificent and comfortable, & the orchestra very good. The night before, I went to a very bad film called 'Something for the Boys', & from now on, there are dances most evenings! This weekend we have a return golf match against the Norwegians, but I shall be very bad as I haven't played for ages, & am busy today

& tomorrow with an Athletic meeting. The hair stuff has arrived but alas, one bottle was shattered: however I am managing fine now & will let you know when I need some more.

I quite sympathise with your desire to get out of England for a few months, & if I can find a good job, say here, or in S Africa, in the Army, I might consider staying on a little longer. Anyhow, I will make enquiries – but I want to be certain that you will all be able to be with me, otherwise we are worse off than ever.

I wonder if you've done anything about the Appleton's – Oct 15 is the big day I believe, so you must try and work something – beside you'd be very good at all that, & it might be a good excuse for getting some extra clothing coupons!! I fear, tho', that it is too much to hope for. I rang up John yesterday, but they told me he was in England, & didn't say for how long so I must try again today. We can talk to each other very easily.

I was rather pleased to get an invitation to dine with Bulgey, as I particularly wanted to see the house, which is superb. To my horror, I hear it is to be an evening of Highland Dancing – my deadliest enemy – so somehow I must contrive to sprain my ankle somehow beforehand!!

Give the babies & Susie lots of love from old Papa & to you also, My Darling,
from Tom

* * *

HQ BLFN
Oct 1

My Beloved Maria,

I've had a very gay weekend, with a lot of fun & quite a few amusing incidents. I got up for early Church, & then at 10 o'clock the Guards Bn were having a service to which Allen Adair & Aylmer Tryon were coming so I beetled off to that. I arrived just before ten, when all the pundits were seated, to find the Padre very woe begone, with no organist! We waited a little, & finally I had to offer my humble services. It was a nightmare – I couldn't practice the stop combinations – & all I could get to start with was a noise like a close harmony trio of mice. However I plugged away & got all set up to play the first hymn. To my horror the Padre announced the National Anthem, which I never have been able to play, & this time I was worse than usual. Luckily during the Confession I pulled the right buttons, & from there on all went well!! I had a long talk with General Allan & Aylmer – John Marriott takes over the Division this week – isn't it wonderful!! I am delighted. After a stiff drink, I slipped back to change, & off to the Palace to sip gin with Miss v-H. She is charming & most amusing, & I took an instant fancy to her, & hope to see her often.

With luck, today will be quiet but tomorrow, lackaday, I have the Highland Fling with Bulgey!

Thank you a thousand times for the golf balls which are a real joy. I have been down to my last for 2 weeks. No letters v lately, but there will be some waiting for me today. I fear I do NOT approve of your ENSA leanings – I've seen something of the conditions they work & travel in – all after years of up-hill struggles 'on the boards' – & I fear a gifted amateur would be as popular amongst them as a pole cat!! No, lady of the bed chamber is the answer – but can it be done?

Mama will have shown you the letter I wrote her – a little gloomy about leave, but as the job may be finished sooner, depending entirely on Foreign Policy, I do not feel too badly. Besides, once we take over supreme charge, in about 3 weeks, there is more chance of a duty flip to England.

I do hope Brancaster is fun & not too difficult: you must be very happy to be on your own again – & I bet Jack will rope you in for choir practice! Give the nit pots oceans of love from old poppa, & a host of blessings on your own fair head, my Darling
from your ever loving and adoring Tom

* * *

HQ BLFN
3 October

My Beloved Darling
The Highland Dancing party last night was really quite fun: the house is magnificent & v comfortable: we had an excellent dinner – about 30 people, including some Norwegian girls who had had a few lessons in dancing reels. General Bulgey is v keen & one of his sons (Sandy, I think) was staying there too. A Russian General & his interpreter were also there, but I don't think either of them cared much for the pipes!

I am still rather enamoured with the idea of the Brancaster Country Club – one could have a very pleasant life organising it, & I think make quite a bit of money. One would be living in the country, and could take part in the local government with a view to politics later. You might ask Jack what the form may be, as it is perhaps quite out of the question. In any case, I want, now, to start fishing for a job, so keep your ears open, will you, & vamp all the big shots of industry, with your large sapphire eyes.

Otherwise I can see myself jostling Feldiman off the first tee in order to carry Frank's clubs, & push his bicycle through the bunkers.

I do hope some of the Norfolk boys are getting back from the Far East – they should be, as all <u>our</u> ships have been sent out there. As you say, you might think the next war was imminent – Heigh-ho, what a world!

No more for now my love: blessings upon you all.

Will write again soon.

From your ever loving Tom

* * *

HQ BLFN
Oct 17

My Darling Maria,

Have just got back from Kristiansand after a very pleasant visit. We left about 10.15 on Monday, to drive down in my Chevrolet. It was a heavenly day, hot sun & blue sky, with all the trees in their autumn dress of golden red: in fact almost too good a day to have to drive so far – 9 ½ hours flat out. One view was followed by yet a more lovely one, lakes one after another, with little red and white villages shining in the sun; then through a winding pass thick with trees to the very sides of the road, & out again into valley of farms and cottages. I was with Duncan Strachan, & when we arrived at 7.30pm we found a cable saying his father was dangerously ill, & telling him to go home at once – so, poor chap, he had to gobble his dinner, bundle into a train, & go back to Oslo. I couldn't face the idea of driving back all the way alone, so I popped the car on to the train yesterday, & flew back this afternoon, with my new servant, Robertson. I have sacked Proffit – he was too terrible for words.

It's shattering to hear that I shall now be in the Army till June, & I am resolved to apply for a job either here or in S. Africa, where you can all be with me. Having only heard, last night, I haven't been able to do anything yet but I am seeing the General tonight, & will find out from the ADC what the form will be. If that shows no sign of promise, I may write to Archer Clive, or failing that, to General Poole, who commanded 6 S.A. Div, & would, I'm sure, try to help me – so don't be depressed, my Darling, as I'm sure I can wangle something.

I'm full of amazement at the Church Times from S. A – I didn't think that I gave the impression of having been ordained, but apparently I must have done – which shows how well I behaved out there!!

No more for now, honey blossom. Give David and Caroline a big hug from me, & show them where I was on the map at Kristiansand – I could almost hear them being naughty!!

Bless you, my most precious Darling, & all my most devoted love

from your ever adoring Tom

* * *

HQ BLFN
Oct 20

Beloved Maria,

The Red X ball went off very well, & was great fun except that I was in a foul temper, my car having broken down. So we were late for the dinner party, much to the General's delight, who adores seeing his Staff discomforted, & roars with laughter & assumed derisiveness – things like that keep him chuckling for weeks!! Our entry was further complicated by the fact that Astrid had damaged her bottom while riding & has been forbidden to sit down for a month!! So we had to collect bundles of cushions, while she perched precariously on the edge of a chair, looking too uncomfortable.

Bridget Lloyd & George Burns were there, tho' I hardly had a chance to see them: also the Crown Prince & Princess, but alas not Miss Von Harnow – whom I haven't seen since our first encounter.

Tonight is the usual local hop & I have 'a blind date' – an English girl, civilian, out here in connection with War Crimes – I imagine a sort of English 'Irma Grese'– but I trust not!!

John rang me up this morning – sounding in v good form. I think he'll be very glad to get back to his job, once the first adjustment is over. I told him to look out for a good civilian job for me.

I wrote Frank G a long letter opposing his 'new hole' so he may come and moan to you about it. But having been elected to the committee I may as well say what I think.

No letters from you recently, but I expect a nice batch today – can you wire Sietner to send me some more stuff today?

All my fondest love, to you, my three pretty Darlings
from your ever adoring Tom

* * *

HQ BLFN
Oct 23

My Beloved Maria,
I am distressed that you are still having these beastly colds, which do indeed make one feel foul and miserable.

I'm writing today to my friends in South Africa just to see if there is any hope of a job out there next year – but I don't suppose there will be an answer for some time. I still live in hopes of being able to slip back on duty one day, but there is, alas, no particular reason why I should. There is no leave for us merely because there is no way of getting back and it will slow down the final evacuation of the country, which heaven knows is a long enough job as it is!

Our hop was great fun on Saturday, tho' my blind date was

not over-exciting. I got George Burns to join us after dinner & we had a good giggle – tho' I didn't dare to mention Hersey. On Sunday I had a quiet day & on Monday (last night) dined with the General, who was giving one of his weekly dinner parties – v pleasant, with a sing song after dinner.

He boomed in yesterday to say that we are to give General 'Bulgey' a dinner next week, & Iain Macleod* & I are to "produce a few tricks" – so we have been busy wracking our brains, & I have written a long ballad describing the Liberation of Norway by Scottish Command. It's not v good, but if they all dine well it should pass muster.

I'm getting desperately bored with Oslo & long to get home – but luckily the time passes v quickly: at all costs I want to avoid going to Germany afterwards: so let us hope that S A comes up trumps.

I will certainly write to David Robarts and find out what he thinks may be going – I agree with you about Jack, he's too vague and unreliable nowadays.

The toys came from Sweden. I fear there are none here – but I will see if I can get anything for the children's stockings.

Bless you my darlings – I long for you all again.

From your ever adoring Tom

* * *

HQ BLFN
Oct 30

My Beloved Darling,
I am so glad you enjoyed your flip to London & saw a lot of friends: & Brancaster too seems to produce its share of local

---

*   Was to become Chancellor of the Exchequer.

gaiety. It's certainly nice for you to have the C-Ws* as friends & neighbours as they are certainly v charming.

I have led a much quieter life recently, having found some amusing books & also having been fairly busy getting ready for the farewell party we are giving to General Thorne tomorrow – a real Halloween party with spooks & turnips & ducking for apples – & also a cabaret in which alas I have to perform more than I care – 2 topical songs, one a skit on Miss Otis, the other on the Stately Homes of England – & finally a recitation called the Ballad of Norway – in fact it will be quite a 'do', with coloured lights, fountains, search lights & the rest, not to mention Snap dragon!

I still don't know for certain what our plans are, but they will have gone wrong if we don't get back for Xmas, for that is the intention. I can't yet say whether I'll get home for a second in November, but something may turn up, or I may find some sort of excuse.

Last weekend I played golf on Saturday pm, danced until about midnight & on Sunday had a quiet afternoon with Damon Runyan & Rufus Isaacs, until I fell asleep turning the pages – & a quiet game of bridge in the evening.

John rang me up the other day, but the line was very bad & I just gathered that he was off about Thursday – also a letter from Brigski sending you, as usual, his most devoted love. He sounds delighted with his new job. As I write streams of fire engines go screaming past in full sail, hooting wildly – how the children would love it! Give them both big hugs from me – I will do what I can about things for their stocking – but most of the goodies come from Sweden.

Bless you angel heart and all my love
from Tom

* * *

———————

*   Cory-Wright.

HQ BLFN Nov 2

My Beloved Darling,
Our Halloween party for General Bulgey was an outstanding success, & voted as the finest party of all time by everyone there. We had a delicious & vast dinner with lots of champagne & then after the King, drank Bulgey's health with Highland honours, i.e. left foot on the chair, right foot on the table. He made a delightful speech, & remarked that tho' he was about to retire it wouldn't be entirely peaceful as he had 6 grandchildren & no dog!! The cabaret, too, was a roaring success, tho' I completely muffed my first song – however the other things went over well, & the timing was very slick. After the Revels began, & two by two everyone had to come & duck for apples, getting soaking wet. Bogey was 3 in 30 secs & those who failed had to attend a defaulters parade at 11.30am when they were made to do such things as laugh hysterically, sing Good King Wenceslas, imitate a hen laying an egg, & dance with each other. Naturally we had most of the senior ones up there & they all entered into the spirit of it.

Poor Bulgey's departure on the cruiser was a little marred yesterday by the fact that he was struck by a car in the street & bowled bottom over apex – so he was limping & very bruised & rather shaken. But he stumped round the Guards of Honour & smiled away at everyone. It was a very striking scene to see the Throne of Norway waving goodbye to their Liberators. The cruiser glided away, first with the pipes playing Skye Boat Song, & then the Marine stand on the quarter deck playing Auld Lang Syne.

It was great fun and now we are all on our own, & faced with most of the tricky work still to be done. I can't write more as the post is off in 5 minutes.

So till next time, all my love, Darling Heart, to you and the nit pots

from your ever adoring Tom

HQ BLFN
Nov 5

My Beloved Maria,
I am distressed about these wretched colds of yours which really
are becoming a curse. I have so far avoided them by having a hot
shower followed by a cold one every morning – but I can't see you
doing that!!

The conditions at Holkham certainly do seem terrible now, and
as you say they ought to live apart. The trouble is that your Mother
really has no women friends to go to, and would be unhappy
alone and away from her position at Holkham. Have any of you
tried to tell them to snap out of it? Surely some of these men
who profess to be such friends of your Father's could tell him to
pull himself together – the trouble is that they're only his friends
because they constantly flatter him. It is a tragic position to drift
into, and made the more so at this time when the memory of
David and all the others is so vividly recalled.

I am sorry that one of my letters should have given the impression that I was in the last stages of gloom – which was not the
case at all, tho' a little disappointed at not being promoted. In fact
that matters little, as I am virtually doing the job & still enjoying
the General's confidence (Or hope I do!) But I've been suffering
a little from inflamed gums (which sounds disgusting) & now
they are better – so please don't think of me as a depression from
Iceland – tho' I'd come tomorrow if I could.

The idea of the Staff Colleges is a pleasant one, but I don't
believe that it is feasible owing to the fact that courses now last
a year, & I would hit the middle of one. However anything in
that line John can tell you about would be most helpful – If as
you suggest, it might be difficult to get you to S.A then I will
not touch it – but having written, I will wait and see what the
answer is.

Must stop & catch 9.30 post.

Lots of love, to you all my Darlings
                        from your ever adoring Tom
                                Did the fizz arrive?

* * *

HQ BLFN
Nov 7

My Beloved Maria

George Pereira has been up from Bergen, on a short visit to see us, & arrived late on Monday – so I had some oysters & champagne waiting for him, much to his delight. The drink situation here is quite fantastic, & I have really got limitless Champagne, Cointreau, & Benedictine, some of which I hope to bring back – so one's consumption is fairly high!! How wonderful if you could be here to share it with me – I may say I am becoming extremely sex-starved, & the presence of all these luscious blondes is by no means assuaging!! We sometimes try and compute the rate, in England, which our present life could cost, assuming it were possible. A bedroom suite, with sitting room & bathroom, limitless champagne etc (here it costs I think 4/- a bottle), my own car, a large Mercedes, & a little BMW as an alternative, a driver, a servant, successions of parties, plus a few 'pickings' for one's luckless wife – & there you have Master Harvey's present existence, for which, far from paying (& in England it would cost at least £5000 a year), he is being paid. So when you realise that I would come home tomorrow if I had the chance, you will see that Blue Tile Farm still holds a measure of attraction for your gay, global husband!

We gave George a little stag party last night, which was v. pleasant, with heated political argument followed by reading poetry – unusual in a military atmosphere. Iain Macleod, one of my confreres, writes v good poetry, & is altogether quite a card, being a professional gambler, & amongst the first four bridge & poker players in Europe – He has an insatiable capacity for alcohol, & a great sense of humour, two very necessary qualities in this place.

I do hope I can manage to get a job in England after this one is over – I imagine that 50 Div will be disbanded when we get home, so with luck I shall get 2 or 3 weeks leave then – and it is at present looking more & more certain that we shall be home for Christmas, which will be wonderful. My two ambitions now are to slip over to London for a few days, and later to Stockholm – here there is no shopping at all, as everything is still rationed & not very good. But if I do go to Stockholm you can expect to see a good slice out of my bank balance! Talking of which, before I came out here I was trying to find out whether we were having to pay tax on the £300 per year allowance that Mother gives us – because as she has already paid on it, I feel that should be enough – would you try & find out about my grandmother's will, & whether death duties are payable again on Mother's death – John will probably be able to tell you – or at any rate find out for you.

I am so glad there is being a little party in Norfolk, & that you manage to see a lot of friends – what is the news from Chobham – is Lord Bob a civvy now, & what of their home. You might ask Jocelyn Hambro whether he could transfer some money for me to Sweden – if he can (£100), let me know when & I'll beetle off straight away – otherwise it is v. difficult to arrange.

No more for now, my Love. I do ask you to talk to John about trying to get me a job in England next year, as I can't bear this blasted separation much longer – particularly in Germany. I would like a job on the committee deciding the future policy for infantry – but there probably isn't such a thing!!

Heigh-ho my pretty ones –
& all my fondest love from your ever adoring Tom

HQ BLFN
Nov 17

My Beloved Darling,
No mail has come for days owing to the rotten weather, & I fear
mine to you must have been equally delayed. So I am a bit behind
hand with your news. Today is better & a plane should be able
to fly in alright, so there should be quite a nice batch. The good
news today is that we are going to get some ships after all, tho' the
one we may come home on will probably not arrive in England
until Christmas Day or Boxing Day. I have however put myself
provisionally down for the Advance Party, which I trust will have
no work, & should be home around the 20. But you know what
shipping plans are – they can change v. completely & quickly so,
as I always say, don't be absolutely keyed up for it, until you see
me tottering into view, an aged, wizened roue from the frozen
North!!
    The General gave a lovely party at Gimle last night, & as usual,
we tried to introduce some novelty, as that is a tradition of the
Division! This time it was a treasure hunt – as they arrived each
guest was given a ticket – the man with the first half of a well
known combination, the girl a second half – e g the Horse, the
Hound – except that they were all muddled up – after supper they
had to find their correct partner, & off they went – all over the
house, down to the air raid shelter, thro' the bedrooms & finally
up to the attic where I was, dispensing drinks which they at once
had to swallow. Then men took laces off, girls their shoes, tied
their legs for a 3 legged a race – & back down again down a tiny
spiral staircase, with everyone else fighting to get up. Everyone
entered into the spirit very well & it all went with a great swing.
As usual the fare was sumptuous, & I fear I did rather more than
justice to it. I drove home behind a Naval Officer who hit the
pavement 4 times in 400 yards!!
    Work is boiling up a lot now & we are going to be pretty busy

until we leave – but that's all to the good. I imagine we'll land in Scotland & go straight on leave, but apart from that there is no news on our future.

Nanny Cory-Wright has always been a divine person, & I'm sure she must love David & Caroline – while with Susie she'd be blissful. I'm sure by now you are quite one of the old inhabitants of Brancaster & excel even Miss R in flights of gossip!!

Give the nit pots lots of Love and kisses from Poppa – & a special one for you my darling – how I long for you!

From your ever devoted Tom

* * *

HQ BLFN
Nov 27

My Darling Maria,
I fear it is a longish time since I last wrote, but as you know I was up at Trondheim last weekend, with the General. We had a v. good journey up there, in sleepers, about 16 hours it took, & so we got there about 10 am on Saturday. There wasn't a great deal of work to do, so we were able to indulge in good meals & sleep it off afterwards. The object of our visit was the Farewell Service in the Cathedral on Sunday – & excellent it was too. It is a superb Gothic Cathedral, with lovely glass, & the ministers wearing rich vestments. The band played the hymns, & the Organ the voluntary – the 4th biggest Organ in the world, with the most lovely tone. There were 1100 troops there, British & Norwegian, & so the service was bilingual. The highlight was the Bishop's sermon, first a passage in English, then in Norwegian – & very charming and sincere sermon, as well as a considerable linguistic achievement. We caught the train back on Sunday evening & got in here about 10.30 on Monday morning. Meanwhile there had been great festivities in Oslo for the King's 40th anniversary – flags,

beacons & fireworks watched by vast crowds. Today I believe there are more festivities, but I have seen little sign of them apart from the decorations.

The papers have been full of your family's doings, lately: first poor Moira's* suicide, which was v shocking – & secondly that fascinating article in the Daily Mail (23 Nov) which you must have seen, giving a beautifully lyrical version of the pandemonium that reigns, from dawn till dusk, in the Audit Room. It was a brilliant stroke & I feel a lot of people may write in and apply for jobs – tho' whether that was the intention or not I can't make out!! Anyhow it must have made you all giggle – & probably delighted (secretly) your Pa & Ma to read it!! I'm only sorry they didn't mention the pre war rice puddings also mildewing all over the house!!

Still no definite news yet about my return home, but be it before or after Christmas I am getting very excited about it. I hope, by the way, that a few parcels have arrived safely – I hope to hear that one has in your next letter, which with luck will be here today. I just daren't think what job I shall get when this is all over, but I feel the General will help all he can. I think some rubbishy thing at London District would suit me well enough. How kind of John to give me his petrol – you must let me know whether to meet you in London or whether to come straight to Norfolk – in which case I would like to be met at Peterbro' if that is possible, as I shall land at Glasgow. But if London is easier I'll go that way. I hope the date will be the 19th Dec – but it may be the 31st. I fear Sweden is off now for good, so I won't be able to get any really decent toys for the children as the shops here are hopeless. Mike Henderson is going with the General later on so he may be able to help me.

Honey Blossom, no more for now – but all my love to you
from your ever adoring Tom

---

*   Moira Coke, aged thirty-four, daughter of Richard Coke.

HQ BLFN
Dec 2

My Darling Maria,
It is, alas, beginning to look as tho' I shan't get back till 31 Dec, which is a bitter blow – the only consolation is that I think I shall get a job which will keep me in the country until I'm demobilised – I may still be able to persuade the old man that it is vital for me to be home for Xmas – but I don't hold up v. much hope. It will mean we'll have to have a second Christmas 'din' altogether – which will completely ruin our stomachs! Last night I dreamt that you suddenly arrived in the middle of a party – but it wasn't quite as idyllic as it sounds, as apparently I had failed to meet you at the station!!

   Two v. good parties – 1st Saint Andrews Night, with whisky & haggis & reels & last night the usual weekly dance – but very cheerful and pleasant. Today I may totter on to a pair of skis, but it is drizzling with rain & I may avoid it – however I have made it quite clear that any movement I may attempt will be very gradual, on a flat surface!

   Must dash off to work – will write again tomorrow.

Bless you, my Darlings
from your loving Tom

* * *

HQ BLFN
Dec 4

My Darling Maria,
My first skiing lesson was quite a success, tho' neither the weather nor the snow were v. good – however I only tried to walk & generally get the feel of the things, & never fell over once – tho' I fear I shall not maintain that virgin record. So I am now hoping

309

for more snow, so that I can try more often, & help pass the time until 27 Dec. Mike Henderson, the ADC, is in London at the moment & he is the only person who may be able to reverse the General's decision – tho' I fear he won't be able to – However when he gets back I shall ask him to try – but meanwhile I think you had better not expect me until the New Year. Normally speaking ten days wouldn't matter much – but it is disappointing to miss Christmas at home.

George Pereira left for home today, I dined with him on the Empire Well and last night – a filthy dinner & pretty uncomfortable & generally "austerity" – but a nice ship apart from that. He was at Bergen with Esmond Baring, who I gather was your host at the dance on the 8.

Again the weather has closed down and there has been no mails v. lately – & I fear you may have suffered in the same way.

I enclose some photographs which may amuse me, tho' I fear my features are less exposed than my activities!!

Bless you, my honeybee
& all my devoted love
from Tom

* * *

HQ BLFN
December 15

My beloved Darling,
What a heavenly 'flying interlude' we had together – & now it won't be long till I'm home for good. I have got a job as G 2 East Kent Sub District & report on Jan 14 – so I shall get home leave & remain in England – I know nothing more about it – but it will be more convenient than Durban.

After that dismal false start, we got to Copenhagen on Wednesday but when we tried for Oslo on Thursday became iced up in a horrible flight & had to turn back – so we caught the night train, plus sleeper & arrived here midday on Friday. Here there is a whirl of activity – & I have hardly had time to breathe – a vast children's party for 500 poor children yesterday – all superb, marvellous toys, chutes from the roof, rocking horses, see-saws, aeroplanes flying from roof to floor, Father Christmas & vast 'eats', the whole thing filmed & broadcast – the party given by the soldiers themselves – the decorations too were lavish – & I will tell you more about it when I am less rushed.

I have to command a hotchpotch company on the King's Parade, which involves endless rehearsals – the General has a cocktail party tonight followed by a dance & there are dances every day next week – so I shall be a wreck. I have a streaming cold!! On top of it all, I rang up Le… [illegible] v. Harrow about Marjorie's letter, delivered it last night, with a covering letter from myself to the King, & have to lunch there today, which is fun but v. inconvenient. So life is a frantic rush as you can see from my writing – having been interrupted about every 10 secs.

No more for now my Darling – give the babies lots of love – it was so divine to be with your sweet self again my Love.

from your ever adoring Tom

* * *

HQ BLFN
Dec 18

Honey Darling,
Again a v. rushed line – am just off to this Royal Parade – which we have been practising day in & day out since I got back – & is still pretty bad. We are all ½ dead now, partly with exhaustion, partly with colds & this week is non-stop. However I take things v. easy in the morning when we parade late!

The lunch party was great fun, I talked to the King solidly from the moment we left lunch until we left. He was in great form & asked after your parents, Holkham & in fact all his friends. He said Aunt M's letter was a v.good one, & much more decipherable than when she is well!!

Another dance at Gimle last night, again v. good, tho' thick snow envelopes everything. We also had our usual treasure hunt, but naturally I got no prize.

Ink all gone. Today we only have a cocktail party, but tomorrow our big farewell dance & Friday & Saturday two more!!

No skiing since I got back as I have been busy with the parade. Iain Macleod is home now & will be collecting the furs & his drink. In case Mail is slow I must wish you all a v. Happy Christmas, my Darlings – how I long for 1946.

Bless you all
from your ever adoring Tom

* * *

HQ BLFN
Dec 21

My Beloved Darling,
Great complications arose yesterday when a signal from the War Office said I was wanted as soon as possible – & we had to decide what to do. Eventually, tho' I longed to be home for Christmas, we decided that the uncertainty of flying, in this weather, plus the fact that one's luggage gets left all over the place were decisive disadvantages. I shall, instead, disembark at Glasgow on 31, I hope, & get straight in the train for Peterbro' – I shall have a ton of luggage, so please send a big car – & don't bother to come over yourself if the train arrives at some unearthly hour! Victor can do all that.

I am so glad you found all well at home, & I do hope that you managed to have a v. happy Christmas – don't plan too much about our Christmas 'din' until you hear when I arrive for certain, as one may always be delayed by fog.

Our farewell Dance went on till v. late, but never really got going, I was rather 'stuffedshirty' all the time. Tonight the Guards have their dance & tomorrow the final KNA party, which will be terrific. Mercifully next week is likely to be fairly quiet, but we look like having a pretty uncomfortable journey on the ship – packed to overflowing, & rolling like a drunken schooner.

Nothing but rain the last few days & all the lovely snow has gone – which is so sad as one would have had a really good chance to get some skiing.

I am now off to do a little shopping – something for Mama, and a few oddments for the children's stockings, but I fear nothing v. great. Will write again soon – all my love, my Darlings – & thank you so much for the lovely letter you wrote.

From your ever adoring Tom

* * *

Letters to his mother from Norway

Nov 11

My Darling Mother,

[…] I must confess I seemed to have conveyed a far more melancholy picture of my state of mind than was the case – here we are incomparably better off than any other British troops in the whole wide world – incomparably. It is the separation that spoils everything, and I hope that that will soon come to an end. We are gradually getting our job finished here, but there are naturally many loose ends about. Norway has suffered little physically, but they seem to have lost a little impetus which is understandable; it doesn't, however, make our job any easier.

The Atom bomb is certainly a headache – but I have great

respect for old Bevin, in refusing to think of it as a "trump card in the poker game of world politics" – not his words really! He is v outspoken and seems to justify the remark made of him in the House, that he must have been reading that famous play "The importance of being Anthony".

Bless you, my Darling,
and all my love from Tom

* * *

Nov 22

My Darling Mother,
[…] Things are getting fairly lively now in an effort to spur the comatose Norwegians into some sort of coherent activity. Charming tho' they are it is a Sysiphean task to get them to take a decision, and so we are just going to leave them to make the best of it. No doubt they will be better once we are out of the way, and they can do things as they like.

Bless you, my Darling,
and all my love from Tom

* * *

Nov 30

My Darling Mother,
[…] As you say, the Earl and Countess cooking and washing up was a fascinating story and caused a good deal of amusement all over Norfolk, I should imagine. Maria had a good giggle over it, and the neighbours too.
  Am having v little work at the moment – so yesterday I went to the War Crimes Trial – v. interesting it was too, tho' on a small scale compared with Nuremberg. Iain Macleod and I have

become sort of court jesters for the General and have now been summoned to entertain the Crown Prince when he dines at Gruisle. We were going to make them all act charades and love scenes from Shakespeare but were told that was undiplomatic – so we must think again.

All my love from Tom

* * *

5th Dec

My Darling Mother,
[…] It is disappointing I can't get back for Christmas, isn't it, but very soon after I shall be back, this time, I hope, for good. Poor darling Maria has many disappointments to bear but I think she realizes that one can't regulate one's own life in the Army particularly for one's own convenience.

It will be a good thing when we can get away from here, as it must be an infernal nuisance to the Norwegians to have us still hanging about. Not that they could ever have managed without us as their powers of organization and enjoyment of any form of work are nil!!

Bless you, my Darling
and all my love from Tom

* * *

HQ BFLN
Dec 18

My Darling Mother,
Have just come off the parade for the King, which went very well on the whole – I had to command the 50 Div Rifle Coy, a splendid collection of veterans, but not as qualified in drill as one

would have wished. I had a most pleasant lunch at the Palace on Saturday, as Maria may have told you and found the old man in great form and v friendly and amusing. She will also have told you of our goings on in London, which were great fun but it was tantalizing not being able to get to Norfolk and see you all.

Bless you, my darling, a Happy Christmas and all my love from your soon returning and very loving Tom

* * *

HQ.
East Kent Sub District Dover Castle
March 14

My darling Mother,
Maria will have told you of our gaieties in London. The dance at BP was naturally the high light, and everyone enjoyed it and looked v sweet, Maria in particular. We whisked round with our respective Sovereigns and I "got" Princess Elizabeth in a Paul Jones, so we had our share of the Family! Apart from that we were able to fit in many other activities varying from Constable to Cicely Courtnedge, and Burlington House to Brompton Oratory! It was great fun and we saw many friends. I have heard nothing definite yet about a job but am in communication and should hear again before very long. Today my demobilisation group begins, a real milestone after 6 1/2 years and the closing chapter of quite a long and varied book. Looking at the papers it is hard to believe that demobilisation is possible – the reverse would seem more appropriate – it is awfully hard to gauge what are the country's views about Russia – angry exasperation, I should say, that our genuine desire for friendship and understanding should be so deliberately trampled on at every opportunity.

The cold is something indescribable again, after a lovely day on Tuesday – and it is really too much to make going out anything but detestable. I hope to be down in Norfolk during the first week in April and I long for nice weather then. I must say I do look forward to becoming a civilian – I realise that everything will be v different and not terribly easy (or cheap!) to start with – but we can really feel that we are beginning the first act, now that the closing notes of the overture are already dying away. Bless you, my Darling, and all my love, from Tom

* * *

Letters to his wife from Dover Castle

EKSD
Jan 18

My beloved Maria,
The cold here is something indescribable, tho' the Mess is lovely & warm, & I have a good fire in my office. But the moment one pokes one's nose out of doors, it becomes a crystallised fruit. I spent most of yesterday driving round to see people, & found George Montague at Hythe – I am always bumping into him, as he was on the boat with me when I went out to Italy. The folk here are quite pleasant, tho' not as nice as 50 Div. One, Angus Charrington seems v. pleasant – he has a little house at Sandgate – about 20 mins away, & has asked us to stay, plus David, if we wish. They have a Nanny who could cope if we went out – their small boy is 18 months. Mrs C. seems v. nice & friendly, so it might be a good idea, as I gather the Grand costs literally £50 per week! Anyhow think it over. The house is quite nice, but v. cold. They feel the cold even more that you do – so we can all huddle over the fire without shame!! I am going to try to get to Oxford again on 2/3 March for the Society weekend, which is a real highlight! There is practically no work to do here – & that of a very dull kind. It seems to be a most inefficient headquarters. I hardly feel it worthwhile trying to ginger things up. Old

Pickering is a nice old boy, who lives completely in the past, having been a subaltern with Wavell, the Auk, Monty, Alex & attributes their success entirely to his advice. He doesn't do a stroke & never gives a decision, so a more startling contrast with Douglas Graham is hard to find. However we jog happily along – & if it weren't so cold I could get plenty of golf!! I rang up Simon this morning, but he still knows nothing definite. I have also written to Norman Gwatkin, telling him that a merely poodle-faking job was not what we wanted.

It was divine our leave, & so wonderful to be home in England again. I do hope we shall be able to get things settled up for the future – it won't be at all easy at first. I have just smashed my mirror – but I am not superstitious!!

Lots of love to the babies, & Susie, and to you, my sweet and adorable Darling

from your ever loving & devoted Tom

* * *

HQ EKSD
January 23

My beloved Maria,
Thank you so much for the letter & cheque – you say that you have become 'very queer' lately, but I certainly have seen no signs of it, and to me you are still your own sweet and adorable self!

I must say it was pretty good cheek of my 'prostitute friend', as you so generously call her, to write to me – another example of my pulverising fascination for women all over the world. It was quite an amusing effort, illustrated as well, & you shall see it when you come down here. Her husband is in England again, & I imagine she consoles herself by thinking of the British!!

I also heard again from Norman Gwatkin who virtually said that the jobs which were going were pretty good hell – but anyhow to go & see him sometime. So I think that is definitely off, & I can't say I'm sorry. Dumps Vickers rang me up yesterday – she is apparently in Dover, very close to the Castle so I must get hold of her. She sounded v. giggly on the telephone, but all the Vickers are rather like that. General Oliver Leese came down for the day yesterday, and seemed in good form – we got rather cold during the inspection, but on the whole the weather here seems better than most places – no fog & not too desperately cold – although Canterbury & Maidstone have been completely blanketed. Your train journey down here is going to be an awful gamble at this time of year – but perhaps we'll get a mild spell.

We went to the LSO concert last night – the orchestra played superbly – I didn't enjoy the Eroica as much as some of the other symphonies, but the Elgar Variations were grand – altho' those too are difficult to understand straight off. I hope you read & digested the 20 point oath administered to her husband by a subsequently murdered wife – it was as good a way as I can think of to ensure that one is murdered sooner or later!! I will ring you up tonight, so we will have spoken before this reaches you.

All my love to the children, & to yourself Beloved One from your ever adoring Tom

* * *

HQ EKSD
Jan 29

My Darling One,
The weekend was great fun, tho' it involved a lot of travelling. I left here at about 10.30 on Saturday, & got to Oxford at 5 – went straight to the Mitre & after some tea went off to see John Bryson at Balliol. He seemed v. well, his usual rather intangible self. I have arranged to stay at Balliol for the Society match. I then went to Vincent's, where I met Gerald Micklem, Neill Fisher, David

Macindoe, & some others, & stayed there until it was time to go to Sonners – no sign of Tommy yet, & whenever I rang the Mitre it was engaged – but he turned up as we were going into dinner, so all was well. Sonners dug out some excellent claret for us – the old boy on my left was due to be 95 yesterday – he talked all through grace, & after dinner got stuck into a large glass of port, and lit a cigar which he stuck into his pipe & puffed at angrily. He became a Fellow of the College in 1877! We gossiped away over our port, & I think Tommy enjoyed himself. We shared a room at the pub, & both slept v. well. Alas, we woke to find thick fog, & our hopes that Southfields being higher, would be clear were premature. We did eventually start off in the fog, but it cleared after 12, & we stopped early to give us time for lunch & the singles. Tommy & I had a most pleasant match, which we halved after a great comeback. In the afternoon it was lovely & we all enjoyed ourselves. I played a nice chap, a freshman from Rugby, & won 2 & 1. I fear they have got anything but a good side. I couldn't be bothered to go back that night, as I couldn't catch a train to Dover, so I stayed with Pat Marston, an old friend with whom Gerald was also staying. He is a schoolmaster there, & has a charming wife & four young children – so it was great fun.

I had a v. short time in London, but had my hair cut & got the shirts. It was nice finding John March & Robert Boothby to travel up with: I feel the Oxford Employment Board has as good a chance as anything of finding me an interesting job – & I will say that I am prepared to go, with family, to America or a Dominion – but I think Europe is better left alone for the time being. I think I shall get a long weekend on Feb 8/11, so I will come down to Norfolk then.

All my love, Darling Maria –
from your ever adoring Tom

South African Royal Tour 1947

HMS Vanguard
31 January

My Darling One,
There is a mail going ashore tonight, so I must send you one
more kiss before the sea comes between us. It was lovely to hear
your voice, and throughout all those last days your cheerfulness
and loving consideration have helped and sustained me beyond
belief. Because it is you who have to bear the burden – I go off in
luxury to the joys of the Tropics, leaving you the drudgery of life
at home and house – moving combined! It was a fine moment
when the King arrived to inspect the Seamen's Guard of Honour
lined up on the quay, with their Colours and with the Vanguard
as a towering gray background, decked with flags, and lined along
her sweeping decks by the crew. Then he walked up the gangway,
the Royal standard was hoisted and the Marines presented arms.
Later in the evening, the band turned out for Sunset and the flags
and White Ensign were lowered as we stood at the salute.

Now we relax, and our thoughts turn to all of you at home;
our love speeds over the snow to be with you, and our hearts and
prayers forever keep us together.

Bless you all from your ever adoring
Tom

* * *

HMS Vanguard
At Sea,
Feb 3

My Beloved Darling,
I believe we may get a mail away tomorrow, so I am writing in
case.

Well, you will have heard a good deal about us, I expect. We all got up early on the 1st and duly at 7.30 slipped, and began to glide out to sea; it was cold and rather dark, but all the Royal Family stood on their little platform to wave goodbye to England, and to acknowledge the cheers of the ships we passed, and of the shore establishments, as they gave a Royal salute. After an hour or so, we repaired to breakfast, feeling rather sleepy, and hung about until 11.15 when we were due to meet the Fleet. They were superb as they steamed towards us led by 4 battleships and firing their salutes, and flags flying and the Ship's Companies on deck. There was a gleam of sun to light up the grey paint; so it was a magnificent scene. The day dragged on and nothing much happened – the Richelieu made a complete nonsense of herself, but I was safely in bed and asleep, the time being 2.30 pm, after lunch. My cabin is v. good, with a porthole, writing desk and three telephones, cupboards, washbasin, electric fire, fans etc. So I can be quite cosy down here. As you know the weather has been pretty rough and yesterday my powers of survival were stretched tight. However I did survive, ate all my meals, and today feel much better, tho' it is just as rough. The Queen is in marvellous form, but the others are seizing the chance of a good rest, and spent most of the time in bed, which is very wise. I took the Queen up to the Captain's bridge this afternoon, to see the Portuguese ship which very gallantly, for she is only tiny, sailed out to salute TMs. She adored it up there, in spite of the many precipitous ladders we had to negotiate. This afternoon I sat and read on the sun lounge which is delightful – warm, sheltered, a colourful view aft, wirelesses, gramophone, deck chairs etc. The Royal apartments are very good too, comfortable, charming furniture, fireplaces, pictures, etc.: we sit down about 20 to dinner and have 4 courses and limitless wine!! We haven't had a cinema yet as early bed, for once, has been the habit! I do so hope all goes well at home, and that the weather is a little warmer. I haven't yet heard the news, but I hope to do so at 6 pm in 15 minutes time. But the wireless is very bad and crackly – as bad I fear as my writing, but we are moving about a good deal still!

I am sending the children or rather 2/3 of them a postcard, which I hope arrive alright. They bring to you all my most loving thoughts and prayers and blessings.

From your ever adoring Tom

* * *

Feb 6
At Sea

My Beloved Darling,
Heaven knows when this will reach you – I hope to talk to you on the telephone later today to find out about these wretched measles – nothing could be more unfortunate and ill timed: I am truly sorry for you. We are out of the rough weather now, tho' today is funnily enough cooler than yesterday, which is a bore, as I am sporting my zoot suit for the first time – and you will be pleased to hear that it is much admired!! Yesterday was the real first taste of joy; we woke to see Tenerife, off the Canary Islands, on our starboard side. A gaunt mass of volcanic rock starting up from the middle of the sea with a few towns notably Santa Cruz, and one vast mountain, an extinct volcano, hidden in low cloud. Later on the cloud lifted a little and there was the Fuji-Yama like peak, 12,000 ft high, speckled with snow. Later on the Implacable started flying off her aircraft and they stooped around us and fired their rockets. It was warm enough to sit in the sun and after tea we played deck games with film cameras whizzing unmercifully, much to the embarrassment of TCH in his ridiculous shorts and skinny legs! You may see it on the films and it was at that moment that your telephone arrived telling me of David, poor little chap. I dread to think how many people must be in quarantine!! There is also 22 Rifle shooting, clay pigeon shooting and the rest. We danced on the ¼ deck after dinner, under a lighted awning and

to the music of the Marine Dance band. Our cabaret was a trio of Marine pipers who played some marches and an eightsome. Unfortunately we were pretty short of female partners – another good reason why wives should accompany their husbands. The Queen is due to visit Implacable one day and we sat up pretty late trying to hack out a suitable effort. However the visit has had to be postponed as it's a bit choppy today owing to the N E Trade Winds which operate in this area.

On board they are all extremely pleasant and we can wander about at will: tonight we have been asked to drinks in the Gun Room (with the midshipmen) and there is a Ship's Concert on Saturday. We cross the line on 10th.

Feb 7th pm Had a good day today. The Royals visited the escort ships, so I stayed on board, pottered, ate and slept. After tea we played deck games and had the usual catastrophes – I sent two quoits overboard (apparently the correct name for them is grummit!!) and one football and this evening we broke 4 bats and sent 4 tennis balls into the sea – but it was great fun although a coldish wind, surprisingly enough. After dinner we had a ship's concert on the ¼ deck. They had built a superb stage with every sort of light and a full theatre orchestra – and it was really awfully good in spite of the difficulties of rehearsal.

My Darling, it was so lovely to hear your voice and to discover that David is really better – though I fear the germs may spread. How wonderful you are to put up with all the trials and tribulations of motherhood in 1947 England. Bless you a thousand times for your cheerfulness and loving devotion, which are beyond praise. I do hope that things will be a little easier soon – you know that all my family and yours will rally round if you want them. Must stop now as the post goes at 8 am and it is now midnight. A million kisses to all my darlings at home

from your ever adoring Tom

* * *

February 14

My Beloved One

It was heavenly to hear your voice again, but I was so very distressed to hear that you and Caroline have become victims. You sounded so cheerful, yet I feel you must be going through hell, & I pray that all your troubles and sickness will pass quickly and safely. I feel helpless, so far away from you: and I long to get news that you are all on the way to recovery. I am sure Silvia must be a tremendous help to you, and I feel most deeply grateful to her for being with you.

We land in 3 days time & then the daily grind really begins. It has been the greatest fun on the ship, & I think we will be sorry to leave her. The worst of the heat has now passed, but the four days round the equator were very hot with temperatures of 86o in the shade & often 96o in one's cabin. I wear my tropical suit in the morning and just a shirt and shorts for the rest of the day – dinner jacket in the evening. There has been v. little work to do & I spend a lot of time reading, sipping iced coffee, & dozing, with deck games after tea. We usually have 4 or 5 guests in the evening & then have a cinema, or charades or just gossip, but never by any chance get to bed early – actually between 12 and 1.30 am. The Ward Room entertained us the other day & we had a very good evening, & guest night sing song. Unfortunately the Bosun, at one stage, squashed my glass in my hand, & I had two bad cuts. They stitched one up at once (1.am) & next morning stitched the other, & had to put two more in the first one – which as you can imagine hurt more than somewhat. In actual fact the cuts interfere very little with my normal activities tho' they prevent me from bathing. I hope to have the stitches out tomorrow.

The crossing the line ceremonies were v. well done and Gillard's broadcast will have given you a good idea of them. The brilliantly funny fanfare, the guard of honour, & the conga procession around the ship were all good & the King offering the main grace got a great cheer. Michael Adeane and I waited in terror for our turn but they had apparently decided to have pity on us – the Princesses enjoyed their ceremony, more perhaps than those who followed them but almost at once, chaos broke out, & there was a general deluge of water from hoses, & the swimming baths were a milling mess of bodies.

There were two baths, just below the Royal platform, & each contained v. polluted water and six monstrous bears, whose duty it was to duck the victims. Each bath had two seats perched above it & into these the victims were bundled; they were given a soap pill, syringed with some awful muck, & their face and & hair lathered in green and blue whitewash – vast razors then shaved them clean. The chairs fell backwards and they were tipped head over heels into the water, where the bears pounced upon them – I was delighted to miss the ceremony! Tho' Neptune finally had his blood sacrifice when I cut my fingers in the evening!! The midshipmen have a high old time with the Princesses and provide an admiring audience, making equally good hosts or guests. They & Meg* each got a Valentine this morning but I don't know who sent them! They are a delightful lot, as are the Officers – and I think they'll have a whale of a time in S. Africa.

I clambered round the engine and boiler rooms yesterday, & I believe that the whole Family is doing so today – tho' I don't envy them the perpendicular steel ladders. The whole ship has fallen in love with them and morale is sky high.

Capetown is getting daily more frenzied & I can't imagine what the scenes will be like. I shall disembark in a top hat, a most unsuitable outfit for this weather – but I shall shed it as soon as I can. This letter won't I fear include the story of that – I shall add to it, up to Sunday night, & then get it sent off at once on Monday, so I hope you will get it by the 22nd anyway: so for the time being no more.

_____

*   Meg Colville (a Lady in Waiting).

February 16

The RFs evening in the Ward Room went off very well, & they had a sing song until midnight with the Princesses giving turns from time to time. We took advantage of their absence to visit the Warrant Officers Mess before dinner, & then to get to bed by 9.30, which was a very pleasant change. Saturday was quite a peaceful day, but we entertained about 50 guests to cocktails, in the Royal Apartments, for it is still too windy on the quarter deck. After dinner we had the rest of the film Notorious, Ingrid Bergman & Cary Grant, but as we had to advance the clock an hour, it was again 12.30 before we got to bed.

This morning, after Church, I had my stitches out & was delighted to find both my fingers healing up well, tho' one has still to be bandaged. Later two RN sloops came out to join escort, but unfortunately it was too rough for them to transfer the mail which they are carrying – so we may have to wait a day or two yet. All is set for tomorrow, & I think that we shall all get up early in order to get a good view of Table Mountain. I know I shall find it difficult to write to as many of the family as I should, but I seem to write the story of the day's events so often, what with diaries, etc that time apart, I would have to go thro' purgatory – I expect you will keep them in the picture, and no doubt, from time to time, there may be odd bits in the papers!

The Queen was desperately sorry to hear of your ill luck and sends much love and sympathy. I do so hope that your attack hasn't been too bad, tho' I fear it will make you very cheap for a bit. Don't forget, when things are a little easier, to let me have sizes of clothes, which you want me to get.

All my deepest love to you my darling, and to David, Caroline, Juliet and Silvia. I think of you constantly and pray that you will soon all be well again.

Will write again soon.
From your ever adoring Tom

Government House
Cape-town
February 18

My Beloved,
Well we have arrived, in top hat & tails & a temperature of 102°
in the shade – so we feel v. limp! It was lovely gliding up to Table
Mountain in the early morning, & I think we all woke up early
with excitement. Gradually as we came nearer, we could see the
detail of the crowds & stands, the vast WELCOME, on one
of the peaks, formed by school children sitting in rows and the
splashes of colour from the flags & uniforms. We duly docked
& then the van Zyls and Smuts came aboard to say Hello. It
was quite sad leaving the ship which had been a happy home for
nearly three weeks – everyone was keyed up & the Queen started
'trucking' around her Cabin, with her parasol over her shoulder.
Naturally it was all slightly formal & the Govt & Co had to be
presented – but as the heat was already so great, we soon set off
on our drive, preceded by magnificent mounted police with their
rifles at the 'On guard'. There was a huge crowd (by S. African
standards but not by ours) all very cheerful, and the Family all
looked very well and the ladies prettily dressed. I recognised one
friend in the crowd but otherwise it was a mass of faces, at least
half of them black or coloured. We eventually got to Govt. House
which is charming, cool, big rooms, shutters, exquisite masses of
flowers everywhere – like a French chateau, surrounded by oak
trees and lawns. But oh! the heat. The King said he wanted to go
home again! The day became an endless procession of formalities
and presentations, but I changed into cooler clothes for lunch
and back into morning dress afterwards. Eventually at about 7pm
everyone left, I did my letters, changed into a Household Coat
and we set off for the State Banquet. It was now lovely and cool
the whole of Table Mountain was floodlit, a pale powder blue.
The crowds were still in the street, & cheered frenziedly at the

Queen in her crinoline, with the Garter & a glistening diamond tiara. All the party, I must say, had lovely dresses and jewels and Princess Margaret in particular was a picture. We had ten courses, of which I nibbled at about half – the whole Hall was decorated with Ostrich feathers, but as there were 500 at dinner, one could hardly see anything. On & on it went, we finally reached the speeches an hour late, and the King's was really excellent. I suppose it was about 1.30 when we were all in bed, & then almost too hot to sleep. Today I did some work, but no functions, & this afternoon we go to a Garden Party, which I fear must be boiling. There's hardly a second to write, but I will do my best. Don't forget to send me a list of your wants and sizes. I do so hope that by the time this gets to you that the measles have been defeated.

Bless you, angels all, from your ever adoring
Tom

* * *

Government House
Cape Town
February 21

My Darling One,
The struggle to find a moment to write is frantic. We never stop from one dawn to the next. However I won't neglect you, and here goes with another narrative. The garden party went off well, in a lovely shady garden, with a cool breeze & everyone dressed up to the nines. I met Kathleen Dewar there and then dashed out to dine with her in a lovely house where she is staying with her sister. High above the sea, you can wander on the terrace & see the lights of Muizenberg below, & the black mass of the mountains behind. Katie was in great form 'doing a little beachcombing' but I left fairly early, & got to bed soon after 11. Next day we

set off through 15 miles of crowds, to Simonstown; it was v well arranged, with a special swing welcome chanted by the coloured children and v good guards of honour. Admiralty House then confronted us with a miniature garden party – to our annoyed surprise – and after that we went to Kenilworth Race course to watch the Derby, having had lunch. It's a very pretty course and again everyone was very smart: I saw Katie again, Tommy Clapham and Tommy Charles – and put £10 on the winner at 3-1 so won £30, which will come to you in due course, in the shape of handbags etc. – but so far haven't seen a shop even. After the race I escaped with Peter Ashmore and watched Bobby Locke play Sam Snead – well worth it and v interesting. Bobby in great form v. v. sorry to hear of your measles. We got back about 6 pm, did the day's correspondence and then with Minner Harlech went to dine with Evelyn and Mary Baring: they are a delightful couple both v. intelligent and great fun. We had a good gossip about the country and the people and I added to my increasing knowledge of local problems. Minner is the greatest fun, very quick and knowledgeable v. entertaining. Next morning we were off early to Paarl and Stellenbosch – 2 very Nationalist areas. However at Paarl there was the holiday spirit & they got a great welcome. It is a delightful old Huguenot town with v few people, straddling along the 7. mile long high street – old white farms and churches and oak trees. It is mostly vineyards around there and the people are farmers. We then drove up the mountains to Mill Stream, high above the town – where tables were laid under the trees and we ate a gigantic tea. All v. homely & pleasant. Then in the cars again, and off to a big fruit farm for lunch. You've never seen such a mass of fruit, flowers and wine – and again we lunched out of doors, the company were again many of them anti-British – but they thawed completely and we all got on famously. Some of them were vast & hugely fat – some gaunt with long droopy beards & whiskers. We ate & drank & talked copiously, then off again to Stellenbosch a hotbed of the Nats.

There were no Union Jacks on the official buildings, but quite a lot in the crowd, and the reception was very good. After the presentations they drove round the arena & then adjourned to the City Hall – a superb new building, built in 1942. There again, 500 sat down to a vast tea, with orchestral accompaniment; I met 2 old friends, and again the informality impressed everybody. By this time we'd already been 70 miles and had another 30 to go so we set off again and got back about 5.30. I then had quite a lot of letters to write – at 6.45 I had to go down to see the Pilot Train which looks very grim – then back, change, dine – pick up the Princesses at Groot Schuur and take them to a dance, given by Mrs Waterson. It was a lovely evening, floodlit flower garden, coloured band, & some v. attractive girls – not one of whom I was introduced to!! I meet nothing but 70 year old boer fraus weighing 25 stone. We got back about 1. Today we opened Parliament and then get into the train at about 4 pm. I was thrilled to get your letters (plus the sizes) & Sylvia's. I just haven't time to write and thank her for all she has done to help you – what a comfort she must have been. I am longing to hear that you are really better. The news of the house sounds very good. I am sorry about the overdraft – I suppose it is the 1st Jan payments – but you might check on any big items, for there shouldn't have been any, unless you paid the tailor and shirtmakers.

I will try and get some postcards for the children today: give them all my love and kisses. I miss you all so much and long to bring you out here – one day it will have to be managed. When we get settled in the train I will try to write a more gossipy letter, but it's physically impossible in this rush.

I fear things must be ghastly still at home: how our hearts bleed for you – I only hope the news from here doesn't rub salt in the wound. How much longer are the country going to stand these things. I'll try and write about some of the people I have met – for they are quite a collection, some of them.

No more for now my beloved. I apologise for my writing, but

time is the enemy. I do hope you get this soon and that it finds you better. It brings my devoted love and kisses to you all. Even in the rush – you are seldom out of my thoughts.

Bless you my darlings
from your ever adoring Tom

* * *

THE WHITE TRAIN
DIE WITTREIN
February 24

My darling one,
I am trying a different technique for this letter – less narrative, and more description, as you hear a good deal of what we do as it is. So here is a nicely tabulated epistle for your approval!

The Train
The Royal Train is really v. good – the air conditioning makes it lovely & cool. Our big sitting room has been rather vulgarly decorated – stinkwood tables & cabinets (incl radiogram) and tapestry covered chairs with tassels! But it is full of beautiful flowers & tolerable pictures. We can sit down 16 to dinner & the food is delicious. The bathrooms' loos are painted blue & fulfil their functions admirably. When we stop, uniformed natives rush along the platform and attach sealed 'thunderboxes' to the drains, so everything is very elegantly concealed and disposed of. We, on the Pilot Train, spend most of our time here, & then, after dinner, get into a huge Daimler and drive till we catch up on the Pilot Train where we sleep. Included in the staff are three highly painted & decorative blondes, who mince along the corridors & get banged into at the most awkward places. They are students who volunteered for the duties of bedmaking & bath cleaning – but they are so dumb that they achieve nothing. However they

cause a good deal of amusement.

The organisation by the Railways has been astonishingly efficient – and whenever we stop for the night the most elaborate arrangements are made. Everything is floodlit, police, moving their feet like guardsmen, step up with specially constructed landing stages – & whole fences & even artificial woods have been erected to ensure our privacy. At every station at which we have stopped (which we do every two hours) the RF get out and walk down, chatting to people – and this is v. popular.

The line on which we are travelling has already taken us through an amazing variety of country – sometimes it might be the Highlands with purple mountains on either side; then Salisbury Plain, then the wine country of Italy and the Pyrenees or the pine covered gorges of Scandinavia. We travel slowly for the twists and turns and ups & downs – are tremendous and often we can see our 2 engines and first 6 coaches apparently coming past us in the opposite direction! The running isn't awfully smooth and I find it impossible to write legibly.

People

We have met many: first the old Field Marshal who towers above all the others: he never gets tired and he discusses, in just casual chatter, such different subjects as the Quantum Theory (mathematics), the Antarctic origin of the Cape geology, the philosophy of the 20th century, Mohammedenism & bird life. We always have a Minister on the train with us – so far Mr and Mrs Sturrock (Railways). He is a fat & cosy old Scotsman, an efficient businessman, who smokes incessant cigars & has a huge tummy. She is also Scottish and very nice tho' not exciting. They hand over to the Lawrences today. They are much younger; he is clever and drinks a bit – she is very pleasant, but a bit 'hostessy' to look at – 'just the right sort of slap and tickle for the King' said Delia*, so I hope she's right. All of us are well: the Queen is having a

---

*   Lady Delia Peel (a Lady in Waiting).

tremendous personal success but the others are now less tired & in excellent form. We are in fact a very happy party and we get a lot of laughs. We had a day off yesterday – an alfresco Service, then lunch & then we laid down on cushions – I went sound asleep and woke to find they had all gone for a walk. So I upped and set off & had a lovely stroll through the forest. Then we had tea and got back about 6.30. It wasn't too hot, as there was no sun; but even so I just wore a shirt & tropical trousers. Today is also cloudy with slight spits of rain – but it will soon be all too hot again.

I am longing to hear how you all are – I daren't listen to the wireless, the news is still so ghastly. Surely it must stop soon. I have bought you 2 handbags & a few rather mizzy little clothes for Caroline – but I will get down to it better at Durban and find you some shoes & stockings. I didn't have time to make use of the size cutting at Cape town.

Give the children lots of love and kisses, will you My Darling, & keep lots for your own sweet self.

From your ever loving Tom

* * *

THE WHITE TRAIN
DIE WITTREIN
March 1st

My Darling One,
Port Elizabeth has been the greatest fun, and we were all sorry to leave. They had built a special station as I described to Sylvia, and there we were virtually on the beach. I bathed three times one day – before each meal, and it was superb. We had surf boards too and dashed about on them, tho' not always v. skilfully. A large crowd always gathered to watch – & my huge bronzed form was exposed to the gaze of a million hungry eyes. Once, the King wanted the

Life Guard to do a practice rescue, & so we towed Meg out to some distance, then called for help. The consternation was considerable amongst those who didn't know – and two swimmers arrived from another part of the sea, before the Life Guard – so we had to send them out of the way. Then the Life Guard arrived with the line & Meg was hauled back through the water at about 15 knots! One evening some of the Railway officials asked Peter T* & I out to dinner which we did rather reluctantly. 5 rather dull men, 2 quite nice women. We motored out to a local Yacht Club, and after some drinks, went to our table where we found 20 dozen oysters, 3 dozen crabs and champagne and stout – so that gave us something to get on with. Our host, an ex Major & v. friendly was a little Yorkshire plumber who's made good. We then trailed off to the Star Dust – a remarkably good nightclub, with an excellent band & air conditioning that really works. We took it in turns to dance around with the gels & eventually got to bed at about 2 am. I was in the sea again before 8. I did some shopping for you – I couldn't get you a good bathing dress – but I found four pairs of shoes, some bathing dresses for the children and that's about all. I will try to send a few of them by air, but I fear they'll mostly have to wait & come back with me. It was such a relief to hear from you that you are really on the mend – what a hell of a time it's been. Everyone here sends you much love & sympathy. I'm afraid the postcards I have sent are terribly dull, but I hope the children like them. There appear to be no toys in the whole country.

We spent about ¾ an hour at the Snake Park one day – they were perfectly foul & disgusting creatures. Then yesterday we motored to Grahamstown, a quiet little town devoted to Colleges and schools with a delightful situation, tucked away in the folds of green scrub covered hills. We had a pretty drive to get there – in fact we were a little early so the King got out and we all walked for a 1/4 an hour ahead of the car – much to the consternation

---

*   Peter Townsend.

of a farmer who'd brought along his boys: when the King walked up & started talking he hadn't a clue who he was – suddenly he realised and his face was a joy to see. I met Judge and Mrs Gardner, Murray's parents – so delightful and charming – they are sending you some butter!

Today we visit a big native College & they sing their anthem. We have had advance copies, and I have been going thru 'it' with Meg and Delia so you can imagine the noise. We have lost our nice Minister, Harry Lawrence & wife –& now have the Watersons – he wet and pompous, she (in Delia's words) the lady's maid one would have <u>not</u> brought on the tour – irresponsible, unsquashable and generally exacerbating. They are with us for some time, & I think we will go mad! My fondest love to you all: a kiss for David, Caroline and Juliet and all my blessings on you all

from your ever loving Tom

* * *

THE WHITE TRAIN
DIE WITTREIN
March 2nd

My Beloved Darling,
Your letter of Feb 22 arrived last night, & I hope that some of mine have reached you by now. We are now at East London, where we arrived last night. You will have heard how much we enjoyed being close to the beach at Port Elizabeth & we were sorry to have to leave. However yesterday was a grand day, because we visited an assembly of native students who sang three songs – 5,200 of them in perfect harmony. I daresay you might have heard the recording of it: it was deeply moving and I am hoping to get a record of the songs, to play to you when I get home. The conductor was a native, Professor Jabaru, who smiled & grinned

throughout the performance, & threw himself about in a most lively manner. His baton was a long ebony walking stick, which he waved very effectively to control this vast & spread out choir, whose members had never sung together before & some of whom had walked since 2.am to be there. As they held the last dying notes, he ran his finger slowly along the stick, to the ferrule, as tho' drawing out the sound, like a piece of elastic. We all enjoyed that immensely. We then got back into the train and moved on to East London. Peter Ashmore, Mima and I were told by the King to find some good beaches, so we didn't drive through the town. Instead we looked at a lovely beach nearby (20 minutes in the car) which would be alright for the evening, as we were bound to be late – & Peter went off to a further one, where we may spend this afternoon. It was a delightful day with high, shrub covered sand hills, reached by a little shady path. The surf is terrific, & in parts dangerous, but we had life-savers and lines all ready – tho' our part of the beach is really alright. We all …gathered for tea on the train, & then piled into the cars and out of it: it was really too rough to swim, but we had a wonderful pounding in the surf. Pr E[*] & the Q[†] didn't bathe, but collected shells. Unfortunately the sun soon went down & it wasn't quite as warm as one would have liked. Today we have Church at 11.15 – lunch on the train, and then off to the beaches. There is a friend of mine here – Sandy Pollock who was with John at Univ, & I am going to have a 'sundowner' with him. It is really wonderful to think that you can start moving on 17th – I shall be feeling terribly helpless & useless being stuck out here – but I am sure you will do it all too beautifully. I have implicit faith: promise me not to get too tired and to slip up to The Maggots' and have a real laze. We will certainly come out here together before long, and have a real holiday in the sun. I must try & make a little mun' on the sly. I shall be thinking of you a lot on the 7th: a day of many ever happy

---

[*]   Princess Elizabeth.
[†]   The Queen.

memories. I hope you throw a little party to celebrate. I have a Press acquaintance on board – Rex Reynolds of the Johannesburg Sunday Times. I was chatting to him last night and it turned out that he was in the RAF & in 80 Squadron with David* – in fact he took over David's Flight after he was missing – and was himself taken prisoner a week later. He spoke in glowing terms of David and said how much he was adored by the 'erks' as well as by his brother officers. I think he wrote to your Mother from his prison camp. Wasn't that a strange coincidence.

No more for now, my Darling. Give the children my kisses – and to yourself my deepest love and many happy returns of the great day

from your ever adoring
Tom

* * *

THE WHITE TRAIN
DIE WITTREIN
March 8th

My Beloved Darling, The Queen & and I drank your health last night, & sent many telepathic messages of good wishes. I hope my cable arrived & also in due course, a couple of parcels – gold shoes have not so far been attainable, but you may be amused with the others. I am waiting till I get to Durban, or even back to Cape Town, for the materials, as the shops are better there. At the moment we are at Bloemfontein, having arrived yesterday. Govt. House is delightful – newly built, on top of a hill with views to North & East of about 60 miles. The long, flat garden, with pergolas, flower beds & a fountain has been cut out of the side of the hill, & one can stand on the edge, silhouetted against the outstretched miles of veld. The functions yesterday were pretty

---

*   Flight Lt David Coke DFC, Mary's brother.

deadly, but it was a good welcome from a town so predominantly Nationalist & Republican. The visit to the Natives was a complete shambles, for a high wind got up & started a little dust storm, making the choir assembled in our honour, both inaudible & invisible. About 4 different songs were being sung simultaneously in different parts of the crowd, & it was a great joy to us all to have a taste of chaos after so many unchaotic banalities. In the evening we went to the Civic Ball, & again some young men were produced to dance with the Princesses. The Queen wore a pearl studded crinoline dress, with Garter, tiara etc. & looked v. well. Most of us are still living in the train as Govt. House is a bit too small – but we are quite happy doing that. Today at 11 am we go by plane to the O.F.S. game reserve, rather a mingy one I believe, but it might be quite amusing. To get up here we have travelled quite hard recently: & I think we all of us were very attracted by the Transkei. We visited Umtata, & the country was green and rolling and fresh. Everywhere were tidy little kraals, & natives in native dress, yellow & orange blankets, rings on their legs, & sometimes white or red paint on their faces. The women wear a funny rather clumsy head dress, not unlike the hat of a fish porter at Billingsgate: they all cheered the train with great enthusiasm. The Indaba, or gathering which we went to, was also most unusual, altho' here the natives were almost all in European dress. There must have been over 30,000 present, and about 1 in 5 had come on horseback – so behind the assembly, on a large, slightly rising expanse of veld, grazed some 5.000 horses. Chief Jeremiah Moaherh led the salutation 'Bayete' – the Royal Salute, groaned out by 30,000 voices, the sound seeming to be the very essence of obeisance. But then we had to retrace our steps back along this v. twisty and difficult stretch of railway – & you will have heard that our equipment train tipped off the line & killed the unhappy driver. Otherwise none of our recent activities had been out of the ordinary.

I wasn't surprised to hear that Edward* had taken to Sonia† – but it's bad luck if he's missed the bus – however that's Sonia's business. Hugh & Lavinia‡ should be a v. good couple and she will inherit plenty of artistic treasures to keep her busy; Norfolk is becoming a sort of family racket now – a challenge to the nationalisation of land. I wish to goodness Tommy could get out of the army and settle down to some farming – I am sure he might keep on trying, particularly now that John Marriott is at London District. He'd far better do that even at the cost of his pension, rather than hang on for 2 or 3 years in these rather second rate jobs. David Stirling is out here planning some great enterprise, & I am anxious to get hold of him, in case he might have some room for me. It would be nice to have an interest out here in Rhodesia, as it would give us a good excuse for coming out here from time to time. Anyhow I am writing to Sario now, as I believe she knows where is he is to be found.

This country seems to be entirely devoid of postcards which I could send to the children, but I am hoping to get some today. I often try to imagine what they are doing & saying – much as usual no doubt – tho' I am sure you must have had quite a time with them when they were convalescing. You might also start thinking about where to go this summer – it's no good going anywhere where sunshine is the least bit doubtful – I feel Italy would be best, preferably by car, but it might be worth your while finding out the form – we could perhaps bring Susie back, if she's still out there then.

No more for now – but my devoted love to you all & many kisses for the nits. Tell David that the Princesses went out riding this morning & saw lots of zebras. I also send them each a medal, commemorating the Royal Visit.

From your ever adoring Tom

---

*   Edward Ford.

†   Sonia Heathcoat-Amory.

‡   Hugh Cholmondeley and his future wife Lavinia Leslie (TCH's cousin).

THE WHITE TRAIN
DIE WITTREIN, March 12

My Beloved One,

We are now in Basutoland, having arrived there yesterday from the Free State. Our stay in Bloemfontein was a great success, for as you know the whole province is v. Nationalist & Republican – but the Royal Family had an amazing personal success, particularly at the 'braaivleis' in the game reserve, where those present are the most ardent anti-British section in the Union. On Sunday afternoon I played a few holes of golf, more to test out the new skin on my finger than anything else, & then had a swim. We set off on Sunday evening, & until Tuesday afternoon were passing thro' the flat, drought stricken & interminable plains that are so typical of the Free State. But gradually we got closer to Maseru, where we now are, & so also to the western edges of the Drakensberg Mountains – trees began to appear, the grass is green and the country is broken with tall flat escarpments, on high sugar loaf 'koppies' – so that in the slanting rays of the setting sun, it seems as tho' we have landed on the moon, & found it friendly & cultivated.

The boundary between Basutoland (which is entirely British) and the Free State, is a bridge across the river and at that bridge the Union police escort of motor cyclists pulled up, & we drove across in British territory. There was a little parade ground, banked, amphitheatre like, by a gentle slope. In the centre where the ex-servicemen, & the guards of honour, mounted & unmounted, & on the other side a little canopy under which Evelyn Baring & Co. made the presentations. The recent Paramount Chieftain is a woman, a widow of 38, & I should think one of some personality – nor is she particularly insignificant physically, & is known unofficially & irreverently as Her Amplitude.

While they were walking round I spotted Katie & had a long chat with her, arranging to dine in the evening.

For days now, the Basutos have been streaming into the town, on foot & on horseback, to attend the 'Pitso' today. Women are not allowed, but they are 50,000 men & about 1/3 come on horseback – so all the green & open fields are black with horses & men, & at night their shrill voices echo across the valleys, & the camp fires, on which they cook some of the 500 oxen which they have brought to slaughter, twinkle & glow across the valleys. So of course, many of them were here yesterday, & we drove through them to the Residency – chanting, singing, groaning, dancing, as varied in performance as in dress – some in straight European clothes, others with gay magenta, black & white or yellow blankets; & on their heads, ostrich-feathers, pork pie hats, caps, waste paper baskets, coloured steel helmets, service dress caps, peacocks feathers or ram's horns. Even as I write, I see from the train window, a few late starters galloping along the horizon to join the others.

We came back to lunch on the train & after a snooze, I went up to the Residency to bathe, which was fun, but the sun was setting low. Then I took Cuthbert White up to dine with Katie, the Beattys & Lady Jones (Enid Bagnold, author of National Velvet). We dined out of doors, by spirit lamps & then the maids came into the garden and sang their native songs in perfect harmony, & with that sighing plaintive drag which plunges into one's heart like a knife. Then I brought them back to the train, joined up with the others (the RF* were all dining at the Residency) & we went up to watch a firework display. Unfortunately we were made to sit far too close, & there were a lot of near squeaks – I caught one flaming missile in my hat!!

I told you in my last letter that I was hoping to get in touch with David Stirling[†] – I have now got a telegram from him asking me to meet him in Jo'burg – so I am very hopeful & excited that we may be able to fix something really interesting.

---

* Royal Family.
† D. Stirling, founder of the SAS.

I will write again from the Natal National Park, where we are going to have 4 days rest – it should be lovely. You must be getting v. busy with the house, & everything so difficult. I see that our shares have gone up again – you might like to check with Dudley Woolland's secretary that he has sold as I suggested for that will bring in a few hundred pounds which I daresay you can use to advantage.

Give my love to <u>all</u> the family & tell them the news. Fun tho' all this is, I am longing to be home again.

Bless you, Darling One
from your ever adoring
Tom

* * *

National Park Hostel
PO Mont-Aux Sources
Natal
Phone: Mont-Aux Sources
Call Office
March 15th 1947

My Darling,
But for your absence, this is Heaven. We motored out here from Ladysmith, 60 miles, on Thursday evening, arriving about 6:30pm. All much looking forward to 4 days of peace and quiet. You will see from the postcards that the Hostel consists of a main dining block, surrounded by little houses and rondavels, for sleeping, all perched on little grass terraces edged with herbaceous borders of cannas, zinnias, geraniums, and flowering shrubs. We are here quite alone except for General Smuts.

We went off to bed early, and on Friday morning, quite a lot of the gang went riding. I had a short swim before breakfast in the large bath at the bottom of the garden – but the water was a bit chilly and I didn't stay in long. It was already beginning to get warm and by the end of breakfast the sun was hot. I must just describe the situation of the Hostel; It lies at the foot of the western end of the Drakensberg, and towering above is a line of jagged peaks, 11,000 feet high. On the left is the Eastern Buttress, a square formidable mass of rock and then to the right the gaunt black Amphitheatre ending in the Sentinel another jagged tooth of rock. Between us and these mountains are the foothills green and fresh fields through which wind gently sloping paths. After breakfast I set out for a walk with the King and General Smuts, a guide and 3 "gestapo" and we had a great time. The sun shone and we could see behind as a view of 60 miles, including the famous Spion Kop. We took our time, going at a steady pace, and stopping quite often to gaze up at the mountains, or to look at some flowers growing beside the path, or at a butterfly hovering and darting amongst us. Every now and then the path led us into a little wood, as cool and shady as you could wish, with a mountain stream tumbling through. In one of these woods the ground was just a mass of wild begonias and without moving from the path we picked gladioli and host of other S. African flowers. Smuts knows them all, being a great botanist. Every now and then he would stop to look at the Eastern Buttress and exclaim to it "Well, my Eastern Buttress, you are a fine fellow. I take off my hat to you" or "Now we are going to the mountains – to the abode of the gods – we are ascending from the human scale to the divine" and all the time, little spurts of philosophy bubbles out of him, like water from a subterranean spring. We got back in time to have a lovely bathe before lunch and then for 2 1/4 hours I slept. Then tea, & two sets of tennis in which I was well beaten by Peter Townsend. In order to get to bed early, we dined at 7/30pm and throughout dinner, Smuts kept up an unconscious, unending stream of fascinating conversation. Apart from his present day experience, his life has spanned a vast space of time & of events and he can speak first hand of almost every major activity in the past 50 years. In the space of 15 mins he will talk of the flowers of Abyssinia, the time-scale of mountains and of stars, the origins and histories of the nation's tribes, the magnificence of Morhesh, the smallness of Molotov, the future of the Empire – and all, with a detached and objective humour of one sitting on a tower watching with kindly amusement the petty problems of the tiny figures nipping about far below. He will then describe how he visited Ireland in 1916, as Mr Smith, to end the war and to urge on them Dominion status – in the next breath he will tell you the story of how he besieged Ladysmith and at the end he will bustle us all off to bed – possibly his greatest achievement!!

Today, alas, is overcast and even chilly, but even that is pleasant over here and I shall miss one of the rare opportunities of sun-bathing. We leave here at 3pm on Monday, and start off again on the multiple activities of the tour. This rest has come at a v. good time; for we were all beginning to get stale and tired, and this gives us all a good chance to pick up again. This should reach you during a v. busy week; how I wish I could be of some help, but I address the envelope with joy to the first real home we have had, to which I long to return. My love to you all; I'm sending postcards to the children at Lingwood.

> Bless you a thousand times
> from your ever adoring Tom

* * *

THE WHITE TRAIN
DIE WITTTREIN
March 18

My Darling One,
I was so delighted to get your letter dated 8th, yesterday, & to hear that you had managed to have some fun in London. I feared that this ghastly, unbelievable weather would postpone getting into

the house, but as you say, it can't be helped. So glad the children are well – Juliet sounds quite a tubster: she should be sitting up when I get home.

We have had an amusing time with Smuts in attendance, & I am writing a longish account of it to Mother, who will no doubt send it on to you – I've hardly written her a line since I have been away. We're now in Pietermaritzburg, & I stayed on the train this morning, & dictated for 1½ hours: then we all go out to lunch, & a garden party this afternoon. Tomorrow is Zululand, which I hope will be fun. I had a telegram from David Stirling suggesting we should meet in Johannesburg, so I am hoping that something may come out of it. I am afraid I never seem to be included in any photographs – my natural modesty drives me to the background – but I will try to do better in future!

I am distressed about Sonia: one doesn't want to make her unhappy, at the same time she might snap out of it if people push her enough – I am sure Sylvia knows her well enough at least to tell her of Edward's feelings, &– then she must make up her own mind – but I am sure a little advocacy wouldn't do any harm. He does sound unutterably dreary, & that won't make for the children's happiness even if she tries to persuade herself that it will. I am sure it's worth one more try.

I am afraid my power to write lyrics has dried up with the advancing years – but I enclose 'The Flat' in case Cunningham is interested – but I am a little doubtful of having my name associated in public with words of questionable taste!! You ought to put him in touch with Freddie Shaughnessy,[*] who's of a v. different calibre, & knows the form.

The Natal countryside is again quite different tho' we haven't seen much of it yet. High hills, covered in green woods, & green fields, with little white & red houses. It is smaller & more enclosed than many parts, and is also sub-tropical, & v. hot: tho' today is nice and cloudy. They have an insoluble Indian problem – but are

_____

*   Writer of *Upstairs, Downstairs*.

much more English than the other provinces – I personally find it slightly tedious; I would rather they were better S. Africans, & less blatantly English – & they're not such a good type of English at that.

I will do some shopping to you at Durban – I do so hope the other things have arrived by now & are OK.

No more for now as it is nearly lunchtime. Bless you all my darlings. I pray the weather is better, & that all goes well. Much love and kisses to you all

from your ever loving
Tom

* * *

KING'S HOUSE
DURBAN, March 22

My Darling One,
Our visit to Eshowe was delightful, tho' the dance by the Zulus was disappointing. Our drive into the town was beautiful, up a winding road, through unending acres of green iris-like sugar plantation. As we climbed higher, the view increased, and the green hills of Zululand rose up on 3 sides, with the sea far below, behind us. Eshowe is full of charm, a small shady hill station, with tropical flowers growing everywhere, and wide clean streets. The morning was spent in civic 'do's', and from time to time we repaired to the Residency, to gaze at the distant ocean, at the Rhodesian flame tree, a big chestnut-tree, with red, pointed flowers or just to relax in the cool of the drawing room. I met, as I had arranged, my old campaigning friend Guy Chennels, who commanded the tanks allotted to my company in Italy, & we had a good gossip together. I later presented him to the Princesses, but his shyness was more acute than usual, & all he could do was to enthuse over the success of the tour, & urged them 'to

keep their pecker up'! After lunch we set off for the dance, which was preceded by speeches, and the presentation, to certain chiefs, of gifts. Here again we had a magnificent variety of dress – the heir presumptive in Commissionaires ceremonial, others in Zulu traditional war 'paint', some in European clothes, one in gaiters, riding breeches, a white dustcoat and a sun helmet with an ostrich feather attached – rather like an inebriated farmer at the weekly fat stock market. Meanwhile, some 150 yards away from the dais, was the great body of Zulus, rank upon rank, some 50,000, of whom the first few ranks were due to dance. They were drawn up, I gather against their will, by regiments, the old way, whereas nowadays they are accustomed to dancing in families and groups. The regiments are really age-groups of which the senior was the over – 70s.

They all then started with a big sweeping movement rather like a surrealistic march past, and then to our intense surprise, the ladies joined in, very excitedly, bowing & singing & generally 'in the groove'. Nature has liberally endowed them all with figures amply capable of nourishing the youngest child, and these fountains of nourishment entered nobly into the spirit of gyroscoping animation. As if all this wasn't sufficiently riveting, across the foot dais kept shuffling, soft shoe fashion, a female witch doctor, yelling hideously, & then suddenly stopping, & walking off quite ordinarily. Another delightful figure was the old gentleman, trotting arthritically behind the warriors scarcely able to move for age and infirmity, but every so many hobbles, stamping his foot gallantly in true Zulu fashion.

Gradually however, things became more and more chaotic, nothing really got going & the monstrous regiment of women kept bursting in on the scene, wobbling deliriously. Then the men started doing their individual displays, similar to a man with six hornets in the seat of his trousers, and acute ear-ache– & so time past & it was time to motor home to the train & get on our way to Durban.

I must say we have had a wonderful welcome here, & it is a beautiful city. It is shaped, as far as one can say, like a horse shoe. The iron ring is a ridge of green & tropical suburbs dotted with pink & white houses: the centre is flat, the shopping & business quarters, wide streets & skyscrapers, and long broad esplanades running along the beach, with the surf of the Indian Ocean thundering down upon the white hot sand. I won't bore you with the details of the functions, which were like all the others – the Civic Hall was graced by even more hideous women than usual. I have absented myself almost continuously and had two games of golf, with fair success & hardly conscious of my now well-nigh cured finger. I had a good morning's shopping too & I hope soon that the results will reach you and be satisfactory. I think now that I shall do a little in Johannesburg for the children – so tell me if there is anything that you particularly want for them apart from shoes. Today we go racing & I am hoping hard for a winner – on the other hand I may be cleared out completely by this evening.

I had a long & pathetically unhappy letter from E F & sent him a wire of which you have no doubt heard: I am sure a second attempt should be made, & can't at any rate do harm. No doubt by the time you get this, the thing will be finally decided once & for all. I feel terribly sorry for Edward & somewhat guilty – but the engagement was so vague when I left, and there was no reason to suppose that he & Sonia would click. I don't know what she feels about him but at least she should be told of his feelings.

The heat here is terribly sticky, & I sweat like a pig and am as a result somewhat spotty, which is devastatingly attractive. However am extremely well, & I think I may have put on an ounce or two of weight. The weather at home I daren't even mention – it is a constant shadow over the S.African sun, and the sympathy for you all felt by everyone here is deep and sincere.

No more for now my Darling – all my devoted love to you and the children

from your ever adoring
Tom

* * *

GOVERNMENT HOUSE
PRETORIA
April 5th

My Beloved,

It seems ages since I last wrote to you, but as you can gather the week has been tremendously hectic, and I have a lot to tell you about. Last Monday we had a big day in Pretoria with an admirable parade in the afternoon, v. smart & moving & luckily without rain, which had been threatening all day. On Sunday afternoon I had played golf with Ian Moore & went round in 72 so that was fun. In the morning we had all been to the Dutch Reform Church, but I believe I told you about that. I am getting so vague in the rush of succeeding events, that I really don't know what has happened, is happening or is going to happen! On Monday night Michael and I went to a dinner given by the Pretoria Regiment – they did us awfully well, & were charming hosts. In spite of promises to the contrary, dinner was followed by speeches, & I was called upon to speak, quite unprepared. Luckily however one of the preceding speakers had said how relieved they had been, on meeting 24th Guards Brigade, to find that the Officers were almost human. So I began by saying that it was nothing compared with our relief in finding that the South Africans were white and not black! Tuesday was spent in Johannesburg leaving here at 9am & finally getting to bed at 12.30am.

They got a tumultuous reception, almost hysterical, but a v. well behaved crowd. After lunch we had a 23 mile drive through a sea of excited black faces, until we reached the races where our hosts were Tommy and Sophie Plapham. Alas we all backed the wrong horse to our disgust, so my powers of shopping will be limited!! However I have sent the children five pairs of shoes, which I hope you have already got. I will see about the veiling & Sarie has already got me 18 yards of elastic!! We got back from the races at about 6pm, & Meg & I took the Princesses to a ball of 'young people' – preceded by a dinner party. I must say it was v.well arranged & we all enjoyed ourselves, in spite of being tired. One never quite knows with this place, particularly J'burg, what horrors of publicity & bad taste mightn't suddenly be showered upon the Royal Family – but luckily all went well, & by judicious watching, we avoided any excesses of that sort. The King & Queen looked in for a short time, I saw quite a lot of old friends, & so it was a good end to a big day. The next day looked like being even worse – 123 mile drive through solid crowds at 15 mph – so I slipped away, did a little shopping, & then went off to play a six-ball at Glendower, with some more friends. Again I played well, & thoroughly enjoyed the fresh air & exercise. After dinner Pr. M* gave an astonishing take off of a contralto (coloratura) accompanying herself – a most spirited & polished performance worthy of Bea Lillie!

On Thursday we flew up to Pietersburg, where we had a v.dull day; & there Delia & I dashed up to a cocktail party at Robert's Heights – in fact we were nearly late for dinner. Then yesterday we went to Church, & then David Stirling came to see me & we lunched at the Pretoria Club. He told me all about his group & its plans and asked me to join him (while still doing this job) as director & 'negotiator' in London. He has got good chaps with him, Freddie de Guingand, Andrew Scott & many others, & the

---

*   Princess Margaret.

scope of the thing is wide & important. I warned him that I was a child in such matters, but anyhow I can learn at the various London Offices – so I shall be coming home later than ever!!

However I hope it will mean that in 5 years time we can have a pied a terre in Rhodesia, which I am told is a jewel beyond price with which even the Union can't be compared. I shall go into all the details with him when I get back, & will then ask permission of H M which I am sure will be forthcoming, as I have already sowed the seeds of approval. So I feel that it is something that we can really look forward to, as a contrast to the unending gloom of England.

I have just this second got your letter telling me of Caroline's accident. Goodness I am sorry – I don't know how you cope and stay so well and cheerful. All the family write in glowing terms of your 'guts' & the party here, to whom I recount all my woes, now speak of you as a byword of female indomitability. I do hope she is better now, poor little sweet – it's inevitable that children should pile themselves up occasionally, but none the less hell when it happens. The nanny you have heard of certainly seems promising, & I wish you every success with her.

I dined with General Poole last night, having spent the whole afternoon swimming, our first chance. The garden here is a dream of paradise, but we hadn't been able to set foot in it until yesterday we were so busy. Sarie & Jennifer came over to tea with shoppings for the Queen, & I am lunching with them today. David S & Ernest Oppenheimer are dining here tonight. Then at 5.30 tomorrow I fly off to Salisbury & I shall be making my Easter Communion in Rhodesia. Anne has also written, & I am going to try & get her what she wants – let me know if you want curtain materials & if so how much, as I may be able to get some in Cape Town.

I find it painful & embarrassing to keep on sympathising with you at home – you are being a perfect brick & God bless you for it.

Much love and kisses to the children & a special one for Caroline: tell her how proud I am that she has been so brave.

From your ever adoring

Tom

VICTORIA FALLS
April 11

My beloved one,

We arrived here this morning after an all-night train from Salisbury. I must say I have taken a great fancy to S. Rhodesia & I liked both the people & the country. It is a lovely country on the whole, & tremendous possibilities, without most of the problems of the Union. I am delighted to think that if my plan with David S. comes off, that we shall see a good deal of it, & perhaps even come here for good if we feel like it. I have already met a lot of the influential people, all of whom are encouraging & helpful – I have even been invited to stay with the Governor General of the Belgian Congo – who said I was the image of Leopold when he was young!!

Salisbury was v. hectic; we never really stopped with the usual 'do's' all day, & a dance one night & a reception the other. It was quite amusing at the dance because while we were in one room with the Royal Family waiting to make their entry, it was being discussed exactly which route they should take – and as soon as a decision was made, some ADC popped his head round the door & said, you can't go that way – it is too full, or not ready, or something. Finally it was decided, & the Governor said, I'll open the door & the band will play the National Anthem. By this time we were all pretty weak – the door opened & the band played Money is the Route of all Evil. We hurriedly shut it again, but we

356

were all hysterical & the Queen was kicking round saying Send him victorious boom de ada. Even then they again opened the door too soon, & everyone could see a convulsed & apparently jitter mad Royal Family framed in the doorway! Anyhow it made the party go.

I got one game of golf at Salisbury, & wrote the Queen's speech for Cape Town (you may hear extracts on the BBC on April 22nd).

Now of course I must try and describe the Falls, which everyone agrees cannot in fact be described. Even as I write – it is now dark, & I have been bathing in the floodlit pool – they are roaring in my ears. For 1 ¼ mile in breadth, & 300 feet in height the waters thunder down in the gorge – the river is in flood, & over a 100 million gallons a minute are crashing perpendicularly to perdition. A wall of spray, like white smoke, springs up from below, not hanging like a mist, but shooting, like steam under pressure, 400 feet into the air – so that the wide panorama of the Falls is blotted out of sight. The temperature by day is 100°, & the spray falls like rain, so you can imagine beside the river you are in a vast greenhouse. The chasm, swirling and foaming, is banded with rainbows, and the weight & fury of the waters stirs up the soil till the water is brown – while the earth shakes as you peer down into a raging hell of foam and turmoil.

Tomorrow I hope to get a good view of the Devil's Cataract. This afternoon we did our stuff in N Rhodesia – stinking hot and rather dull, but now we have two days off – little enough on top of so much. By now you might really be in the house – I do hope you haven't had too ghastly a time. I was so relieved to hear that little Caroline is better & that scar is unlikely – provided they did it properly, she should be young enough to avoid one. I can't wait to hear about the Nanny – I do hope she's alright. I have sent a few more parcels, but will probably bring the household things and Anne's with me on Vanguard. What do you think my Mama would like – I am also bringing biscuits, lard, olive oil etc: but not, I fear, an awful lot. Anyhow my contacts are good!! Must go and change for dinner.

Bless you, my angels four – not long now before I am home!

From your ever adoring
Tom

* * *

Government House
Bulawayo
Southern Rhodesia
April 15

My darling one,

Got a letter from you dated 7th this morning, & was so glad to hear that all goes well. We left the Falls on Sunday evening, having had a delightful tho' short rest. It was tremendously hot, but I bathed a good deal, and managed to keep fairly cool. We got to Bulawayo yesterday morning, & Tommy, Michael Cuthbert White and I are staying in a house, at the gates, belonging to the Chartered Company – we are v. well looked after by a couple, comfortable, quiet and on our own, so we are very happy. Yesterday was quite a pleasant & easy day – and we had a reception in the evening. Tony Combe rang me up & came up here for a drink before dinner, & I hope to dine with him tonight. Then we are off tomorrow, and it becomes one hectic rush till we embark, particularly with Pr E's birthday in the offing.

This afternoon we got to a Native Indaba, which should be good, & later on to visit Rhodes grave, in the Matobo Hills. Seeing the Rhodesians one begins to get some idea of the achievement of the man, & the tremendous drawing power which made him able to do what he did.

If we do eventually want to come out here, I am sure it could be easily arranged but we will have to talk it over at length when I get home. I daresay we won't want to move for some years anyway. I have heard nothing of Edward and Sonia – I take it that she is definitely marrying Roddy – I am sorry, as I think she will be awfully bored with him. Caroline will love being page to Lavinia: I hope we can all get down there.

I am afraid I am bound to be pretty busy when I get back: there won't be much of a chance of getting away for long until August. I quite see about the £75 & the car, tho' it would be a great help. I wonder if I could wangle a car from one of the embassies – I have got so used to travelling in comfort, we really must do something!!

Must go to lunch. All my love my darlings.

From your ever adoring
Tom

With Princess Margaret
in Italy 1949

The Princess goes bathing with a man in shirt-tails

PRINCESS MARGARET, in her light blue two-piece swim suit, is helped over the rocks by Major Thomas Harvey, the Queen's Private Secretary, before setting out in a small boat for a swim off Capri. The major is wearing his shirt loose over his shorts in the now-popular fashion of Continental resorts.

THE Princess, holding her cartwheel straw hat—her first purchase in Italy—is helped into the dinghy by the major and the boatman.

"I see your wife's read about this new Continental fashion for men."

362

MORGANO TIBERIO PALACE CAPRI
29 April

Darling one, this is the first chance to write since I left for I have naturally been busy before the Princess arrived, and things have been hectic since. I had an uneventful flight out, dull because of cloud and at Rome the weather was very beastly. I went straight to the Embassy where everyone was charming and helpful: We had a series of discussions and conferences and finally finished up very sleepy bridge at 11pm: however I won 7/- so my guardian angel was still on duty! Next day we flew down to Naples, and again it wasn't too nice but after we arrived the weather got better and better and finally gave HRH a perfect welcome. Everything was hectic at Naples because there were 150 reporters and photographers all poised for action, all ardent individualists, all seeking a scoop, all being prodded and goaded by their editors. The joy (or sorrow) of Italy is that all arrangements break down at the last minute, and of course the Princess hadn't been out of the plane 2 minutes before she was completely swamped by photographers and all the pompous presentations took place in this melee – poor Cecil Howard, who is the prettiest and fascinating wife of Mondy Howard, bumped her head on a camera when rising from her curtsey! Finally we got to the Hotel, and then by way of appeasement, had another short "session" on the roof this time – 68 photographers all diving and ducking and darting and hammering and rushing forward and even going faster backwards, into each other, backwards and forwards, upwards and downwards, with many exclamation and jester of alternate joy and despair. Later still we went for a short drive round the city and after a dinner in our own sitting room, tumbled into bed, too sleepy to talk any sort of business. It was too much to hope that one would sleep well but it might have been worse and we were totally fresh next day. The local Admiral, a charmer, had but his launch and crew to take us. We went in great comfort and high speed to Capri, followed by a Corvet with the luggage. In Capri one can only go as far as the Piazza; the rest is walking through narrow but deliciously smelling and cheerful streets with a posse of charming but not always sufficiently firm Italian plain clothes police and pattering and panting photographers who "snap" and then run like mad for 30 yards and then turn and snap again. Now my friend from my last visit, M. Cerio has lent us a delicious villa for picnics and bathing and we have the Admirals yacht, so we can have a little peace. But it is all great fun and I think both the ladies of the party are thoroughly happy and enjoying themselves.

Much love, darling – do pass this round the family and friends as there is not much time for writing. All love from Tom

* * *

British Embassy Rome
8th May 1949

My Darling
A heavy thunder storm has just descended upon us, and forcibly cancelled our drive to Villa d'Este and Hadrian's Villa. So I will snatch this chance of bringing you a little more up to date with our progress, and, I hope, with slightly more accuracy than it is accorded in the Press. In my last letter, I left you in Capri, where we stayed on until the 3rd. Except for one wet day, we had a delicious time, peacefully lying about in the Cerio Villa and eating a delicious lunch, and a hopping on and off the yacht which we were lent. Sometimes we went out to sea, when it was really quite rough, and had to cling with both hands and feet to the masts, as we swayed and plunged round the cliffs. We went for a longish walk too, one afternoon, but the Princess picked up some blisters so we didn't try again!

The Italian Navy provided a Corvet to take us to Sorento and the Princess was duly piped aboard, and treated with great respect and kindness. They set out some chairs and a table on deck and we sat sipping orange juice as we glided across the Bay. It only takes about 35 minutes so we were at our new hotel in good time for lunch. The hotel was not so nice as the one at Capri, being rather late Victorian and pretentious, but they did us pretty well on the whole. That afternoon we motored to Pompeii and spent two fascinating hours being shown round by the two leading professors who made everything most interesting and amusing. Next day, we had a long but thrilling drive round the Amalfi – Ravello coast road to Salerno and onto Paestum, where we ate a picnic lunch. Then another super professor took us round the Greek Temples and the museum. These three superb temples stand on the plain, about 500 yards from the sea. The centre and lay out one is honey coloured with the afternoon sun slanting onto its pillars looked exquisitely beautiful. The "Finds" in the museum were also wonderfully early Greek and Roman friezes and a superb collection of pottery made in 2400BC and discovered by U.S. Bulldozers when making the air-strip for the Salerno landing.

On the way home, we stopped at the military cemetery and laid a bunch of Paestum roses on one of the graves.

Our last day at Sorrento was spent at sea on the yacht. It wasn't as nice a day as we would of liked, but we were determined to sunbathe. Goose pimples or no goose pimples, and in fact the weather got better though there was always rather too much wind. We picnicked on board and altogether had a delicious time, looked after by Salvatore, our beloved boatman. We returned after about 5 hours and in the evening they danced a tarantella for us before dinner, they all looked handsome and danced very gaily, but the orchestra in spite of having a leader with a face as distinguished as Beethoven himself, were pathetically bad. The accordionist kept grinning at the princess and saying "you like?" And therefore getting even more out of time than his colleagues.

After dinner they sang a serenade from lighted boats, gliding on the sea 150ft below the hotel terrace. Unfortunately distance and the usual Italian crowd noises made them factually inaudible – but later on they advanced on land and sang their local songs, while the children stripped and dived into the harbour, and one by one the lights on the boats caught fire and everyone screamed until they were safely in the water, there again, it could have been much warmer – but it was typical of the welcome the princess has had and the gay childlike way in which the Italians do such things.

It is, of course, a long drive to Rome and we left at 9.30am, and motored with only half an hour for a picnic, until we got here at 2.45 (via Cassino which has "picked up" amazingly). We had sent the luggage on ahead, and had to change in order to watch the jumping at the Horse Show – there was a British team taking part – and we all enjoyed it, though three hours is a bit long. The usual Italian "bog" at the end telling us to go before the president and then finding the presidents car, instead of ours, and having to fight inch by inch through a vast and excited crowd, until we finally did get to ours. Then in the evening we had a dinner party of 46 and a dance here till 2am – a very good party with lots of nice Italian boys for the princess to dance with. Saturday morning was hairdresser, press photographs and presentation of 200 Embassy staff. In the afternoon laze and bathe, while I played golf – then a vast noisy Roman cocktail party at 7.45 – to 8.45 (with Princess Torlonia) then dinner at 9 in a restaurant. The plan was after that to go to the Howards flat and relax. Not a bit – we were then told that all Rome would be insulted if we didn't go to the ball so at 11pm we solemnly changed, arrived at the ball at 11.45 in a turmoil of noise and heat, and squash and fury and bright lights which suddenly went mauve or green (so flattering) and photographs and detectives and there we sat, like sweating sardines until 1.15am when we went home. Today Church and a museum before lunch – our drive was cancelled, cocktails at the Canadian Embassy at 6.30pm and then our evening with the Howards, out of which we were cheated last night. So you can see there hasn't been a great deal of time for writing, particularly as there is always a certain amount of work and planning to do. However we are all V. [missing material] and engaging ourselves tremendously. Things won't be so hectic again after this, at any rate until Paris.

I know you will pass this round the various families – I hope you can all read it.

Much love to you all, from both of us
Your very loving Tom

14 May
Grand Hotel Firenze

My darling one,
It is I fear, ages since I last wrote to you and I have so much to say that I hardly know where to start. This innocent holiday has become like a triumphant Royal Tour, and we have not had one single second in which to write home. Today, for the first time, we have all wilted, and have remained in doors, incapable of movement. I will however now try and describe to you some of the highlights of the Rome visit – but you will, I know, forgive the gaps, and the illegibility. It was a long and horrid drive to Rome, and we reached the Embassy at 2.45, in order to change and visit the International Show jumping, where we stayed for 4 – 7pm. The jumping was lovely to watch and the Princess sat beside the President. We had the usual muddle when we left because the cars were in the wrong order and we had to charge thro' the crowd but I must say it was the only sign of muddle really that we saw in Rome. That night there was a drinks party of 46 and a very nice dance at the Embassy till about 2am and we had left Sorrento at 9.30. Next morning sight-seeing, lunch at the Embassy, I then played golf with H E and then a cocktail party with the Canadian Ambassador, then, at the last minute, this fearful public Ball. And so we went on visiting some lovely pictures in the Borghese Gallery, the Forum, Villa d' Este and Hadrian's Villa, and parties with our Minister to the Vatican, our Counsellor, Jackie Ward who gave a splendid dance (his wife was Daphne Mulholland) and the South African Minister. But the big day was Tuesday and that I will try to describe in more detail. (I have forgotten a garden party – 600 people!).

We started off at 10.30 (after a 3.am dance) to visit the Capitol, a group of buildings designed by Michel Angelo, and now the

Municipal Offices and Museums. We were shown round by the Mayor and a Professor, and we saw so many beautiful things, ancient Roman and Greek sculpture. The Capitoline Venus, the boy taking the thorn from his foot and many other well known things – unfortunately both the Mayor and the Professor had very bad breath so the whispered comments were at times unwelcome. We spent 2 hours there and nipped back to the Embassy in order to tidy up for lunch with the President at the Palace of the Quirinale. On driving into this Palace we found a Guard of Honour and all the Royal Guards in full scarlet and black, with Roman Helmets. We were led up a long staircase and through a series of 17th Century saloons, in each of which stood 4 of the vast Palace Guards. At last we reached the President and later again sat down to a charming lunch – beautifully sent by about 20 liveried footmen. Marguerites and roses decorated the table and at the end of lunch the President made a charming little speech of greeting, to which later on H E replied. After lunch we proceeded to walk round all the State Apartments and then the whole of the garden, both as big as at B P, with very fine tapestries but nothing else of great note. Finally we got home at about 4pm. Now it was already time to prepare for our visit to the Pope.

Before that, HRH and Mary had been busy collecting suitable garments, black dresses and lace veils, and I must say they both looked very sweet. The Minister came to collect us, and we drove into the St Peter's Square and round behind the church, under a series of medieval buttresses and archways, until we felt we had passed back through half a dozen centuries. We were met by Papal Chamberlains and the Swiss Guard, in their blue and gold uniform (with scarlet lined pleats), helmets and pikes. Each of us flanked by two guards, we then began a long climb to the second floor – at each turning, there was a click and a rattle, as a new guard presented his pike to the Princess. Slowly we glided upstairs, with only the click of the "Present" to break the shuffle of our feet. When we got to the top of the stairs, we had to walk through a long series of rooms, each with its complement of guards, Swiss in some, Palatine in others, and finally the Noble Guard. We passed by them all and finally came to the Ante-chamber, where we waited, with our escort of one Cardinal, one Monsignor and two Chamberlains. HRH had said she wished to be alone with the Pope, so when his bell rang, the Minister took her in and then came back to us. The instructions were that he would be sitting at his desk on the right of the door, & we should bow or curtsey 3 times. After 20 min the bell rang again, the sign for Maria and me to join HRH – we duly entered and made our obeisance to the saintly figure, who smiled so sweetly and bade us sit down – he gave us each a little medallion and spoke in English about our visit to Rome, and said how much he had enjoyed seeing HRH and hearing all the news about the Royal Family and the baby Prince. He then gave us his Blessing and we withdrew. It was most moving and lovely. We were then escorted with the same pageantry (plus a little photography) to the doors of the Vatican and then we began sight-seeing still in our black. With a charming lady professor, we examined, detail by detail, the Raphael Loggia and Rooms, the Sistine Chapel and the Borgia Apartments – no mean feat in itself. We then walked to St Peter's and inspected some of the more outstanding features; then only then did we get into the car, driving back via the Janiculum Hill, to see the view. We got back to the Embassy at 7.10pm, I only hope you are not too tired reading about it.

In fact, the visit to Rome was a great success and HRH has done her stuff beautifully, so that a lot of good has been done: it has necessarily altered the nature of her trip, but that was inevitable in a Capital City. Here we are now relaxing for a day or two, otherwise we would burst. If you send this to John, ask him to let Edward Ford see it, as he has been so kind to write and hadn't had a decent answer from me.

Bless you, my darling, and all our love.

From Tom

* * *

Most lovely creature.
Welcome to Capri's shores.
Meet all our foreign boars.
Wolfing spaghetti.
Looking so pretty.
La prin ci pessa Margarita

Swayed in a gondola
We also fond of her
Asti Spumanti
Have some more Chianti
La bella donna
Whoops! She's a goner.
La Principessa
Poor Margherita

Far from Stoke Poges
Hemmed in by Doges
Singing a melody
On the laguna
O bella Napoli
O for a cup of tea.
Singing unhappily
Poor Margarita

And when in Tuscany
Down on the Arno
She found material
For her piano
Gay songs & serious
Love songs so various
Sing songs uproarious
La Principessa

MISCELLANEOUS

"Lord Buxton"*

The Day Ennoblement was born
You should have heard the fauna fawn
Upon their greatly loved Protector
(as well as Anglia's Director).

Three cheers rang out from Crete to Cos
And on to the Galapagos
Where Turtles' spirits used to droop
At prospect of becoming Soup.

Across the Serengeti Plain
There spread, like wildfire, the refrain
'Tell it to all, noise it abroad
Our friend has just become a Lord'.

Mammoth and Rhino, Mink and Mouse
Have access to the Upper House,
Where all our hopes and all our fears
Can be presented to the Peers,
Leaving them so aghast and stunned
They'll all support the Wild Life Fund.

Alas? There is one wicked Beast
With memories of a famous feast
Who read somewhere in the 'Express'
The details of the Aub's address
And checking up in the Directory
Confirmed it was the Stiffkey Rectory.†

---

*   Aubrey Buxton: great friend and neighbour in Norfolk.
†   Harold Davidson, once Rector of Stiffkey, was mauled to death by a lion.

His grandsire told him, ere he died,
It should be in the Good Food Guide.
'You'll never get a better meal
From Beef, or pork, or Ham or Veal
Or Blackberry and Apple Tart,
Than Mousse de Cure a la Carte!

Frocked or unfrocked, the lion won't care
Once he has picked your bones all bare.
The Danger that you have to face
Is common to the Human Race;
E'en with a handle to your name
To Lions you'll always taste the same.

* * *

The Forsaken Wives of Humble

Any young Lady who knows Aylmer Tryon,
will share the anxieties of Mrs. Bowes-Lyon
and will realise the reason is perfectly simple,
for running in tears to Mrs. Dalrymple
and spending a hurried and weepy half hour,
with an equally lachrymose Mrs. Balfour.

Their husbands go Southwards on one of those benders,
that is otherwise known as the Holkham tail-enders.[*]
From which they'll return with their eyes and heads
        swimming
from an excess of wine, song and absence of women.
And after long days and late Bachelor nights,

---

[*]   Tail Enders was a great shoot (cock pheasant and woodcock) Tommy
        Leicester had at Holkham at the end of the season with the same friends
        every year.

they'll be thinking of naught but their conjugal rights,
which is why the poor Ladies of Humble, East Lothian,
regret they were ever talked into betrothing.

* * *

In reply to Tom Harvey who wrote out one day
a verse in his office when old Mullens was away.
And he sighed for our loved ones left far in the North,
cooking our porridge or stirring our broth.
But I think that his logic is faulty in parts,
we are busy all day – not just fiddling with tarts!
And when we return all our manhood restored
one hopes that our darlings will cease to be bored.

For if mussels and onions are good for the gun,
this short interruption should double the fun!
And reward for their waiting is likely to be
on the scale of the shooting near Wells-by-the-Sea.

* * *

MacHumbies Reply:
Yes, I left my beloved deserted at Humbie
though I knew in a month once again she'd a Mum be,
for the cry of the cocks in the Old Barn Plantation
compelled me to make it a lovely gestation.

As that bold rhymer Harvey was invoked by Lord
        Leicester
I'll awaken my muse and most thoroughly test her,
to visit me when I walk through the Obelisk Wood
and make me a poet e'en one half as good.

So don't worry the shooters at the fam'd Golden Gates
by making them think with remorse of their mates.
Rather heed the advice of the marksman Mark Turner,
that a woman won't fash at what doesn't concern her
and follow the lead of the brave Tryon Bros,
that not to shoot woodcock's the only real loss.

So hearken to me each East Lothian tail ender
a sojourn in Norfolk's the best marriage mender
and Holkham excitements and bachelor nights
the best preparation for conjugal rights.

* * *

Lines written on hearing that the Earl Marshal
is ill with Chicken Pox

Why do the Heralds shake in fear,
And timid Mittens in his socks?
Because to their dismay they hear
The Earl Marshall has chicken pox.

Black Dragon Pursuivant turns pale
And bites her fingers in remorse;
What will befall if she should fail
To shelter Ascot from Divorce.

But Bernard, languishing in bed
Cares not a tittle, nor a jot
In spite of all the life he's led
He's never been in such a spot.

The Coronation Stakes were tough;
No steeplechase their strain can match.

Most people would have had enough,
But Bernard never wished to scratch.

But now, dear Heaven, how he pines
To end that soul destroying itch.
Yet if he does, his facial lines
Will deepen into one long ditch.

So, please, your Shadow's warning heed
Even if you are kept from sleep.
Last Easter I did scratch and bleed,
And now my face is pitted deep.

Cast back to '53 your mind
Recall the panoply and pomp.
Alas, what is it now you find?
Bed-pan oply and stomach pump.

Yes, Norfolk, cannot so far tell
How long the pain, how soon the cure,
I.T.C.H. alone can spell
The miseries that you endure.

* * *

Many Aussies, every Pom',
Know the dangers of the Tom.
Norfolk birds in some disorder
Flee away from this marauder.
Signorinas down in Roma
Mutter darkly "Cave Thoma".
When to Africa he com'
Signal DANGER with Tom-Tom.

For Geoff Todd on his 70ᵗʰ birthday

At Ladysmith and Spion Kop
The musket spits, the Cannon roars,
At home a baby's whimpers stop
The hideous noise of crashing Boers,
The watching World is stricken dumb
"Ain't he the image of his Mum?"

In his layette his beauty tears
The heart-strings of his loving kin
The Golliwogs and Teddy Bears
His sweet and captivating grin,
His air of being 'oh so happy'
In spite of that confounded nappy!

Our Hero grew to manly strength,
Plastered with Perfumes and pomades,
And when the War broke out, at length
He joined the famous Irish Guards
Giving the Social Whirl a miss
Until the final Armistice.

Pacific though he was by birth
He quite enjoyed the years of War,
Fortified by his sense of mirth
And by great draughts of Croft's '04
Until in Peace he was deployed
To Join the famous house of Lloyd.

The Firm of Saville, Bough & Hay,
Insured the richest in the land,
There is no Duchess live today
With rings of Diamond on her hand

Who cannot now afford to laugh
Thanks to Todd's toil on her behalf.

Thus life proceeded, smooth and sweet
Full of extravagant Delights,
All centred round St. James's Street
And – need I really say it – Whites.
His many friends were quite agreed
That Geoff had all that he could need!

Sensation struck the Social 'swim'
When it was suddenly announced
Felicity had chosen him,
And vows of marriage had pronounced,
And Punters groaned who could have won
At odds of 28 to 1.

Such friends as might indeed have been
Surprised but all agreed on this
That they have very seldom seen
Such rich and rare connubial bliss,
No, nothing like it have they met
Since Romeo and Juliet.

Seventy years have thus elapsed
Since first these tiny cries were cried
And tiddler toddler Todd collapsed
As those first baby steps he tried.
A movement that he'll still repeat
Whenever he drinks Whisky neat.

To envy Blind, to Flattery Deaf,
Of Malice totally devoid,
The birthday of our Hero, Geoff

Gives us all pleasure unalloyed.
That's why we join in thanking God
For being friends of Geoffrey Todd.

* * *

*Lines written from Buckingham Palace to commemorate the
presentation of a Gold Snuff Box to the Senior Common Room at
Christ Church Oxford, by Her Majesty the Queen on 24/11/46.
She was the FIRST Woman to dine with them.*

My Womanhood you did not deem a fault
Though Dons prefer to dine with sterner stuff
You took my presence with a pinch of salt,
Now take my present with a pinch of Snuff.

* * *

A Birthday Verse

Dear Gracious Lady. Thank you for your life
Long years of service and your lovely smile.
The courage that you lent to our dear King
Reluctantly exalted to his throne.
So that in peace and War he won our hearts.
What richer legacy could he bequeath,
Or any mourning nation dare expect
Than a Queen Mother verily adored
And a Queen regnant precious beyond price.

* * *

To Sir John Marriott after a minor 'op'*

Everybody in the City
Is exclaiming what a pity
That the General's little titty
Has gone white.

For they say the slightest snip'll
Take the ripple off a nipple,
Be it single, double, triple,
Left or right.

But it's thanks to the Hospittle
That your tit'll feel less brittle
When they whittle just a little
Off your skin.

And to know you've had that snickle
Make you want your mouth to tickle
With a trickle of Veuve Clikle
Or some Gin.

For the most primaeval Chimp'll
Quite admit it's not too simple
Hiding dimple, or yet pimple,
'Neath your gown.

So a Breast long use't to bullets
(tho' as tender as a Pullet's)
Must just learn, at last, to pull its
Bra well down.

---

*   John Marriott was a General in the Scots Guards and an old
     family friend.

384

To Victor on his 60ᵗʰ Birthday *

Maxi Ha Ha, laughing Edward
Thought, one night, when going bed-ward,
"Who's the Man to save the Nation,
By intensive cerebration?"

By the morning he had picked a
Winner in the Mighty Victor –
U Think Tank, no Burmese Leader,
But a Bio-Physics Reader
Master of those tiny Cells
Which the Mammal frame dispels,
Golfer, Cricketer, self-taught
Maestro of the Piano-forte.
Not for him Lafite of Clay
As he greets the dawning Day;
But at Night a Dinner – suit on
(Even though not drinking Mouton)
Knitted brows, both low and high
Force him now to wear a tie
While the nightly hours of toil
Swallow up the Midnight oil.
Even worse (and thanks to Solly)
Bowler Hat and well-rolled Brolley
Now replace the Cap and Club.
What a dream! Ay, there's the rub.
While all your friends are truly grateful
We hope you will not find it hateful
Or redolent with grief and pain
To Think and Think and Think again.

* * *

---

*   Victor Rothschild's birthday (the first line refers to Ted Heath).

385

Sometime in 1950 the "Taylor & Cutter" featured me as one of the five best dressed men in England!

It was not long before Mike Parker and Martin Charteris (who had just joined Princess Elizabeth's household and was helping with her speeches etc.) sent down to my Office an elegant spray of 'Pansies' in cellophane.

I replied in verse as below:

> On the Altar of Fashion the most recent martyr is
> Colonel the Honourable Martin C. Charteris.
> With nothing to do but to gaze at the Press
> He found he'd forgotten on which side to 'dress'.
> So hurriedly casting an eye down his breeches
> He saw what reminded us all of his speeches
> The pattern he saw – and Oh how it appals –
> On the one hand all Cock, on the other all Balls!

* * *

Lines addressed to the Duke of Norfolk on winning the Gold Cup

> Emerald, Ruby, Topaz, Jade
> Are Stones whose value does not fade,
> And can be bought for Decoration
> (or as a hedge against Inflation)
> But now, I'm glad to say, the Duke
> (And this is clearly not a fluke)
> Has proved that Ragstone is The Thing –
> Far better than a Diamond Ring.
> (Of course a scintillating Rock
> Has great attraction for a 'Jock'
> But I am speaking for the Duchess
> Whose views don't coincide with Hutch's.)

Thus all his many friends cheered up
Seeing him win that famous Cup.
A just reward for years of toil
In making Ascot truly Royal.

* * *

For Sylvia Combe on her 70th birthday[*]

Never was a lighted candle
She has voluntarily missed.
Getting there by ski or sandle,
Through a Sandstorm, snow or Mist.
Be it Munich, Minsk or Methwold
Burnham Thorpe or Tel Aviv
She is first across the threshold
And most always last to leave.

But it gives her greater pleasure
To be Hostess, not just Guest,
And to raid, in massive measure,
Budge's well-filled Deep Freeze Chest
So that she can feed her neighbours
With the goodies she has bought
To revive them from their labours
On her lovely tennis-court.

But the very least suggestion
That a friend is in distress,
Risking Tilly's indigestion,
She's away like an express
And her car, much used to pressure,
But less used to oil and water,

Roars from Norfolk up to Cheshire,
Back to London to escort'er.

To St. Paul's for Emma's 'Debut'
Then away, just like an arrow,
Or a super-modern Jehu,
To her grandson still at Harrow.
Trodden are the Beeston tough lines,
Cricket watched till drawn are stumps;
Who has ever equalled such signs
Of a 'Granny come up Trumps'.

By her family surrounded
And her three score ten completed,
May her joy be quite unbounded,
Unalloyed and undefeated.

So when Roger, Emma, Simon,
Lucy, Silvia and Carey*
Are the Grooms and Brides of Hymen
They'll give thanks to that Good Fairy
Who has shown the art of Living
Is the Precious Gift of Giving.

* * *

Portrait Painters – 1951:

Annigoni get your Gunn, and arm yourself with speed.
They say a Lion is on the run, a Mann is what we need.
A frond foot doesn't help a bit, nor yet the fleetest Walker,
A Jagger p'raps would make a hit, used by a Birley stalker.
No Grimm reproof, nor even mild, nor yet a Bishop's blessing

---

*   Sylvia Combe's grandchildren.

Can make this animal less Wild, at Best it's Tone's depressing.
The Devastation from the north, to Sa-lis-bury southwards,
The Lambes that Leo in his wrath has masticated
    mouthwards,
A Temple-Bird, a lovely Swift, a Martin quite enchantin',
A whiting with its Scales adrift, and more types from
    La Fontaine
Only their Tombs survive to show, thanks to the
    Mason's Penn,
Watt epitaphs the Fates bestow, on R.S.P.P. men.
The words are these, and Markham well,
"We seldom equal Simon Elwes."

P.S.
Who is this Lion, I hear you shriek, that caused such fearful
scandals?

* * *

Prince Charles was born 14ᵗʰ November, 1948,
at Buckingham Palace.

"Good Evening – Sweet Prince"

The only activity that I was aware of at 7.30 p.m. on Sunday November 14ᵗʰ, 1948, was the thumping of my heart, jerked out of its normal monotonous lethargy by game of squash. Four of us, the Duke of Edinburgh, Patrick,* Mike† and myself, had been playing singles, a l'Americaine, and the expectant father had beaten each of us in turn. I then creaked off to have a bath in the downstairs household bathroom, which was later to become the seat of so much discomfiture.

---

*   Patrick Plunkett.
†   Mike Parker, Private Secretary to Prince Philip.

I was gracefully allowed to dine in my disreputable grey flannel suit and chewed and crumpled flannel shirt, and so we sat down four in number, Mary,* Edward† and Patrick all in evening dress. I think we were all tired of waiting for things to happen, and could picture ourselves hanging about in this way for days. But at 9.15, as we were finishing our coffee, Mary was called to the telephone, and a glint of anticipation slipped into our eyes, or certainly into Edward's, which shone like a greyhound's when its head is stroked. This is it, we said, and trooped off towards the Equerry's Room.

Mary we found telephoning in Edward's room – "They've taken her downstairs, and it's not expected to be long now – I've telephoned to Tommy and Joey,‡ and they're coming over, I am still trying to get Richard".§ Mary was soon whisked away by some other call, so I hung around trying to get Richard. He had arranged to notify the Press that things had started, so that the papers could start bringing out their special editions. He wasn't easily found – he had just left the Ritz – he had come in by the Electrician's Gate – "Oh yes, Sir, he's in the house. But where? Oh, where?" Needless to say, Wulff and Nickolls¶ had appeared like goosepimples on on Eskimo fan-dancer, their nostrils dilated like drain-pipes to catch a whiff of anaesthetic, their ears stretched to catch the chink of a hypodermic, their eyeballs on stalks to see all there was to be seen. Still no sign of Richard, and yet the Press must be told as soon as possible – crisis or no crisis? No crisis! Richard appeared, and all was well. Not till next day did he admit that he had crept into his bedroom for an early night, and was intercepted by Mike who broke the news. If this was not one of the great encounters of history, its non occurrence might have shaped one or two destinies.

---

*	His wife.
†	Edward Ford.
‡	Tommy Lascelles and his wife.
§	Richard Colville.
¶	Dogs.

Meanwhile, members of the Household came in and gathered in the Equerry's room. Four of us tried to play bridge, and got as far as cutting the cards – but suddenly in came someone, (and I can't for the life of me remember who) and said "It's a boy – but nothing is to be said for half an-hour." Then Tommy came in, then Richard – "I knew she'd do it, she'd never let us down", and down to business; filling in 'Prince' on the telegrams, and ringing up the Home Office. Out went the news over the tapes and we got the wireless ready to hear the announcement. On droned the ten o'clock news, though none of us heard a word of it: Richard stood beside the wireless, telephoning to the B.B.C. News Editor – "Have you had the tapes? – No, the News Editor, God, they're slow – ah, News Editor, have you" – and before he could finish, we heard the news reader's voice go up a semi-tone, and he read the announcement.

Patrick and I then went to hear the crowd's reaction – but clearly they still knew nothing – so I sent Childs to tell the police-man, who passed round the good news. The cheers rolled along the railings – and the gates had to be quickly shut against the pressing and delighted crowd. Tommy was meanwhile despatch-ing telegrams, and telephoning to the Prime Minister and Mr Churchill. Queen Mary drove over from Marlborough House, bringing with her the Athlones. Her Majesty was clearly thrilled by the safe arrival of her first great grandchild: Uncle Algy* was less demonstrative, muttering half-audible and faintly disconso-late phrases such "Glad it's all over – all for the best, I suppose – horrid business" – as if he were Mr Jingle at the deathbed of his mother. Still apparently inconsolable, he was hustled upstairs in the lift, there to repeat his inarticulate lamentations over the unsuspecting Prince.

Glasses and Champagne were being brought to the Equerry's room, while Ainslie tidied the table with one hand, and with the other telephoned for "any spare Pages to put their flippin' skates

---

* Prince Alexander of Teck, 1st Earl of Athlone.

on and come to the King's door". Another purposeful bustler was, as usual, Mrs Ferguson, whom I found weeping for joy in the bathroom, and filling a hot water can for Sir John Weir – "Ay, it's great news", she said, jogging off along the passage at a good triple.

In a few minutes, the King and Queen, with them Queen Mary, came in to the Equerry's room bringing with them the three doctors, who seemed quite fresh after their exertions, and Sir John Weir, who was a good deal more tired than any of them – possibly as a result of struggling to get his name on the Bulletin. However, he had a large glass of champagne, and later confided to me, in a loud voice, that "he'd never been so pleased to see a male organ in all his life" – a sentiment I would have echoed with fervour had Queen Mary been more than a foot away from us.

Amid the comings and goings of this cheerful gathering, a trained observer would have seen more in a minute than I saw in an hour. The delight felt by Their Majesties can be imagined – The Queen, beaming with happiness, while Queen Mary sat in the straightest-backed chair we could find, and cross-examined Gilliatt from A to Z. The King, who was simply delighted by the success of everything, particularly after the disruption of his normal routine which had necessarily taken place. I think everything seemed a bit unreal to him, even the little red baby upstairs but a Prince had been born, his daughter was all right, and after all, what is habit on such an occasion.

Something else the trained observer would have noticed – the disappearance of Princess Alice* – made at a pace and in a direction that dispelled all doubt, though not, alas, all anxiety. This same observer would, however, have been somewhat overtrained had he detected any signs among those present of either sympathy or attention. Indeed, the laughter rose in pitch until the word 'oysters' was mentioned, and even then no-one seemed anxious

---

*   Princess Alice, Countess of Athlone.

to help. Gradually the focus shifted to one of the least glamorous but most necessary corners of the vast Palace – this Palace which was, at that moment, the centre of world interest and good-will. It is not to be supposed that the imagination of the world pictured the happenings inside the Palace as in fact they took place.

Bending over a cot is one thing but bending over a figure prostrate with indigestion is another. Floored by the treachery of a bearded bivalve, poor Princess Alice was suffering the twin tortures and revulsions of food poisoning.

No face bore a darker shadow, no brow a more worried frown than that of the Master of the Household; nor was the former lightened or the latter smoothed by hearing these words from Sir John Weir, "The wumman'll nay leave the hoos tonicht – she a' cold and clammy". Joey's look would have withered an oak tree. Tommy leaped to his feet and made off, saying "When people start going cold and clammy, this is no place for me". As the ghastly truth spread across the Master's brain, like spilt ink, he began to telephone to the housekeeper. I can't remember what he said; all recollection was dimmed by the brilliance of his final sentence – "Well, look 'ere, we can't leave her for another hour in that lavatory".

Still the groans rang out, still the passage was filled with anxious people – Uncle Algy muttered even more hopelessly, "Such a pity, so uncomfortable – bad oyster, so seldom get 'em nowadays – noticed they had longish beards – pity".

After an age, which to the Master must have seemed many ages, it was decided by the Princess's own doctor, who had arrived in all this mêlée, that she should go home to bed – and off they went, uninvited protagonists of the Great Anti-Climacteric.

The next excitement was the baby, who was brought down to the Ballroom: I was allowed to go and see him at 11.45 – just a plasticene head emerging from a cocoon – with Nurse Rowe proudly standing guard: a simple, little cot, with white blankets

– smaller than I had imagined. So, poor little chap, 2 1/2 hours after being born, he was being looked at by outsiders – but with great affection and good-will.

The crowds were still outside, and remained until Richard and Mike walked along the railings asking them to go home. It was a good idea for all of us, and we gradually drifted away, to our beds, a little tired perhaps, but tremendously pleased that the Princess had had a son. So we left him to sleep in peace, beautifully unaware of the excitement he had caused. Perhaps the oyster was, too!

* * *

Index

Printed in Great Britain
by Amazon

54291c6b-3a57-4272-b2b6-ed7073e82f59R01